Sports Architecture

Sports Architecture

Rod Sheard

London and New York

First published 2001 by Spon Press
11 New Fetter Lane, London EC4P 4EE

Simultaneously published in the USA and Canada
by Spon Press
29 West 35th Street, New York, NY 10001

Spon Press is an imprint of the Taylor & Francis Group

© 2001 HOK LOBB

Typeset by M Rules
Printed and bound in Great Britain by Butler & Tanner Ltd, Frome and London

British Library Cataloguing in Publication Data
A catalogue record for this book is available from the British Library

Library of Congress Cataloging in Publication Data
A catalog record for this book has been requested

ISBN 0-419-21220-5

Contents

Acknowledgements

It is thanks to a great many people that this book made the transition from just a good idea into reality. That transition has been helped, encouraged, assisted and pushed by people outside our firm including Caroline Mallinder, Simon Inglis and Maritz Vandenberg and many people inside our firm including Geraint John, Barry Lowe, Janine Graham, Richard King, Ashley Munday, Sean Jones, Derek Wilson, J. Parrish and Mike Crook from our London office and Paul Henry, Alastair Richardson and Michele Fleming in our Australian office.

We can be so enthusiastic about our work that at times it is important for us to stand back a little and see our efforts as others see them, Caroline, Simon and Maritz all helped greatly in providing that perspective and in giving insight into how to get our message across.

It would only be part of a message if we were not able to illustrate our ideas by using photographs of our work and illustrations of our designs and we would like to acknowledge the wonderful photographers whose work appears in this publication.

Ian Lawson – Reebok, Alfred McAlpine, Cheltenham;

Patrick Bingham-Hall – Stadium Australia, Millenium, Colonial, WestpacTrust.

Their work is complementary to our own and we feel their understanding and interpretation of our designs assists enormously with our message. Also Iain Graham Photography – Arsenal, Chelsea; Kevin Nixon – Kempton Park; Philip Locker – Robin Park; Huddersfield Town AFC Ltd and Kirklees Stadium Development Ltd for Aerial and Panoramic photographs of Alfred McAlpine respectively; Olympic Co-ordination Authority (OCA), National Rugby League (NRL) and Trends Publications for permission to use additional photographs of Stadium Australia. Finally, we would like to thank our clients, many of whom have been consulted on the content of the book and some of whom have contributed to its writing.

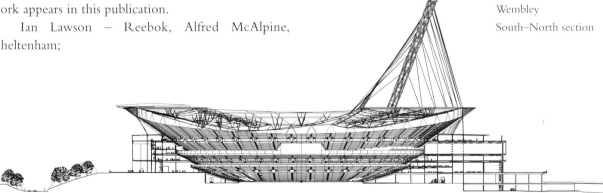

Wembley
South–North section

Foreword

Simon Inglis

(Author of *The Football Grounds of Great Britain* and *The Football Grounds of Europe*)

From the moment the citizens of ancient Greece first settled their Hellenistic haunches on the rough slopes of Olympia, some 2,780 years ago, spectators have harboured expectations, and made demands. Will they be able to find a place to sit or stand? Once in place, will they be able to see properly? Will their favourite athlete, charioteer, matador, football team or batsman perform to their satisfaction? And will they be able to find a toilet without missing any of the action?

At Olympia the first attempt to cater for spectators was to provide earth embankments for up to 45,000 spectators. To quench their thirst, aqueducts and wells had to be built. As the number of spectators and events increased, a larger stadium was laid out on the site, adjoined by an even larger hippodrome. For greater comfort, the VIPs were given stone benches, or *exedra*. Several centuries on, at the Coliseum in Rome, designers created a technological masterpiece; a multi-storey, multi-functional venue perfect for viewing, with a sophisticated crowd circulation system and a retractable canvas cover to keep the Empire's elite cool under the burning Mediterranean sun.

Ever since, while millions of tourists have gaped in awe at the Coliseum's ruins, stadium designers have been busy vying with each other to achieve equal sophistication. They ask, how could the people of the Roman Empire possibly have enjoyed the spectacle of lions tearing apart defenceless human beings? But they seldom imagine the tourist of the year 4098 trailing through the ruins of a Giants Stadium or a Wembley, wondering how on earth twentieth-century society could have allowed humans to risk life and limb in pursuit of an inflated piece of leather. Hadn't these primitive folk ever heard of virtual sport?

As we approach the new millennium, it is all too easy to assume that today's sports are forever, that today's spectators have unique and unprecedented demands, and that modern designers have finally – hallelujah! – learned how to meet those demands. Instead, something new always crops up, and if the spectators like it, they turn up. If they grow bored, they find something else. Such is the perennial challenge for event promoters, and, rather less often, for designers. For the latter, always seeking to build the modern-day Coliseum, a building which will long outlive its original purpose, the chance to sparkle comes but rarely. But when it does come, as in the current generation, all in a rush, they have to be at the cutting edge.

It used to be enough to know how to build a stand, raise an embankment and add roofs. Now, sports architects must be highly specialised in consumer trends, turf technology, safety legislation, environmental issues and, not least, the politics and machinations of high finance and planning procedures. Yet despite all these demands, there always lurks the age-old caveat: facilities alone are never enough. Cruel, but true.

Greek and Roman sportsmen performed on sand – for which the Latin word was '*arena*' – because it needed little maintenance, was readily available and, when the sport turned ugly, as it so often did at the

Coliseum, absorbed blood. Early twentieth-century athletes ran on cinders or shale. Now they run on impeccable, synthetic tracks. Similarly, turf technology has advanced so rapidly that when viewing videos of football or rugby matches which took place only as recently as the late 1970s, one is amazed by the often appalling quality of the playing surfaces. Nowadays, even the merest hint of a bare patch seems to invite scorn. But despite these advances, for the spectator the thrill of the chase has not diminished. As long as each runner runs on the same surface, the race is on. Individual performers like Michael Johnson or Ronaldo can each fill a stadium. But the stadium itself is never top of the bill. The average Coliseum regular would find many aspects of attending a bullfight in Pamplona or Barcelona today familiar. Most spectators still sit on bare stone benches around a sand-covered ring. The rich still grab seats in the shade. Arcaded but sparse concourses circling the arena offer a shaded place to promenade, meet friends and buy snacks. Even the result of the event itself is usually a foregone conclusion. As in Rome, the underdog seldom wins. Yet the punters still turn up, so the show goes on.

Conversely, take the example of speedway and greyhound racing. Both were 'invented' during the 1920s and, within a decade, were so popular that the administrators of more established sports such as football and rugby became seriously worried. Speedway and dog tracks, usually staged at the same, purpose-built stadia, were thoroughly modern. They had track-side lights, timing devices, Tote boards and glass-fronted restaurants. By 1932 there were 220 dog tracks in Britain. In the late 1940s, attendance reached 50 million per year. Now the figure is nearer 4 million and there are barely two dozen tracks left. In short, in sport, the event is all, and no event is immune from the vagaries of public taste or changing fashions. The best stadium in the world would struggle to attract spectators to a sub-standard contest, while primitive facilities matter little if the public sense a cracker in the offing.

If this would seem to indicate that design plays no part in the popularity of sport, it might be supposed that the staff and partners at HOK LOBB – and their ilk – should pack up their stadium blueprints right now

and try pitching for more lucrative commissions involving shopping malls or office blocks. After all, some of the most popular and successful sporting clubs in the world play at venues which are little more than what Robert Venturi has dismissed as 'decorated sheds'. Besides, what does the average fan care for aesthetics so long as his or her team is winning? But that would be to reach a false conclusion. Good design is indeed of crucial importance, quite simply because it enhances the event. Even more importantly, it honours both athletes and spectators. Why does this matter? Because to the participants and their audience, sport matters.

To stage an event in a nondescript setting is to dull its aura. As for the spectator, for much of their lives most people live and work in unremarkable surroundings. All the more reason therefore that the stadium should be their Xanadu, their Hollywood, their Never-Never Land and dream factory all rolled into one. It follows that good stadium design is more likely to emanate from designers who both understand and share such dreams, who know the thrill of a live sporting event and who are themselves captivated (and so motivated) by the experience. The Romans understood this: *Panem et circenses* (Bread and circuses). That, according to Juvenal, was what the populace desired. Bread nourished the body. But spectacles fed the spirit. Ergo, sports architecture should add spice to that feast. To cook this metaphor a little further, however, we must remind ourselves that the architecture itself is not the feast. It is the palace in which the delicacies are served.

For some designers – architects and engineers alike – this can lead to a recipe for over-elaboration, or, as it has been called, structural exhibitionism. Munich's Olympic Stadium is but one example of this phenomenon. A stunning piece of engineering artistry, completed in 1972, its famous tent-like roof structures and adjacent television tower form the city's second most popular tourist attraction. And yet the stadium, often a cold, uncomfortable environment, is certainly unsuited to the extremes of a Bavarian winter, and it could hardly be developed further without compromising the integrity of the original design. Meanwhile its main tenant, Bayern Munich Football Club, is keen to develop a more modern facility and is threatening to depart. Similarly, Turin's Delle Alpi Stadium, completed in 1990, offers a finely tensioned cat's cradle of steel, concrete, cabling and aluminium. But the effect is wasted because it somehow leaves both players and spectators unmoved. After only a few years in use both of its tenant teams, Juventus and Torino, have expressed a desire to move.

So stadium design is no simple matter. Designers are playing with people's dreams, and in many cases treading upon hallowed grounds. State of the art has to respond to the state of the heart. Another role for the designer to take on, therefore, is that of a dream leader.

Sporting clubs and organisations are, by necessity, fairly closeted institutions. Their executives harbour few aesthetic sensibilities. Usually they confine their expectation of design to what they may have seen elsewhere (as in 'we'll build one like that') or, more often than not, to what they hope they may get away with without being pilloried (as in 'the team always comes first'). This is not a criticism. In the sporting world most new stands or developments are greeted with rapturous acclaim simply because they are new.

In a number of cases, however, as shown between these covers, Rod has demonstrated how a dream leader can usefully harness the otherwise untutored aspirations of an ambitious organisation. The award-winning stadium in Huddersfield resulted from precisely such a process. Here was a town of dowdy repute with an ailing football team and a dying rugby club. To seek to build a new football ground was radical enough in the straitened circumstances. To build one for both clubs to share, in the context of West Yorkshire sporting tradition, bordered on the reckless. But to build such an innovative form of stadium – in mill-town Huddersfield of all places – required a real leap in imagination. Huddersfield would no doubt have comfortably settled for less, and no doubt still pronounced it good. Instead, a handful of the town's sporting and political leaders fought for excellence and, just as commendably, trusted in their designers to deliver. The praise since heaped upon the design and its now famous banana truss roofs only confirmed what many sporting aesthetes had argued for years – that stadia and sports facilities are as important to the self-image of a community as a town hall, war memorial or public library. And they need not look like the back end of a railway shed.

But why do some modern designs achieve this acclaim, while others merely function unnoticed, and often unloved? Remembering as always that the event is the thing, we now turn to the spectators. No live sporting event can exist without spectators (even hushed ones such as at snooker tournaments). They are as much a part of the spectacle as are the athletes. This is partly why television embraces sport so enthusiastically. If 50,000 fanatics have paid for the right to roar on their heroes inside the stadium, 50 million viewers at home are more likely to stay tuned. In the future, as digital television comes on stream and access to events becomes ever wider, that live presence will still be required by the programme producers. Italian media mogul Silvio Berlusconi has predicted that this trend may turn the stadium into a vast television studio in which spectators are invited to attend, gratis, as if they were extras in a crowd scene. But crowds there must always be. This begs the further question – what sort of crowds?

It is taken as read – or at least should be – that good design provides safe conditions for spectators. But good design can also encourage individuals to become better spectators. It does this, not by social engineering – though some make this accusation because of hikes in admission costs, which are beyond the remit of the designers – but by elevating the spectators' spirit and sense of occasion. Put more crudely, good design has the power to make spectators feel special. Taking HOK LOBB's design for the North Bank Stand at the Arsenal Stadium in Highbury, London, as an example, one can easily track the seduction process, which its creators have so subtly stage-managed. Their first trick is to positively identify the structure as a sport building. Why is this important? As a building dedicated to the pursuit of human excellence and endeavour, the stadium should, in itself, have presence. It should announce itself, and rejoice in its celebratory function. The fanned glazing bars screening the wings of Arsenal's two Art Deco grandstands are, for example, potent images of an institution which achieved world renown during the 1930s. One glimpse of them is enough to proclaim 'Arsenal'. Hence the new North Bank Stand borrows and adapts this simple, but effective imagery in its own glazed screen ends.

As we move closer to the stadium, instead of disguising its structure, the North Bank Stand's upper rows of red seats, its outer roof columns and lateral truss are also plainly visible. This exposure adds to the sense of expectation, but has a secondary value too. It helps to reveal the basic format of the stand so that visitors feel more comfortable as they begin to negotiate their entry. And so the seduction process begins. Beckoning next are the uplighters, positioned above the turnstile blocks like beacons at the entrance to a magical kingdom. Once inside, leaving the real world behind, the public enters a wide, covered concourse, flanked by bars, kiosks, a souvenir boutique and food counters, each decked in the corporate colours and emblems of Arsenal. Television screens relay images of Arsenal in action; an appetiser before the main course. An oval-shaped mezzanine gallery allows other match-goers to watch the throng below, reminding us once again that the spectators have come to enjoy not only a match but also a gathering of like-minded spirits.

Many match-goers will spend up to an hour in this private street before the actual event begins – a sure sign that they feel comfortable in the environment. Furthermore, by providing this environment, both the club and its designers have extended the parameters of the event, enhancing its value as well as its earning potential. There are those traditionalists who resent this extension of the stadium's role as a form of manipulation. But surveys of Arsenal fans reveal a high level of satisfaction with the facilities on offer. Typically, North Bank Stand regulars regard the stand as a reflection of their club's exalted status and stature. Of course it is a fine stand, they say. It is an Arsenal stand, and only the finest is good enough for Arsenal. The penultimate stage of the seduction process leads the public up through the vomitories and onto the overlapping decks of seats, where at last the secret garden – that perfect rectangle of green in the midst of the city – unfolds before their eyes, until finally the spectator arrives at his or her seat.

Even then, there is still much for the designer to consider. HOK LOBB was among the first architectural practices to use computers to calculate precise sightlines for spectators. They went further by developing the first ever program – now *de rigueur* for all new stadium

developers – to provide would-be ticket purchasers with an on-screen image of the view to be had from each seat. In the North Bank Stand, the seats themselves are padded, and with sufficient leg-room to accommodate most builds. Again, the practice has always been a forceful advocate of generous dimensions for all categories of spectators. Even their toilet designs at Arsenal have won an award. What happens down on the pitch is, of course, beyond the control of any architect. But there can be little doubt that it is the designers' understanding of the event that has enabled them to create enhanced conditions for its enjoyment.

Not all is clear cut in this rapidly evolving relationship between provider and user, however. At Arsenal, where there are two giant Sony Jumbotrons relaying live action, edited features and public messages, and a live band playing in the North Bank concourse before matches, there are mixed views as to the presentation of the event. In a recent survey of 20,000 supporters of Premier League clubs (the Carling Survey, conducted by the Sir Norman Chester Centre for Football Research at Leicester University), roughly a third of Arsenal fans endorsed the club's new approach to match presentation. Yet Highbury has also been dubbed 'the library' by those who feel that both the greater levels of comfort and the changing profile of spectators (towards those willing to buy tickets in advance, and at higher prices) has compromised the atmosphere at matches. For this reason, shortly after the North Stand opening, the club experimented briefly with the designation of a section of the North Bank Stand as a 'singing area'. Had supporters become so passive that they needed cheer-leaders, albeit from amongst their own?

But the early signs are that the measure seems to have worked, and now the Premier League has set up a special panel to study other means of helping to restore some of the atmosphere which appears to have been lost in the modernisation process. The irony of this cannot be avoided. For years spectators complained bitterly about the physical conditions prevailing at football grounds in Britain, conditions which played no small part in the rising tide of hooliganism throughout the 1970s and 1980s. And yet, once greater levels of comfort and amenity were provided, the complaint came back that now, perhaps, fans were too comfortable to be able to participate fully in backing their team. Like prized birds in gilded cages, their songs had become muted. Quite how this conundrum can be resolved is open to question. But it is yet another example of how modern designers have to be constantly alert and in touch with the hopes and aspirations of both clients and their customers.

As dream leaders, Rod's team have continued to seek new ways of celebrating sport in their architecture. Later chapters will show how recent commissions for Bolton Wanderers Football Club, the Welsh Rugby Union at Cardiff, the Sydney Olympic Committee and the city of Melbourne have already prompted further advances from the distinctive forms seen at Arsenal, Huddersfield and elsewhere. Clearly, they are designers who combine a love of sport with a faith in the tools of technology to provide ever more exciting environments.

Stadium Australia, the venue for the Olympics, will command their biggest audience yet, as billions of television viewers across the globe survey their work in the year 2000. This compares with only a few hundred onlookers at the first Olympiad over 4,000 years ago. In those days there was only one event on the programme. It was a race along the length of a single track measuring 600 feet, a distance known to the ancient Greeks as a 'stadion'. In many respects, it is a race, which has never ended.

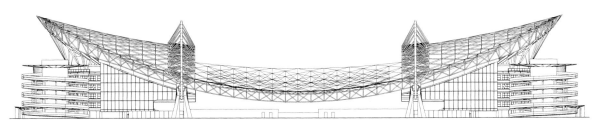

Stadium Australia
section

Introduction

For centuries the term 'architecture' was accorded with such gravitas that it was usually applied only to structures identified with our cultural, religious or governmental heritage. Architecture with a capital 'A' shaped our great theatres, museums and palaces, our churches, institutions and town halls. Most other structures, particularly those in the fields of industry and commerce, were usually dismissed as mere 'buildings' – utilitarian, unimportant and unworthy of serious recognition. Fortunately, that limited and often elitist view has diminished in recent years, with the result that many fine factory, office and retail buildings are now, at last, receiving the recognition they have long merited.

Buildings for sport and leisure have faced a similar struggle to gain the status and credibility they deserve within the architectural establishment, although again, in the past few years, some encouraging signs seem to indicate that entrenched opinions are softening. One major breakthrough came in 1995 when, for the first time ever – and no doubt to the surprise of many traditionalists – the Royal Institute of British Architects granted its coveted Building of the Year Award to one of our stadia, the football and rugby Alfred McAlpine Stadium in Huddersfield. More recently, in 1997, following the opening of another one of our projects, the Reebok Stadium for Bolton Wanderers Football Club, *The Times* described the venue as a 'triumph of high-tech architecture and engineering'. The newspaper further contended that such

buildings looked certain to become 'the dominant landmarks of Britain in the twenty-first century'. Naturally we agree wholeheartedly with *The Times*' statement, but only if the word 'Britain' is replaced by 'the world'.

As we hope this book will demonstrate, we share a passion and a commitment to buildings for sport and leisure. So much so, in fact, that for the last twenty years we have deliberately concentrated exclusively on such buildings. However, Howard V. Lobb CBE founded the company as a general architectural practice in 1935. A gifted man whose career was both busy and distinguished, Lobb 's most notable appointment came in 1948 when the British Prime Minister, Clement Attlee, appointed him to a prominent role in the management of the 1951 Festival of Britain. This honour, and a string of other commissions for schools, power stations, factories, banks, offices, mechanical car parks and recreational buildings, made Howard V. Lobb & Partners one of Britain's leading firms of modern architects in the post-war period.

Thanks to the introduction of the Betting Levy Board in 1959 – a measure that helped finance a number of developments at racecourses – the practice developed a new area of expertise during the 1960s and 1970s. Our first sports-related commissions were for grandstands at Dublin, Doncaster and Newcastle, and so great seemed the potential of this growth area that after Howard Lobb retired from the practice in 1974, the firm's new generation of partners took the momentous decision to focus entirely upon sport and leisure.

As the youngest partner at that time, I wholeheartedly endorsed the decision, and have never regretted it for one moment since. For despite the poor image of sports stadia and arenas, particularly among the architectural establishment, we could think of no other building type so powerfully able to touch the hearts and minds of the 'common man'.

Physically, a stadium can accommodate the inhabitants of a town or part of a city for a few precious hours. Emotionally, it can captivate entire cities and countries, and, for certain events, hold the attention of up to half the world for days on end. Stadia are buildings which change lives, furnishing us with folklore and memories that remain ingrained within our collective culture for years and years after the events that gave rise to them. Stadia and the activities they encompass can lift the individual to elation and evoke a euphoria that may never be forgotten. Equally, stadia can be the scene of enormous disappointments and heartbreaking moments. As a number of academics and writers have noted, in several respects stadia have in effect become the social 'cathedrals' of our time: hallowed places where we can all be at one with our community, where we share a common bond with friends and strangers. They are venues in which we can sing, yell and express ourselves in a manner quite different from that governing our lives beyond the stadium gates. No other building type affects us in quite the same way, which is why we at HOK LOBB find the task of designing them so infinitely exciting.

At the same time, as architects, the almost limitless design possibilities of sports and leisure buildings offer us a fascinating and forever changing series of professional challenges. They possess an inherently complex range of technical criteria to solve and a surprisingly wide range of forms to explore. Every week sees new technological developments. Every town and city has its different demands. Every sport has its own social milieu.

As symbols of a region or a nation, as icons of popular culture, stadia are never viewed in isolation. From the moment they are completed, in tandem with the teams and athletes who perform in their midst, stadia are vigorously competing for praise and attention with their counterparts elsewhere, and inevitably with many more stadia, past, present and future. In order to meet these ongoing challenges more robustly, in 1993 we changed our status from a partnership into a limited liability company. In the following year we established an Australian practice. Since then our expertise in racecourse design (which began in the early 1960s) and football stadium design (starting in the late 1970s) has been augmented by commissions from clients in the worlds of cricket, tennis, rugby, basketball, motor racing and athletics. This was followed in 1996 by the commission to design what will become the largest stadium ever to stage an Olympic Games, Stadium Australia, for Sydney in the year 2000. But we could see that the future of design and of sport was global and we responded to our clients' needs in January 1999 by merging our firm with HOK Sport to become HOK LOBB, the world's first true global sports firm. Using the type of digital information and design technology which was only dreamed of a few years ago we now cover the world and are able to offer a service to our multinational clients wherever they wish to build their vision.

We are often asked why we chose to specialise in sports and leisure. After all, architects are trained to design most types of building, and emerge from university firmly believing that they can and will do precisely that. The answer lies not with us, as architects, but with the clients we serve: clients like David Dein of Arsenal Football Club, whose passion for football and belief in Arsenal is infectious, and Paul Fletcher, previously at Huddersfield, then with Bolton Wanderers and now helping to create the new Wembley, whose positive attitude and tenacity is awe-inspiring; clients like Gareth James at Melbourne Park Trust, Australia, who has an obsession for well managed venues, Glanmore Griffiths of the Welsh Rugby Union in Cardiff and Edward Gillespie in Cheltenham, whose focus on producing results was inspirational. All of these individuals possess a single-minded determination to make their own projects extra special and, most importantly, a reality. They, and fortunately many others like them, share two characteristics in common. First, they hold a vision of a future for their venue, which is both positive and progressive. Second, in order to fulfil that vision, they will do all they humanly can to ensure that their venue becomes a reality. Without such vision or commitment, no stadium could ever be built.

So it was, and so it remains, that the passion of our clients has motivated us as architects to specialise in the design and documentation of a specific type of building. Quite simply, we realised that in order to design the best sports and leisure buildings in the world – the buildings our clients demanded – we would have to match our clients for vision and commitment, that meant committing ourselves totally to one single pursuit. Baron Pierre de Coubertin, founder of the modern Olympic movement in the 1890s, coined the games' motto of 'swifter, higher, stronger'. It is a philosophy that, over a century later, continues to inspire all sporting endeavour. We would just add one word, for we are also driven to be 'better' as well.

In practice our decision to focus specifically on sport and leisure has allowed us to study the genre at a level of detail that would have been quite impossible had stadia been just one among a range of building types worked on in our design studios. As we hope this book will show, our studies have been prolonged and extensive, involving research and development into all aspects of sports buildings. This includes such issues as crowd management, passive design techniques and, increasingly, methods of achieving Environmentally Sustainable Development (ESD) through the sensitive use of materials, advanced fenestration techniques, the design of environmentally positive spaces and the implementation of power management design. Technology allows us to design stadia that are not only more environmentally friendly in their construction but are also able to monitor their own energy performance on a daily basis.

During the course of our studies we have been led beyond sport into the analysis of other related public facilities, such as theme parks and airports. For example, at EuroDisney, near Paris, we observed that people waiting to sample the 'Orbitron' – a simple ride lasting around 1.5 minutes and repeated in a 4.5 minute cycle – will generally queue for around 45 minutes for their short but intense dose of excitement.

Put another way, they will wait for ten ride cycles to pass by before enjoying one of their own. This behaviour fascinated us. If people are prepared to wait for 45 minutes for 1.5 minutes of pleasure, what are the implications for buildings designed for the use of much larger numbers and offering much longer treats? It suggested to us that if the force of people's expectations could be understood, analysed and, moreover, catered for by appropriate design, our sports buildings could begin to take on quite different forms. These new forms could be less dictated by the circulation patterns of thousands of people and more geared towards projecting an image of comfort, order and calm. We have already learned that the main factor in any safe emergency evacuation plan is preventing panic and maintaining order. If we can now go on to design sports buildings that embody these principles for routine use, surely we can further prise open the envelope of conventional wisdom, so that our efforts will more fully meet the expectations of the public. But we have to keep on observing, keep on researching and, above all, keep on learning. This applies not only to developments within sport, leisure and society as a whole, but also to our own management philosophies and techniques.

Management

Compulsory reading for all architectural students should be Ben Rich's *Skunk Works* book. It tells the story of a department – the Skunk Works – of the aircraft designers and manufacturers, Lockheed Martin, where particularly difficult commissions are handled. The department's list of achievements in aircraft design is awe-inspiring. It includes prototypes for the world's first supersonic fighter, the world's fastest aircraft, the world's first stealth fighter and the world's first fully returnable spacecraft. But what makes these achievements even more impressive is that each one has been accomplished within tight budgets and short time programmes. Indeed, most have taken the same period of time required to design a simple sports venue. So how did they achieve this? As a direct result of the firm's advanced management technique of using small, select teams of specialists, provided with the very latest equipment and operating within an environment which encourages free thought and hard work. That same philosophy informs our own work and is perhaps best summarised by the saying, 'The best people, with the best tools, in the best environment, produce the best results.'

The idea is to create and nurture an atmosphere of creativity within our offices, yet at the same time retain a clear focus upon defined time and cost targets, whilst also ensuring total management and administrative support. Beyond the achievement of our ISO 9000 status of quality assurance, this means that we strive constantly to improve and modify our management systems, particularly when it comes to supporting the problem-solving element which lies at the heart of so much of our work.

Into the twenty-first century

We believe that buildings for sport and leisure are not only likely to figure among the leading architectural genres of the twenty-first century, rather as cathedrals and railway stations were to previous ages, but, more emphatically, are destined to become classic icons of the new millennium. Already our more modern 'Cathedrals of Sport' have brought with them a whole new approach to the simple exercise of watching an event. Far from being basic shells in which to gather and watch sport, they have evolved into sophisticated entertainment centres, multi-experience venues capable of being enjoyed in many diverse ways. Sport, and increasingly music, may still provide the core attractions, but the experience goes far beyond them, as do our perceptions. Our aim as architects is to change the perception of sports buildings; to sweep away the common image of crude, concrete monoliths and replace it with the promise of exciting, stimulating and uplifting venues of enjoyment and entertainment. In stating this, however, we do not refer to the straightforward, direct experience of the paying spectator, viewing the live event, nor even the experience of spectators in the stadium alone.

The onset of the age of digital information, particularly in respect of television and flat-screen technology, looks certain to change that experience quite fundamentally in the twenty-first century. We already know for sure that, with the arrival of hundreds of digital channels, there will be a phenomenal increase in the amount of televised sport available to the public. This will be in tandem with a greater diversity in the ways that signals may be received and packaged for the viewer, via terrestrial, satellite or cable television, and of course via the Internet. This diversity will also be reflected by enhanced services offered to spectators within the stadium itself, either at their seat or in other public areas. As a result, the next generation of stadia will become audio-visual studios in their own right, offering broadcasts of sport, music or whatever other events they might host. Indeed, one might go so far as to predict that for certain stadium operators with high-profile sports clubs in residence, television programming might soon become a major element of their core business. Thus the stadia of the twenty-first century are destined to become more multi-functional than ever before; their roots firmly planted in their host communities, welcoming spectators from all over their region, while at the same time relaying their wares to a potentially vast audience around the globe.

The more advanced venue operators will be able to attract, and therefore produce, a range of programming which goes far beyond coverage of a single event, using their arena floor (with or without its removable turf covering), various adjoining studios, plus any other open spaces designed within the venue. Furthermore, via handsets, both live and remote audiences will be able to interact with the venue's information and marketing services: to watch highlights, to call up statistics, to order tickets and merchandise, and generally to tap into the stadium's resources at any time of the day or night. The venue will, in effect, be designed with two distinct functions in mind: as sports and entertainment centres playing host to live audiences, and as sports and entertainment studios serving the viewing and listening requirements of the remote audience.

Change, flexibility and complexity

As the commercial strains upon operators become ever greater, so venues have to be designed to accommodate different events, a concept sometimes referred to as the 'overlay'. For example, the stadium we have designed for the Sydney Olympic Games in the year 2000 – an event that is estimated to attract around 50 per cent of the world's television viewing audience – will metamorphose after the games into a quite different venue. Around 2 million people will visit the building during the Olympic year, when the stadium's capacity will total 110,000. However, immediately after the games' closing ceremony, the athletics track will be removed and the seating decks reconfigured to create an 80,000 seat venue around a standard rectangular pitch. Those are the changes that will be most visible to the casual observer. But behind the scenes a whole host of other alterations will have been made too. For example, the spaces provided to accommodate all the extra personnel and equipment required during the Olympics for the opening and closing ceremonies, for accreditation, security and media, together with the additional facilities required by the 35,000 extra spectators attending Olympic events (including toilets, food and beverage outlets) will all be adapted or removed when the stadium transforms into its post-Olympic mode. In effect, we have designed two stadia on the same site, one an adaptation of the other, offering quite different solutions to their quite different day-to-day needs.

Complex commissions like the one for Stadium Australia have led us to adopt more fluid ways of thinking; in a very real sense to adapt Edward de Bono's concept of lateral thinking to the problems of design, and particularly in the case of stadia, to the ever-present question of financial viability. Taking a sideways view has also proved fruitful when tackling other, more socially oriented issues (for, in addition to the inherent complexity of designing sports and leisure buildings for a diverse range of events, designing for the broad range of people likely to use them is equally challenging). In his book *The Lost World* – the sequel to *Jurassic Park* – Michael Crichton begins with a summary of the 'chaos' or 'complexity theory', from which he draws up a theoretical platform for the eventual self-destruction of the dinosaurs. Although drawn from a popular novel, the theory is nevertheless relevant to patterns of behaviour observed in many a complex system. These complex systems can be the neurones active in the human brain, the behaviour of the stock market and even, perhaps surprisingly, the movement and circulation of crowds around and within a stadium.

As architects, we need to understand the most basic of principles which determine the way people behave, and then cater for this behaviour as best we can, and wherever possible, as simply as we can, in our design solutions. To illustrate this, consider one seemingly mundane issue, that of young teenagers attending rock concerts. Because most concerts finish late in the evening, parents are often reluctant to allow their children to attend. Therefore, by providing a comfortable area specifically for parents, where they can wait and meet up with their children after the event, we can partially ease some of the social concerns which might otherwise contribute towards negative attitudes towards the venue. Providing a telephone hotline may further ease these concerns, so those parents can enquire about the event's finishing time. These may seem like minor considerations in the much larger, overall picture. But by understanding such issues we can, as architects, help our buildings to be successful long after we have completed our designs.

Stadia and the city

Buildings for sport and leisure, and the happiness and sense of community they generate, touch all aspects of our lives, economic, political and social. We strongly believe, therefore, that stadia should form as integral a part of towns and cities as those other supporting pillars of modern, urban society: local government, education, religion, commerce and industry. We would go further, moreover, by arguing that in order to play this role most effectively, such buildings should form part of our city centres. Fortunately, a noticeable increase in the partnerships forged between governments and private enterprise, and between local authorities and sports and media companies, has resulted in this belief being put into practice all over the world.

We have participated and continue to be involved

in a number of successful examples of integrated city stadia, for example at Huddersfield, Cardiff and Melbourne. These venues at the very least provide a point of reference in the wider cityscape. Everyone knows where the stadium is located. But beyond its physical presence, the stadium also provides a tangible focus for community consciousness and social bonding, a place representing urban pride, a place in which one feels part of something important, a place to share and enjoy with one's neighbours. It has also been shown that city centre venues also help to generate revenue for surrounding businesses and services as the secondary spend from these venues can be considerable. Economic impact studies conducted in Britain and the United States indicate that for every pound or dollar spent inside a stadium, between five and ten are spent outside, in the city itself. Indeed 'stadium tourism', now a recognised phenomenon in itself, is regarded as big business not only when the building is complete but even during its construction. Each year, a major stadium typically attracts visitors counted in their millions, to attend events, of course, but also to see around the building itself and to visit the stadium museum and its associated dining, leisure and retail outlets. For example, the second most popular tourist attraction in Munich is its Olympic Stadium, while in Barcelona more tourists visit the museum at the Nou Camp stadium than the much-heralded Picasso museum.

Commercialism of stadia

Quite apart from tourism and the value these buildings can contribute to the renewal of our often-neglected inner-city areas, stadia also generate significant revenue themselves. Sport, as we are so often told by the media, is now a big business. It is, furthermore, a business in which gate receipts (that is, income derived from event ticket sales), once the mainstay of any professional sporting operation, form an ever decreasing percentage of overall revenues. The income from televised events is clearly one major form of income stream. More recently merchandising has shown itself to offer huge potential. To draw an analogy with airports: approximately 40 per cent of the total revenue

generated at airports derives from merchandising – a figure which is increasingly being met by leading sports clubs and stadium operators. Airports are similar to stadia in one crucial aspect, and that is the amounts of time people spend inside them, typically between two to four hours. That represents 'spending time' in a very real sense. Even a single Automatic Teller Machine (ATM) at an airport or stadium can yield for the operators a profit of several thousand pounds per year. Just as the layout of airports has changed radically in recent years to take this phenomenon into account – notice how so many of them now resemble shopping malls with airports attached – so too will stadium design evolve.

Aesthetics and social order

Books about architecture often adopt such a theoretical and impenetrable stance that the lay reader is all too easily deterred, with the result that architecture itself is seen as an elitist and alien subject. In line with our views on the social function of sports and leisure buildings, we want this book to be accessible to all readers, professional and lay. Just as any member of the public should be able to enter and enjoy one of our grandstands or stadia with no previous knowledge, so we hope that you will find pleasure and interest in our words and pictures. There will therefore be no place between these covers for obscure theories of aesthetics, nor any room for densely argued but purely academic debates on design or construction methods. Behind the laying of the concrete, steel and glass, we hope that all will be clearly and comprehensively revealed and understood.

All of us in HOK LOBB have worked hard to achieve quality in our work over the years, and while we all believe in the benefits that good quality architecture can bring, we recognise that aesthetics is in the eye of the beholder and that social concepts are better acted upon than talked about. You will no doubt form your own opinion of the aesthetic approach we bring to our buildings. But the fact that our designs have won the Building of the Year award from the Royal Institute of British Architects and many other awards, encourages us to believe that our work is appreciated.

Although Huddersfield was the first stadium to be honoured in this way, just as importantly it suggests to us that the path has been cleared for more sports and leisure buildings to be similarly honoured in future years.

As far as our social philosophy is concerned, if you ever attend an event at one of our buildings and enjoy yourself, perhaps even irrespective of the result, then our social principles will have proved their worth and nothing further needs to be said.

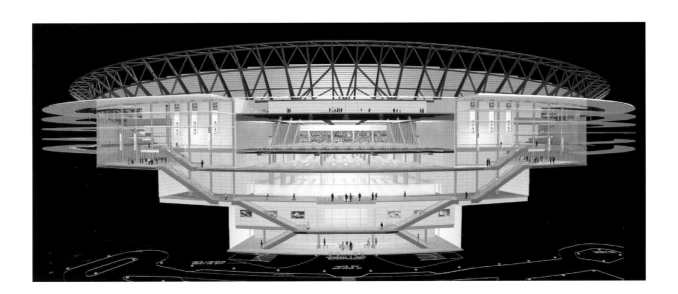

Wembley East
elevation

Designing for Success Part I

Sports architecture

'We were there!'

Stadia are special buildings. They are the only structures designed to bring whole communities together so that they can interact with each other and as one with the event. We gather inside them to celebrate a unique experience. Yet so often the buildings themselves are dull and uninteresting. Sometimes they lack even the most basic of amenities and can be so bleak and unfriendly as to be almost frightening. The good news however, is that these outdated, inhospitable concrete bowls of the twentieth century are gradually disappearing.

A new generation of stadia is in the making. Mediocrity in design, management, catering, safety or comfort has no place in the new sporting cathedrals. Designers and clients are, at long last, waking up to the fact that the long-term health of any venue is directly dependent on two factors, the quality of the event and the quality of the spectator experience.

No one, surely, would doubt that the average living room provides a higher level of comfort and amenity than most stadia, or that televised coverage of a sporting event generally provides a better view of the action, with its close-ups, replays, commentary and interviews. But the critical ingredient which sets the live experience apart from its televised replica is the sense of 'community' a stadium creates, that gathering of people, focused, as one, upon a single transient show of human endeavour. This physical and emotional experience is the 'product' a stadium sells, a product quite unique in modern life. There is simply no other opportunity to be part of the crowd, to yell and jump and wave our arms at the same time as thousands of other people. The Mexican wave, the national songs or the club chants we perform with so many thousands of other strangers provide us with a deep, bonding reassurance that we are not alone, that we are part of a whole, part of something great. In going to the stadium rather than staying in our living rooms we can say, 'We were there!' (fig.1.1)

From sports grounds to sports stadia

The sports stadium as we now know it today largely evolved in Britain's industrialised cities during the nineteenth century. A number of factors created the need. The codification of a number of sports, particularly association football and rugby, had imposed a much-needed uniformity which allowed rival teams to compete in fair contests, bound by agreed rules and easily understood by those watching from the sidelines. Meanwhile, the development of the steam railway network enabled both teams and their followers to travel the country in pursuit of new challenges.

Inevitably, as the public demand increased for more meaningful, competitive games, the sporting authorities established regular league and cup competitions, which in turn increased the team's need for higher quality players. Such players had to be paid, and

1.1

so it was that sports grounds were enclosed so that money could be collected at a 'gate'.

Whilst these early structures started as minimal wood, brick and steel compositions they were often elegant and articulate. But with the increasing use of concrete by the mid-twentieth century, the majority evolved into a forbidding building type, and a less useful one too. In their early days, many stadia were designed for field sports, athletics and sometimes even cycling. Eventually, however, the tracks were removed and the

1.1 The opening of Stadium Australia, Sydney, was an opportunity to use the main truss as a base for a spectacular fireworks display (photography courtesy of the National Rugby League)

1.2

1.2 The Alfred McAlpine Stadium, Huddersfield, hosts the Eagles concert out of the football and rugby season

1.3 The Houston Astrodome, one of the first multi-purpose stadia, in use as a rodeo venue

1.3

1.4

1.4 Spectators arriving at Stadium Australia, Sydney with a sense of expectation (photography courtesy of the Olympic Coordination Authority (Bob Peters))

stadia became single-purpose facilities, serving a single-purpose crowd for a limited number of events each year. The rest of the time they lay unused, without function or patrons. Beyond a few hours' sporting use every few weeks they were, in effect, dead buildings.

That hardly mattered as long as mass spectator sport remained one of the few forms of entertainment available. But in 1937 technology struck the sporting world for the first time when the BBC experimented with the live television broadcast of a football match from Arsenal Football Club (which happened to be near to the studios and transmitter at Alexandra Palace, in north London). It took a few years for the effects of broadcast sport to be felt, but by the late 1950s, television had penetrated so many homes that leisure patterns would never be the same again.

Faced with extra competition from television and the many other leisure pursuits that arose to satisfy the appetite of an increasingly affluent customer base, stadia were forced to adapt in order to survive. This change began in the USA during the 1960s with such pioneering venues as the Houston Astrodome, in 1965, one of the first sophisticated, multi-purpose and multi-user facilities which sought to attract a range of spectators beyond the hard core of sports fanatics who would attend events whatever the conditions. (Fig. 1.2, 1.3)

The contemporary stadium

To succeed in the latter half of the twentieth century a stadium must appeal to and be accepted by many different interest groups, not only the customers, participants, officials and event holders, but such diverse groups as local residents, local authorities, business sponsors, advertisers, concessionaires and media companies. All of these groups have needs. All can play a role. But it is important not to forget the three primary interest groups whose requirements are paramount. These are the spectators, the owner/operators and the participants, or the SOP, as they have come to be known.

–   The spectators expect an enjoyable, safe day out in a stimulating environment. They are the primary group, without whose support the entire enterprise will fail
–   The owner/operators expect to make a return on their investment. They will do this by attracting spectators to the venue in sufficient numbers and by managing them in a safe, efficient and organised manner. If they cannot manage the facility in such a way as to make it pay, either by operating income alone or by operating income + subsidy, the venue will close
–   Without participants there are no events. Participants expect a good and safe standard of playing or performance conditions, ideally with large audiences and, in certain circumstances, good television and media coverage

These are the bare bones of a complex subject. As outlined more fully in Chapters 5–7, it is only by designing for each of these groups – by thinking through logically what each requires from the facility – that we have a chance of achieving a higher standard of design. For now, however, let us look more closely at our three primary interest groups.

The spectator

A happy spectator is one who looks forward to a special treat and whose expectations are not disappointed on the day. Spectators should be able to reach the stadium

1.5 Concourses at Stadium Australia, Sydney

1.5

without undue difficulty; experience an agreeable sense of anticipation as they make their way to their seats through efficient entrances, safe ramps or stairways and pleasant concourses. When they have arrived they should be able to sit in comfort and safety with a clear view of the game. They should be fully informed and entertained during quiet moments by means of information displays, action playbacks and other devices that are better than what they would have seen on television at home. (Fig. 1.4)

After the game spectators should not feel obliged to rush to the exit in order to avoid the crowds. They might, for example, prefer to linger in cafes, stay on at the stadium for a meal, or perhaps go shopping or spend time with their families in the stadium museum, games arcade or cinema. If they have come a long way or wish to stay in the area they might even like to spend a night in the stadium hotel, perhaps in a bedroom whose window overlooks the pitch (a room which, earlier in the day, might have been used by other spectators as a private viewing box). (Fig. 1.5, 1.6)

Successful stadia design requires that this entire sequence of experiences be clearly imagined by the client and his design team. The vision must be firmly cemented in their minds if it is to become a reality. Yet few clients have the knowledge or insight to conjure up this vision alone, which is where an experienced design team such as ours comes into play. Getting it right requires a sound knowledge of the motivations and desires of spectators, not as a monolithic mass but as a diverse collection of different kinds of people. Some may be sports enthusiasts for whom physical closeness to the game, to the players and to their fellow supporters is probably more important than comfort. At the other extreme, some may attend the games primarily for social reasons, or to entertain business associates. To them the game itself is less important than the overall experience of being pampered in an ambience of excitement, comfort and perhaps even exclusivity (in other words, making the occasion more 'special' than merely dining out at a restaurant). Between these two extremes are various intermediate types of spectator; for example, fans who take a real interest in sport but only attend stadia if they can take their families without feeling threatened by boisterous crowds or by the stadium environment itself.

1.6

1.6 Brightly coloured concourses at Chelsea Football Club

The owner/operator

Until recently the owner or operator's prime source of revenue was ticket receipts or income collected at the gate, hence the importance of what has been crudely described as 'bums on seats'. (There is an old story concerning a London gentleman who arrived at a Yorkshire cricket ground early and so placed a newspaper on his preferred seat while he went to enjoy some pre-match victuals. On his return he found a local man sitting on his newspaper. When he complained, the man replied some-what equivocally, 'It's bums what reserve seats round here.')

Although ticket revenue remains important, evidence from stadia around the world shows that it is gradually decreasing as a percentage of the owner/operator's total income. Rather, it forms a base for other types of revenue generation. Such 'non-gate income' tends to fall into one of two categories: that derived from the event itself (for example, game sponsorship, advertising and broadcast fees), and that earned from the audience attending the event (including catering sales, private box rental and club seat sales).

1.7

1.7 Crowd at the opening rugby match at Stadium Australia, Sydney which broke all records and exceeded the business plan (photography courtesy of the Olympic Coordination Authority (Bob Peters))

1.8

Merchandising sales can come from either category.

The ability to maximise both types of non-gate income has become vital to stadium viability, and thus has a significant impact on the design and operation of the venue. However, there has to be a balance. Over-commercialisation can drive away certain types of spectator, so that long-term loyalty is sacrificed for short-term gain. Similarly, if there are 20,000 spectators in the stadium and 20 million viewers watching the event on television, the owner/operator may be strongly tempted to stage the event in a way that suits the remote audience rather than the live one. This staging might affect both the venue design (for example, the location of TV camera positions) and the event organisation (perhaps the timing of the start to suit television schedules). Indeed, if this were taken too far, the live audience might become increasingly alienated, leading to a decline in live attendance, which in turn could result in a gradual desertion of top players, sponsors, advertisers and eventually (and ironically) even the media. Skilled strategic planning is therefore vital to attain a balance between gate income and non-gate income, and between the needs of the live crowd and the remote audience. Both need to be considered in the design.

A third design factor, which often needs to be considered by an owner/operator seeking funds for a stadium, concerns the requirements of any grant-awarding body or major public patron. State or local governments may be willing to offer overt or covert financial support, but there are usually stringent conditions attached. These conditions could be a requirement that the stadium be designed as a multi-activity centre for use by local communities, or that the stadium itself is strategically planned to form a catalyst for urban regeneration.

Public funding for stadia is more widespread than is often thought. In the USA, for example, one would imagine that the spirit of free enterprise would have been sufficient to create a large number of profitable, privately funded venues. Yet the reality is quite different. Local or State government finances the vast majority of US stadia. Moreover, despite their owner/operators' commercial expertise, few can demonstrate that they make a profit when one takes into account the capital cost of their development.

By way of illustration, Table 1.1 reproduced from *Sports, Convention and Entertainment Facilities*, by David Petersen shows ownership of the USA's major league stadia and arenas.

But wherever stadia are located, and whatever the chosen means of generating non-gate income, one generally agreed principle is that, unlike their predecessors, today's stadium owner/operators now plan to run their facilities at a profit, and can therefore attempt to attract various forms of capital financing. One such example from our portfolio of design work is Stadium Australia in Sydney, home of the 2000 Olympic Games (see the case study in Part II). This was partly funded by a share issue on the Sydney stock exchange and underwritten by a group of banks and brokers to the value of A$300 million. Without the ever-increasing potential for 'non-gate' forms of income, it would have been almost impossible for such an issue to succeed.

Table 1.1 Ownership of major league stadia and arenas in the USA

	Stadia		Arenas	
CITY	BASEBALL (MLB)	FOOTBALL (NFL)	BASKETBALL (NBA)	HOCKEY (NHL)
Anaheim	Public			Public
Atlanta	Public	Public	Private	
Baltimore	Public			
Boston	Private	Private	Private	Private
Buffalo		Public		Public
Charlotte		Public	Public	
Chicago	Public/Private	Public	Private	Private
Cincinnati	Public	Public		
Cleveland	Private	Public	Public	
Dallas	Public	Private	Public	Public
Denver	Public	Public	Public	Public
Detroit	Public	Public	Private	Public
East Rutherford		Public	Public	Public
Houston	Private	Private	Public	
Indianapolis		Public	Public	
Kansas City	Public	Public		
Los Angeles	Private		Public/Private	Private
Miami	Private	Private	Public	Public
Milwaukee	Public	Public	Private	
Minneapolis	Public	Public	Private	
New Orleans		Public		
New York	Public (2)		Private	Private
Oakland	Public	Public	Public	
Orlando			Public	
Philadelphia	Public	Public	Private	Private
Phoenix	Public	Public	Public	
Pittsburgh	Public	Public		Public
Portland			Private	
Sacramento			Private	
St Louis	Public	Public		Public
Salt Lake City			Private	
San Antonio			Public	
San Diego	Public	Public		
San Francisco	Public	Public		
San Jose				Public
Seattle	Public	Public	Public	
Tampa	Public	Public		
Washington		Public	Private	Private

Patently there is no easy formula or foolproof method for success. But if there were one key element to aim for it would be this: to ensure that the initial capital cost of the venue's construction is funded and under-written with a minimum of borrowing. If this can be achieved then there is a good chance of also getting the operating revenue in line, provided that the stadium's investors, designers and managers evolve a tailored solution based on the following two principles:

– A true understanding of the psychology of the proposed facility's users. Who are these people, where are they, how many of them are there, what attracts them to events, and what factors might deter them from using the facility?
– Thoroughly researched design, financing, management and marketing solutions that will satisfy the users identified above

If this procedure sounds obvious, it is surprising how many stadium projects have gone ahead without employing such a basic methodology, proceeding instead on a basis of wishful thinking about spectator numbers and fashionable ideas about planning and design. Once such stadia have been built, they are often copied the world over, without anyone knowing for certain if or how their designs are valid.

It is by no means wrong to look at existing facilities. But it should be recognised that, first, no two sports developments are ever the same, and, second, that whilst it is useful to draw on the experience of other examples, indeed this book features many of them from our own portfolio, they can provide only signposts, not final destinations. For example, a number of our designs have been modified by other architects and constructed in different parts of the world. But their success, both architecturally and commercially, has been mixed.

To conclude, clients should be aware that in sports venue design it is absolutely essential to question *all* conventional assumptions, to check each fact pertaining to an existing model, and then to develop and evolve a custom-made solution.

1.9

1.9 Stadium Australia, Sydney: partly funded by share issue on the back of the world's largest sports event

The participant

If spectators and owner/operators are to derive the maximum benefit and enjoyment from a stadium, it follows that the needs of the participants must be considered with extreme care and attention during the design process. This includes provision for their safe and trouble-free arrival at the stadium, and their facilities for changing, bathing, warming-up, treatment, meeting with the media and post-event socialising.

But most important of all for participants is of course the pitch, track, court or stage, the focal point of the entire venue: its quality, dimensions, security and lighting levels. This is where the participants put into practice their months and years of training and preparation, where their dreams may be fulfilled or their worst nightmares realised. Attention to detail is therefore absolutely vital. With this in mind one of the first issues a design team must agree with the client is that of the type of playing surface (or surfaces) to be installed at the stadium. This issue and others relating to participants' facilities are covered in more detail in Chapter 7. (Fig. 1.10)

The environment

As we approach the beginning of the twenty-first century there is an additional factor to consider beyond those of the direct users of the venue, that of the environment. Environmentally Sustainable Development (ESD) involves the responsible use of all the natural resources absorbed by a building, both in its construction and operation. It also requires controls on harmful effluxes such as gases and effluents and, of course, energy efficiency. This last area is a particularly important aspect of ESD for sports stadia, owing to the considerable energy needed to power floodlighting, the illumination of public areas and mechanical ventilation systems often installed for spectator comfort.

The sensible approach is a design strategy in three parts:

- the venue should be designed to use as little energy as possible
- energy demand should be supplied as much as possible from renewable sources

- if non-renewable energy sources are necessary, the least polluting fuel available should be used

Stadium Australia is a pioneering example of how ESD can play a fundamental part in the design of a building (see case study in Part II). The principles we established in Sydney can, however, be applied to any size of venue in most situations.

Generations of stadia

If the emerging sports venues of the late nineteenth century constituted the first generation of stadia, and those that began to supersede them in the post-war period were the second, many of the structures we see today may be considered to represent the third generation.

The first generation developed a reputation for being uncomfortable and sometimes dangerous places, where spectators were denied basic amenities. The second generation sought to win back the hearts and minds of the general public by offering a level of comfort, service and view of the game that could compete with what was available in their own living rooms. They provided more comfortable seating, more seats under cover, toilet facilities for men and women and access to a basic range of food and beverage outlets. In 1955, at the opening of Disneyland in California, Walt Disney announced portentously, 'all who enter here will find happiness and knowledge'. With those words he cast the mould for leisure and entertainment venues for many years to come. In effect, Disneyland was the precursor of the third generation of stadia, which started to emerge in the 1960s and 1970s, places where efficient management, attention to cleanliness and a widening range of spectator facilities for the whole family were on offer, and, most importantly, these were supplemented by information and communication systems which purported to spread knowledge. The successful third-generation stadium, effectively the stadium of today, has become a sophisticated, capital intensive and often profitable installation.

Nevertheless, for all its supposed sophistication, in most cases it still remains vacant for most of the year, and still only caters primarily for its live audience. Indeed, of the many stadia built around the world during the last thirty years, few can claim to be truly multi-functional. Thanks to owner/operators who are either inexperienced or amateurish in their outlook, they have been designed to satisfy poorly drafted, unimaginative briefs. Meanwhile, the construction and design industry has typically seen stadia as crude engineering structures. But there have been improvements. In recent years a huge stock of knowledge has been established in the design, finance and management of sports buildings, so much so that now there is simply no excuse for the ill-informed, ill-conceived developments of the past to continue. In short, we are ready for the fourth generation of stadia.

Visions of the future – the fourth generation

It is never easy to predict the future, but on the basis of the earlier analysis some of the developments that will help shape the sports facilities of the early twenty-first century, the fourth generation of stadia, can already be discerned. As we have already suggested, the spirit, camaraderie, emotion and atmosphere of a great sporting occasion is enhanced by a great venue. The stadium is not a passive backdrop but a theatre set which can only enhance the experience through its design and management. Selling an 'experience' is the core business of any stadium, and will remain so for many years to come.

Nevertheless, the likelihood is that in the fourth generation of stadia, television and the Internet, the 'secondary experience' as it were, will play an increasingly important role, not as an enemy, but as a partner (for clearly the media cannot sell their own packaged sports experience, without a venue to host the event). In 1996 it was calculated that 90 per cent of people with access to a television set watched at least part of the Olympic Games from Atlanta. With television ownership increasing rapidly in the developing nations, it has been estimated that 50 per cent of the world's total population will watch the Sydney Olympics.

Yet it is also worth noting that of the 3,400 hours of Olympic events recorded by television production teams at Atlanta, only around 200 hours was actually broadcast. Logically, therefore, the challenge for the future is to offer more detailed, or specialised coverage of events to a wider, or more specialist audience.

In this respect there is no doubt that the future of sports coverage is digital. The vast majority of spectators in the future will experience sport as a series of 'bits' rather than see the real atoms of the event. These bits of computer information will be distributed around the world by a whole range of methods, from traditional television companies via satellite and cable to clandestine 'ambush' broadcasting ventures utilising miniature cameras, mobile phones and the Internet. This growth in broadcast methods will not necessarily deprive the venue of its core business. Rather it will provide a secondary core business for the owner/operators of the future. In effect, as outlined in the Introduction, stadia will become studios in their own right – centres of television programme making and programme packaging, using both the arena floor and a range of studios and activity spaces designed as part of the overall stadium structure. Indeed, certain broadcasting companies have already recognised this potential and in some parts of the world are already investing in new stadia to ensure that their interests are protected.

In effect, they intend to create two buildings: one a sports and entertainment centre providing action for the live audience, the other a sports and entertainment studio serving the remote audience. One audience will be sitting in stadium seats wired up to fibre optics, through which a number of services will be delivered. The other, much larger, audience will be sitting at home receiving the transmitted digital signal. One intriguing consequence of this arrangement, already discernible in a variety of sports around the world today, is that although the funding of new stadia will no doubt continue to be borne by the live audience through traditional membership, club, bond or private hospitality sales, once the venue is up and running its financial future will rely on the remote audience. In effect, the live audience, though providing useful income through the gate, will itself become increasingly part of the backdrop. After all, half-empty stadia do not make for good television.

For this reason alone, owner/operators will have to work hard to make sure that they can continue to attract as many spectators as possible. This brings us back to the so-called 'SOP'. How will changes in the future affect these three, vital interest groups?

1.10 High quality turf on the pitch at the Reebok Stadium, Bolton; natural turf is still an intrinsic part of some sports

1.11 Giant video screen at Chelsea Football Club to communicate with the crowd

1.10

1.11

1.12 Hand-held receiver to communicate with the individual

1.12

The brief

Good buildings don't just happen. They are the outcome of a two-stage process:

- The first stage is the brief. This is the process of analysing the clients' requirements and all issues associated with those requirements and then laying them out clearly and comprehensively in the brief document. In the USA this stage is often called 'programming'
- The second stage is called design. This is a separate process, though the two stages may run partly in parallel. The design stage brings into play an accumulation of knowledge and experience, aimed at meeting the issues identified in the brief

The brief is therefore the foundation of all subsequent work. For the final design to meet the optimum needs of the client, the brief needs to be as thorough and comprehensive as possible. No matter how much hard work is done at the design stage, should the brief be flawed, or inadequate, problems will almost certainly arise later on. Indeed, whenever a building turns out to be problematic the chances are that the design team will subsequently lay the blame on the client for providing a poor brief. This may or may not be justified, but it is the main reason why we strive to take an active role in the briefing stage, acting as a catalyst in the process and using our experience and a range of standardised facility brief documents to identify and develop the specific needs of the client. There have been studies that suggest 80 per cent of the decisions that will affect the building will be taken in the first 20 per cent of the life of the project.

Compiling the brief document is a collaborative exercise in which the client and architect, aided by specialist advisers, investigate and record every requirement that must be satisfied. The process begins by establishing goals, for example, why does the client wish to build, and what are they hoping to achieve? It then moves on through the determination of needs and the collection and analysis of facts, for example, how many spectators must be accommodated and how much space will they need? The final component is a definitive statement setting out a range of requirements to which planners and designers can respond with solutions. While working through this progression from vague questions to precise answers it is helpful for the briefing team to keep in mind the four basic considerations which govern any building project. These are:

- Function – how must the facility serve its users?
- Form – what physical form the facility might take?
- Economy – the costs involved in constructing and operating the facility, and the expected revenues
- Time – the duration of the design and construction processes (which may be broken into a sequence of phases), and the subsequent life of the facility (Fig. 2.1)

1.16 The pitch at the Millennium Stadium, Cardiff, is completely removable in 1 metre square pallets

1.17 The Alfred McAlpine Stadium, Huddersfield, staging a Bryan Adams concert

1.17

the staging of a variety of different sports with varying demands. First, by incorporating a retractable roof, the stadium of the future will be able to operate both as a closed building (like a dome) and as a conventional, open-air stadium. Second, by adopting flexible turf systems, it will be able to offer a natural surface for field sports, yet be quickly and easily converted so that the turf is temporarily removed to reveal a hard surface underneath. This can in turn be covered by whatever other surface is required, such as carpeting or even surfaces for other sports, such as tennis, indoor athletics, hockey or basketball. We are already working on several projects incorporating this type of flexible technology. True, these systems are relatively expensive. Nor have they yet been fully proven by experience. Nevertheless, the indications are that they will become a practical proposition within the next few years.(Fig. 1.16)

Similarly, the stadium of the future will be able to offer a much higher standard of playing surface. For example, removable cricket wickets are already in limited use and will undoubtedly be seen more and more as technical expertise improves. Meanwhile, several new grass species are being developed that are less susceptible to

damage by roof shadowing and reduced air circulation, and more tolerant to being covered for periods of concerts or exhibition use. Another important development is the combination of natural turf with artificial elements, such as plastic mesh root reinforcement, plastic turf support, and plastic granular growing media for natural grass with computer-controlled nutrient injection. By these means it may be possible to combine the playing characteristics of natural turf with the resilience of synthetics.

We are also seeing the first full-scale use of mechanically movable pitches which are kept in the open fresh air for most of the time and moved into the playing position only during matches. All these exciting developments in roof engineering and turf technology hold out the promise of stadia being able to stage far more events than has been possible in the past. In conclusion, stadia are rapidly evolving so that the owner/operators of the future will more easily and imaginatively be able to protect their core business by integrating other leisure and entertainment uses and thereby ensure that their venues become self-sustaining destinations in their own right. But, as the next chapter reveals, technology alone is not enough. (Fig.1.17)

relationship between the players and spectators. But technology is set to challenge even that assumption, so that the stadium of the future will be able to switch comfortably between the needs of athletics and field sports, without compromising spectators' viewing standards. For example, both Stadium Australia and the Colonial Stadium in Melbourne (see case study in Part II) are designed to have movable lower tiers to allow for football, athletics and even Australian Rules Football (AFL), which is played on a large oval pitch. We are also currently designing what is believed to be the world's first purpose-built combined cricket and rugby stadium in New Zealand. Wellington's Westpac Trust Stadium (see case study in Part II) will appear to be a normal rugby stadium, yet it is designed to accommodate athletics, if required, at a later date. To achieve this multi-functionality is not easy and requires a great deal of careful thought during the initial design process. But the fact that it can be done surely means that there will be fewer single-purpose venues in the future. (Fig. 1.14)

Another means of ensuring that the stadia of the future are used on as many days as possible is to design them in such a way as to make them more attractive for hiring out, as a whole or in part, for non-sporting events. This approach is already well established worldwide when it comes to the wider use of stadia's support facilities, whereby, for example, car parks are made available to general users, restaurants are hired out for functions or, as mentioned earlier, private boxes are converted for use as hotel rooms. In the future, all stadia will follow these principles. However, apart from occasional pop concerts, usually during the non-playing season, a stadium's spectator accommodation and playing area rarely forms part of this equation. That too is set to change quite radically. The process began in the United States in the 1960s, with the building of stadia, or domes, with fixed roofs covering the entire playing area. Although this type of building could be used to stage all kinds of events, such as exhibitions, conferences, concerts and entertainment, the design of the roof allowed only the installation of artificial playing surfaces (the first of which, it will be recalled, was called Astroturf, because it was developed originally for the Houston Astrodome). Such surfaces are not acceptable for most sports in other parts of the world, however, which is why a new generation of stadia is set to evolve. (Fig. 1.15)

Roofs and pitches – new technology

Thanks to further advances in technology, the stadium of the future will be able to offer a much wider range of conditions suitable for both non-sporting use and for

1.16

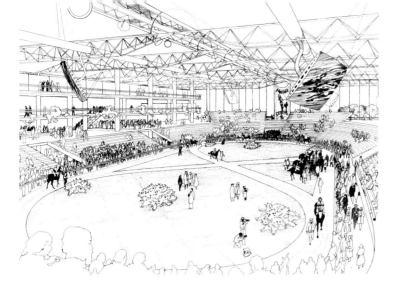

1.15a

1.15b

1.15c

1.15 Sketches showing
a scheme for a covered
parade ring at a
racecourse,
alternatively used as
arena and exhibition
centre

Huddersfield (see case study in Part II) where our award-winning stadium shares its site with a multi-screen cinema and golf driving range while a swimming pool, gym, dance studio, offices and private boxes convert into hotel rooms within the stadium structure itself. In short, the stadium of the future will become an agreeable place of entertainment where people (some of whom may only be mildly interested in sport) can take their families or business acquaintances for an enjoyable afternoon or evening. (Fig. 1.13)

Extending the boundaries

An idle stadium earns no return on the considerable sums that have been invested. Idle time must therefore be reduced to a minimum. In marketing jargon this is referred to as maximising the number of 'use days'. Stadium owner/operators today are already facing up to this challenge, often by adapting their existing facilities. However, the stadium of the future will be designed precisely with maximum utilisation as a fundamental

principle. The most obvious means of achieving this is to make the stadium a base for more than one tenant club. This is an area where Britain has lagged behind certain other countries. Traditionally, it was assumed that if stadia were to be shared, they would be shared by clubs of the same sporting persuasion, as in Italy, for example, where four of the country's largest stadia in Rome, Milan, Turin and Genoa, are each shared by two football clubs. However, as the experience at Huddersfield has shown – and at other British venues which have since followed suit – with pre-planning it is easily possible for one stadium to accommodate two different field sports, football and rugby (three if one includes American football). This is simply because those particular sports require similarly sized rectangular pitches and spectator configurations.

It is more difficult to combine, for example, football and baseball, since they require contrasting pitch layouts and spectator configurations. Similarly, combining athletics with football or rugby has long been regarded as an undesirable match, because the presence of an athletics track around the pitch harms that close

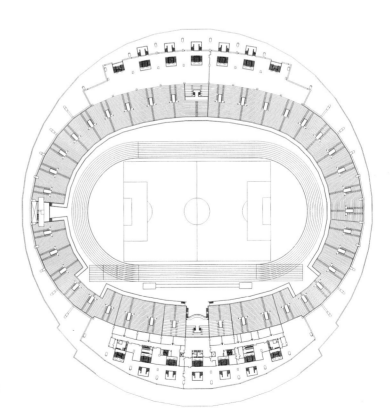

1.14 Plan of Sarawak Stadium, Malaysia, showing comparative distance to football pitch from seating when an athletics track is included

1.14

Keeping ahead of television

We have already noted how modern stadia increasingly need to offer a range of ancillary, non-sporting attractions, ranging from restaurants, cafes and hotels to retail centres, cinemas, video-game arcades, ten-pin bowling alleys and business centres. Undoubtedly the range and sophistication of these additional facilities will continue to expand during the next century. However, an even greater leap forward for spectators will concern their own interaction with the actual event, via a flow of visual and aural information which promises to surpass even that which can be provided by a modern televised broadcast. This advance will come about thanks to spectacular progress in the digital processing of vision, sound, information and communication. Physical closeness to the event, being part of the crowd, will remain the primary attraction, the experience home viewers cannot possibly sample. There will still be close-ups and action replays relayed on huge video screens within the stadium. But in the future these signals will also be narrowcast to small personal receivers provided to spectators at their seats. Furthermore, the range of images and sounds provided will be enhanced by the use of miniature cameras, highly directional microphones and, eventually, personalised virtual reality equipment. In addition, expert commentary, analysis and interviews will fill those stretches of a game when nothing much is happening on the pitch, to form a seamless mix of live action plus entertainment that will rival that of any television broadcast. (Fig. 1.11, 1.12)

However, the spectator will not remain a passive receiver of these services. Instead, he or she will become an active participant. Using a handset which is either integrated within the seat or rented out by the venue operator, spectators of the future will be able to place bets, order drinks and snacks or advance tickets, or call up whatever information they require, be it statistics, records, scores from other venues and so on. After the game music and other attractions will be on offer, all designed to keep the spectator on the stadium premises for as long as possible, thereby providing additional useful revenue. Every class of spectator will be catered for. A family of five, for example, will be able to arrive and leave together but do different things in between. While the parents watch the live game the children may prefer to experience the game from a virtual reality studio where images from in-pitch cameras provide close-up action. Some of the family may wish to spend time in the stadium museum, shop and entertainment arcade or food outlet, ranging from simple fast-food counters to luxury silver service restaurants. Spectators will be able to stroll along concourses resembling high streets, circumnavigating the event bowl, which lies just behind the first row of shops. A business group could use the same stadium as a meeting venue, having access to the sort of facilities usually offered by a conference centre (including a hotel for staying overnight), but with the addition of a top-class sporting event thrown in to give the venue a competitive edge over its less exciting rivals. These principles can already be seen in a modest way at the Alfred McAlpine Stadium in

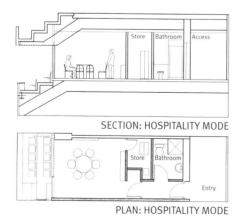

SECTION: HOSPITALITY MODE

PLAN: HOSPITALITY MODE

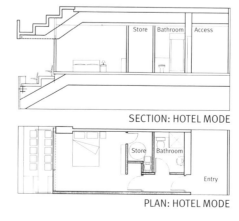

SECTION: HOTEL MODE

PLAN: HOTEL MODE

1.13 Plans and sections showing conversion of a hospitality box into a hotel room at the Alfred McAlpine Stadium, Huddersfield

1.13

Brief development

The brief for a modern sports facility is usually too complex to be compiled all at once. Rather, it should develop in stages, first asking (and getting answers to) the most fundamental questions. In their simplest form, these questions are:

2.1

- Who are the proposed customers? What kinds of people are they? How many of them are there? What are their basic requirements?
- What type of event is the venue intended to stage?
- Who are the likely participants in those events? How many of them are there? What are their requirements?

2.1 The Alfred McAlpine Stadium, Huddersfield, conceived as a phased development which dictated its form – each stand is structurally independent

– What other services, such as restaurant, shopping or business facilities are proposed?

– What provision for storage, service access, parking and so on must be provided on site for spectators and participants and their vehicles and equipment?

– What provision must be made for future developments in all these areas?

Once basic questions such as these have been answered the design team can commence feasibility studies and the masterplanning of the site. From that point onwards, the brief will develop into a continuous process of further investigation into increasingly detailed issues, leading from there to the design development of physical solutions to these issues (although in practice both strands often run in parallel).

Briefing aids

To draw up a brief for a building type as complex as a sports facility, subject as they are to such stringent criteria for functional and economic success, is no easy task. Experience is vital if the right questions are to be asked and their relative importance ranked accordingly, so that matters of high priority do not get lost in a forest of detail. Moreover, because the vast majority of clients who commission sports buildings very rarely become involved in such projects more than once or twice in their lifetimes, few of them can be guided by their own past experience. It is doubly important, therefore, that such clients use designers who have a stock of practical experience and knowledge to draw upon.

In the course of researching and evolving designs for hundreds of sports facilities in twelve different countries, covering all the major sporting types, we have gained extensive experience of developing and drawing up briefs, experience which we have distilled into a set of computerised aids to assist clients. Collectively these briefing aids amount to more than 200 sheets of information and data, divided into four categories, three of which reflect the needs of those groups we referred to in the previous chapter as the SOP, the spectators, owner/operators and participants, together with a

Table 2.1 Business aims table

EVENTS	SPECTATORS	FINANCE	FACILITIES
Core Events	Customer Base	SWOT Analysis	Site Options
Multi Use Events	Ideal Customer	Business Plan	Master Plan
Limitations	Competition	Funds Analysis	Access
Management	Demographics	Capital & Debt	Revenue Sources
Operations	Isochronal	Grants & Gifts	Environmental
Events Calendar	Age Groups	Life Cycle Costs	Town Planning
Promoters	Marketing	Debentures	Authorities
Contracts	Hearts & Minds	Hospitality	Design
Return on Effort	Public Perception	Advertising	Documentation
Community	Ticket Packages	Naming	Procurement
Greater Good	Enjoyment	Cost Control	Commission & Monitor

Platinum members	Fine dining	Themed retail	Stadium travel
Gold members	Themed restaurant	Parent facilities	Event experience
Silver members	Dining lounge	Mail order	TV production
Private hospitality	Executive dining	Conference centre	Digital production
Loge hospitality	Club dining	Supporters' club	Themed retailing
Club members	Members' dining	Exhibitions	Photo studio
VIP	Silver service	Customer care	Museum
Visiting VIP	Club dining	First aid	Video arcade
Affiliated members	Stepped restaurant	Hire shop	Betting shop
Executive	Food court	Retail outlet	Theatre
Member seating	Fast food	Programme sales	TV screens
General seating	Snack bar	Child care	Interactive displays
Public seating	Drinks bar	Ticket sales	Tours
Bench seating	Confectionery stall	Telephones	Multi sports
Perch seating	Mobile stall	Toilets	Lounges
Standing	Hawkers	Business centre	Picnic area

2.2

2.2 Matrix of event experience to be considered in the briefing process (20,000 spectators of 20,000 different requirements)

fourth category covering general matters. The main areas covered by the briefing aids are as follows:

Spectators

- Capacity – project analysis and calculation of maximum capacities
- Sightlines – 'C' value calculation, section profiling, optimum bowl analysis
- Seating position – possible tread widths, seating centres, fixing methods
- Movable seating – assessment of need, extent of provision, configurations
- Private boxes – space requirements, services required, configuration options
- Club-type facilities – space requirements, services needs, configuration options
- External circulation – space requirements, distribution, layouts
- Turnstiles – numbers calculation, typical arrangement, size requirements
- Stairs – numbers calculation, size requirements, relationship to ramps, positioning
- Ramps – numbers calculation, size requirements, relationship to stairs, positioning
- Lifts and escalators – numbers calculation, size requirements, grouping, positioning
- Internal circulation – space requirements, distribution, layouts
- Crowd control – analysis and arrangement of control and safety measures
- Timed exit analysis – calculation and design of exit routes to meet specific exit times

- Exit gates – numbers required, size requirements, general distribution
- Toilets – ratio of male to female, numbers required, grouping, flexibility for varying events
- Information systems – general requirements, locations, appropriate technology
- Communication systems – requirements, possible locations, technology
- Transport – parking required, operational requirements, road and public transport links
- Security – general provision, strategic location, typical facility arrangements
- First aid – numbers relating to spectators, space requirements, positioning
- Signage and graphics – strategic information, numbers required, positioning
- Child care – typical space requirements, positioning, general layout
- Customer care – total numbers relating to capacity, space requirements
- Betting outlets – outlets required, space requirements, positioning
  (Fig. 2.2)

Owner/operators

- Stadium administration – space requirements, relationships, positioning
- Advertising – numbers of boards and panels, positioning to pitch, in-house locations
- Broadcasting – space requirements, servicing, positioning, general layout
- Media facilities – numbers, sizes, relationships, flexibility for different events
- Media support – vehicle park, signal relay positions, temporary services provision
- Stadium control – space requirements, servicing, positioning, layout
- Snack concessions – numbers, space requirements, relationships
- Fast food concessions – numbers, space requirements, relationships
- Beverage concessions – numbers, space requirements, relationships
- Speciality concessions – numbers, space requirements, positioning
- Vending and ATM machines – services, numbers, positioning
- Catering – catering operations, typical layouts, space requirements
- Ticketing (advance sales and match day) – numbers, space requirements, positioning
- Retailing – numbers, space requirements, relationships, positioning
- Programme sales – numbers, space requirements, relationships, positioning
- Cleaning and maintenance – operational methods, space requirements
- Operators' storage – space requirements, access, positioning
- Public safety systems – requirements, locations, appropriate technology
- Fire safety – approach, methods of minimising compartmentation

Participants

- Changing facilities – space requirements, relationships, positioning
- Medical facilities – space requirements, relationships, positioning
- Participants' storage – numbers, space requirements, positioning
- Concert facilities – space requirements, special services, positioning
- Activity area – general pitch and track design, construction, servicing necessary
- Activity technology – sports operation technology, measurement, recording
- Security – general provision, location, facility layout
- Pitch lighting – lumen requirements, fixture location, general strategy
- Participants' social facilities – space requirements, positioning
- Support facilities – space requirements, services, positioning

General

Programme – typical time-scales, construction elements sequence

Materials – selection, detailing for public safety

Building control – general approach to applications, supporting information

Sub-contractors – specialist sports sub-contractors' involvement, strategic roles

Construction safety team – safety strategy for site, supporting information

Construction – typical sports details, methods, sequences of construction

Roof coverage – design approach, extent, percentage of coverage (Fig. 2.3)

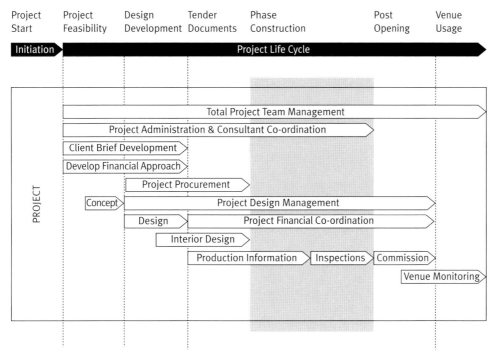

2.3 Project life cycle design approach

2.3

Feasibility studies

The cycle of success

The process of making a building is a clearly defined sequence of analysis, assessment and then design, starting with 'the big picture' before gradually focusing upon the details. Part of the big picture, before agreeing the masterplan, is the analysis of feasible options. In practice the two stages will often overlap, with various outline designs being developed and tested for feasibility before a final version is firmed up to become the formal masterplan. This chapter and the next should therefore be read in this context.

To make a sport development 'work' in all its forms, four elements essential to its eventual financial success must be progressed together. These four elements – facilities, events, spectators, finances – we call the cycle of success.

In the cycle of success all four elements are interdependent. If the finance can be raised there is more chance of building the correct facilities. Creating the right facilities will attract the right events, which in turn will attract spectators. By demonstrating that the building will attract sufficient numbers of spectators, the client has the optimum chance of raising the necessary finance. And so the cycle of success goes round. Equally, if just one link in the cycle were to prove weak, or to be overlooked, the whole project would be placed in jeopardy. For this reason, the involvement

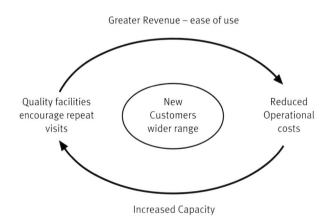

3.1 New facilities outline diagram

3.1

of financiers in design matters and designers becoming involved with event scheduling can be of benefit to the project's overall chances of becoming a successful reality. (Fig. 3.1)

Facilities

At an early stage in the briefing process, once the client's wishes and desires are known but before any party becomes too deeply enmeshed in fine detail, the actual physical viability of the project needs to be assessed. Only then can a realistic decision be made as to whether the project is viable. Some pivotal questions that need to be answered at this stage include:

–   Is the site in the right location?
–   How compatible is the surrounding environment?
–   Is the site suitable in shape, area and topography?
–   Are its critical dimensions adequate?
–   Can it actually accommodate the proposed facilities and allow for future possible expansion?
–   Does the site have adequate access and links to public transport?
–   Are there sufficient public utilities available?

These are only a few of the key issues to be addressed. To assist in determining some of the answers a range of physical tests will usually be required, such as a topographical survey of the site, soil investigation, tree species analysis and a search of the site's legal status. Other more complex investigations will then follow, to determine, for example, the proposal's acceptability to local planners and the highway authorities, before preliminary discussions can begin towards the attainment of outline planning consent at feasibility stage.

Issues relating to facilities are usually the responsibility of the architects and their fellow consultants. But as we emphasised earlier, it is unwise to separate issues relating to facilities from the three others within the cycle of success.

Events

It is crucial to determine the type and the number of events, which might realistically be staged at the proposed venue, rather than plan for possible events only. To determine this requires combinations of common sense, thorough research, expert knowledge of the local markets and, never forget, a touch of vision too. In drawing up a project's 'event schedule' it is advisable to categorise each event in terms of the likelihood of it being staged, expressed as a level of risk: low, medium or high. Typically, a low level of risk will be attached to those events that are certain to be staged. For example, if the main client is a football club, it knows for certain that all its team's home games will be staged at the new venue. Similarly, the proposed venue may be a direct replacement for an old one, in which case it is more likely to inherit the old venue's event schedule.

Medium-risk events might include new or additional events, which the proposed venue might well attract, dependent upon the building's suitability. A financial judgement then has to be made as to whether it is worth designing the venue to accommodate such events. Other events might fall into the high-risk category. These could be events for which several other established venues are competing (for example, major international sporting events, rock concerts or exhibitions). Until actual contracts are signed between the venue and those responsible for such events, any inclusion of those events within the event schedule must remain a matter of speculative assessment. Each project will have its own set of questions concerning the event schedule, but a few key issues are as follows:

–   Are the events established in the area or would people in the catchment area regard them as a new 'product'?
–   How much marketing will be required for the events to be a success?
–   What special demands will these events place on the design of the venue?
–   What special demands will these events place on the management of the venue?
–   Is critical infrastructure required for a particular event to be a success?
–   What is the minimum attendance needed at an event for it to be financially successful?

3.2 The business plan highlighting the public demand for a greater diversity of facilities

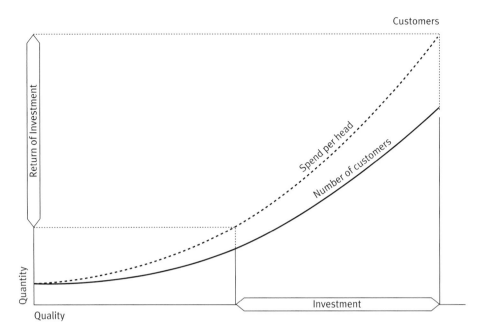

3.2

Spectators

Different events attract different types of spectators. During the feasibility stage it is important, therefore, to assess exactly what type of spectators will be using the venue so that the facilities are designed to cater for their different needs. For example, a football match might attract a predominantly male audience with perhaps only 15 per cent of the total being female. However, a rugby match at the same venue might attract twice that number of females, with a pop concert attracting an equal number of males and females.

Those attending a sport event in the afternoon may have different demands from those attending a concert staged in the evening. The feasibility study should not only take the needs of potential spectators into account; further consideration might also need to be given to the requirements of a local planning authority, which might, for example, demand the provision of additional accommodation for young children, for the elderly or for spectators with disabilities. The feasibility study might also have to take into account the likely objections of local residents. Among the questions which arise with respect to

spectators are the following:

– How easily can the target audience get to the proposed venue?
– What is the local competition in both venues and events?
– Does the local population fit the customer profile for the project?
– Is there support for the project in the local area?

Finance

If the site, its location and the proposed facilities seem viable and the event schedule demonstrates that sufficient spectators will attend sufficient events at the venue then the next step is to put together the financial plan necessary to complete the project's overall business plan. The business plan will take into account all the elements already discussed in this chapter, but especially the two finance-related elements of cost and revenue. The projected costs of the proposal should be estimated along with the projected income. From this information a cash flow analysis can then be prepared to determine whether the two can be balanced successfully. (Fig. 3.2)

An accurate determination of the proposed facility's cost is a relatively straightforward matter once a detailed design has been prepared, its specifications completed and a Bill of Quantities prepared. However, that point in a project invariably comes quite late in the development programme, certainly too late for the owner/operator or client who wants a reasonably reliable cost assessment at the initial concept or even masterplan stage. For this reason capital costs are usually estimated at an early stage by referring to the known costs of earlier projects. In this respect it is usual to express stadia or arena construction costs in terms of a 'cost per seat' equivalent. The cost per seat will vary dramatically between projects, depending on the extent of fit-out, the quality of finishes and, of course, the number of seats designed into the facility. One general rule, however, is that the more seats in a venue, the more expensive will be the cost per seat. This is owing to the greater height of the structure, the more sophisticated safety systems required and the greater range of service facilities which will be needed. (Fig. 3.3)

Thus costs per seat can range from around £500 for a relatively simple, single-tier grandstand to over £2,000 for a more sophisticated venue featuring additional tiers, complex roof structures and a full range of amenities. (Note that the cost per seat for arenas can easily exceed even that figure, because of the additional information

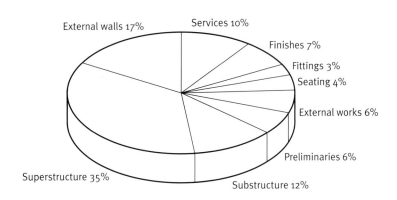

External walls 17%   Services 10%
Finishes 7%
Fittings 3%
Seating 4%
External works 6%
Preliminaries 6%
Superstructure 35%
Substructure 12%

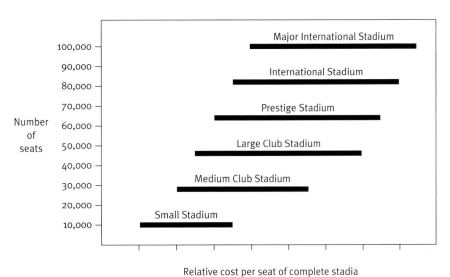

Number of seats

100,000 — Major International Stadium
90,000 —
80,000 — International Stadium
70,000 — Prestige Stadium
60,000 —
50,000 — Large Club Stadium
40,000 —
30,000 — Medium Club Stadium
20,000 —
10,000 — Small Stadium

Relative cost per seat of complete stadia

3.3 Cost comparison diagrams reflecting the increased costs of stadia proportional to size

3.4

3.4 The sale of the
naming rights of this
stadium to Reebok
was used to raise funds
in an increasing trend
to more commercial
venues

and communication systems required in such venues and
the extent of 'back of house' facilities provided as a proportion of the overall floor area.) Operating costs are
usually worked out as a percentage of the capital cost and
the total number of spectators to be accommodated.
Revenues are calculated by determining an anticipated
'spend per head' on concessions and merchandising.
These figures are then combined with the anticipated
revenue from ticket and other sources of income, related
mainly to the venue's event profile and the anticipated
number of spectators. From these projections a business
plan can then be constructed. The whole subject of
financial planning is both daunting and complex but at
least some of the issues are as follows:

- Is the venue to be a 'clean' venue – that is, available to event holders without revenue claims from other agencies, such as broadcasters, sponsors or concession holders – or are there pre-sold elements which will reduce the event holder's potential income?
- Have the venue's advertising and naming rights been sold?
- What outside funding or grants are available?
- If there is a shortfall in revenue, what level of borrowing is possible, based upon the revenue projections?
- Can the potential revenue be increased by an increase in event scheduling?

So we can see that by a detailed feasibility study into all the above elements, a picture emerges of how viable the project is likely to be. Often, it has to be said, the enthusiasm of clients for a particular sports-related project blinds them to the harsher realities. On the other hand, few great stadia have ever been built without vision. Thus the purpose of a feasibility study is to provide a balance between enthusiasm, vision and sheer common sense – to determine whether that all-important cycle of success can be realistically attained, before further time and effort is expended on the next stage of the process.

Masterplanning

Outline concept

If the feasibility study confirms that the project is worth pursuing, the next stage is for the design team to firm up the masterplan. This deals largely with the overall site layout, the relationship between buildings, and their relationship with the site. In sports architecture the masterplan usually takes into account the outline design of individual buildings and the organisation of the site plan in terms of vehicles and people. The masterplanners' basic tasks will generally be as follows:

- To fix a size and orientation for the event area pitch or track. Pitch sizes and layouts are generally prescribed by national and international governing bodies (details of which are held on our database). Orientation must be such that players and runners do not have the late afternoon sun in their eyes. Pitches and tracks are therefore normally orientated on approximately a north–south axis, although there are some notable exceptions to this rule of thumb, including Wembley Stadium (Fig. 4.1)
- To surround the pitch or track with one or more spectator seating areas. The positioning and layout of these areas must be planned to accommodate the required number of spectators, locating them as close as possible to the event while ensuring that they will enjoy acceptable sightlines (measured in terms of 'C' values) without any viewing restrictions or obstructions
- To serve the above areas with the appropriate standard and number of supporting facilities, such as players' and officials' changing rooms, toilets, food and beverage outlets, shops and amusement facilities, offices and media facilities
- To ensure that access and facilities for spectators with disabilities are provided as required

Because of the numerous issues and options that invariably emerge during the masterplan stage, we have developed a set of computer aids to facilitate a rational, step-by-step approach. Among the selection of aids available are the following:

- Field and track layouts for the majority of internationally recognised sports (including racetrack layouts)
- Stand capacity analysis
- Sightline generation and computation
- Stadium profile generation
- Seating space parameters
- Venue management and operation provisions (including back of house areas)
- Food and beverage planning parameters
- Concession computation and layout
- Toilet facility calculation

4.1 Orientation diagram showing A as the best common orientation for many sports, B as the range acceptable for football and rugby and C as the best range for track and field events and pitch games

4.2 Directional signage in clear open concourses at (a) Stadium Australia, Sydney and (b) the Alfred McAlpine Stadium, Huddersfield (Trends Publishing International, photographer Michael Nicholson)

4.2a

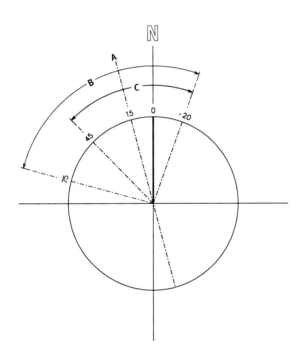

4.1

4.2b

Planning for spectator circulation

The arrangement of circulation routes for vehicles in and around the stadium site is obviously a key element of the masterplan. In addition, the plan must consider access routes to all service and delivery points, plus adequate parking for all potential users, spectators, staff, event and media personnel. But these matters are secondary to, and will only follow on from, the masterplan's primary issue, that of spectator circulation.

At any stadium or arena, this must be the overriding priority of any masterplan. The site's layout and the arrangement of buildings must make allowance for clear access routes from the site entrances (from public roads or from public transport nodes), through the gates, leading into designated circulation routes and onwards into the spectator areas. (Fig.4.2a, 4.2b)

At the end of the event the flow needs to be reversible, allowing safe egress back to the public realm. It is this network of access and egress routes, which

4.3 Vertical circulation via escalator and stair at Stadium Australia, Sydney moving large numbers of people in short periods of time

4.3

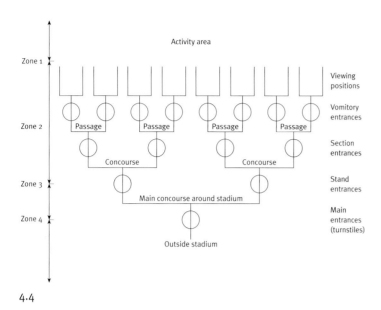

Zone 1

Activity area

Zone 2

Viewing positions

Vomitory entrances

Passage   Passage   Passage   Passage

Section entrances

Concourse   Concourse

Zone 3

Stand entrances

Main concourse around stadium

Zone 4

Main entrances (turnstiles)

Outside stadium

4.4 Spectator flow diagram representing the movement of spectators through a venue

forms the framework around which the body of the venue is built. Crowd circulation is, by its very nature, a complex issue. When the public gather and act in groups, particularly at sporting events, they are often unable or unwilling to make clear decisions. It is absolutely necessary therefore to plan circulation routes in such a way as to present them with simple, clear options. For this reason, wherever possible, access and egress routes tend to be planned as a series of 'Y' or 'T' junctions, offering simple 'yes' or 'no' choices, leading the spectator directly to where they want to be and avoiding the need for complex decision making. Even large stadia can be planned so that this sequence of 'yes' and 'no' decisions is reduced to between four and six key points. Equally, within this network it is important to allow spectators who do take the wrong route to be able to find a logical route back. These secondary 'correcting routes' are almost as important for efficient flow and safety as are the primary circulation routes. (Fig. 4.3)

In addition to planning for circulation in normal conditions, clear and reliable circulation routes are a matter of life and death in emergencies. In this respect, the preservation of life inside a facility must take precedence over the preservation of the building itself. One crucial measure of a stadium's level of safety is the length of time spectators need to move from their seat, first to a 'temporary safety zone' and from there to a 'permanent safety zone' outside the venue. For design purposes, this so-called 'emergency exit' or 'evacuation time' is expressed as a maximum, and is prescribed in advance by the relevant planning or safety authorities, depending upon the nature of the building and the materials used in its construction. The range of times varies from country to country – usually between 5 and 10 minutes – but the method of calculation is the same in all situations. We refer to the calculation method as the 'Timed Exit Analysis' (or TEA). It is based on agreed assumptions as to how many people per minute can safely pass through a particular width of passage, gate or turnstile. A clear width of 600 mm is regarded as the minimum sufficient for one person. A width of 1,200 mm would allow two people to pass through, side by side.

Zoning for safety

The safety of spectators in a stadium is of course paramount. Yet by their very nature, stadia are caught between two conflicting requirements. Fire safety planning requires that the buildings are easy to escape from, yet security considerations dictate that the building should be difficult to get into. The only way to resolve this conflict between circulation in emergency conditions and circulation in normal conditions is to plan the overall site in terms of four concentric zones. (Fig. 4.4)

At the centre is Zone 1. This is the pitch, field or track where events are staged. In certain situations the

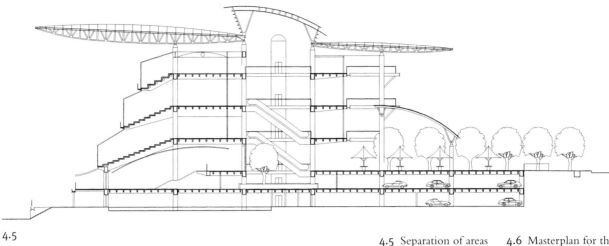

4.5

4.5 Separation of areas through use of a central atrium at the Royal Selangor Turf Club, Malaysia

4.6 Masterplan for the Alfred McAlpine Stadium, Huddersfield, and associated developments

evacuation of spectators onto Zone 1, deemed to be a 'temporary safety refuge', may be acceptable, providing spectators can then be directed to the 'permanent' safety area of Zone 4. Immediately surrounding the activity area is Zone 2, consisting of the spectator seating areas. Encircling the seating areas is Zone 3, the venue's main circulation area, whose outer edge is the stadium perimeter, containing the gates and turnstiles where entry and exit are controlled. Beyond the perimeter fence is Zone 4, the final point of 'permanent' safety, usually a public space or, in some situations, the stadium car park.

In the event of an emergency, spectators must be able to escape from Zone 2 either to Zone 1 or Zone 3. However, as mentioned above, both these zones can only be considered as temporary refuges, where people may be safe for a defined period of time only, before they exit from these areas to Zone 4, the final safety zone. It follows that Zone 4 must be completely safe and large enough to accommodate the entire capacity of the venue. Zoning safety areas in this fashion might seem obvious, but tragically hundreds of people have died in older stadia (such as at Bradford, England, in 1985) because the escape routes and safety zones were not adequately planned or managed to allow for emergencies. Yet even with clear zoning, planning sufficient

escape routes of a specified width and with adequate refuges can be an extremely complex matter, particularly in large scale stadia consisting of several levels and featuring a network of normal circulation routes and holding areas. The masterplan should therefore take into account a number of key issues:

–   The site must be sufficiently large to accommodate each anticipated use
–   The site must be sufficiently large to accommodate the required safety zones
–   The site should be fully zoned from the beginning
–   Related uses should be kept together
–   Incompatible uses should be kept apart
–   Each facility within the overall site should have the necessary access points, parking areas and servicing
–   Provision should be made for future development

Planning for multiple use

All too often owner/operators commission new sports facilities and then discover that while they may have planned adequately for their own core business, that is, for the main sports event, they have failed to plan for

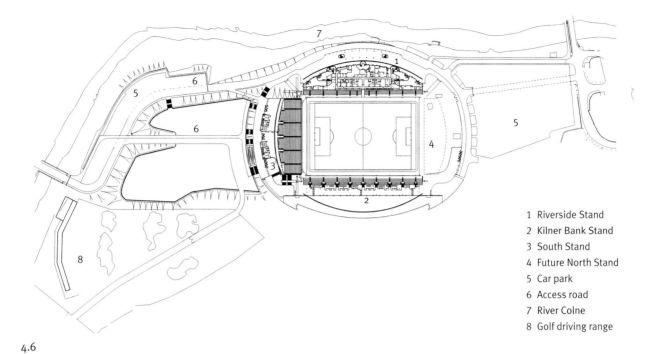

1 Riverside Stand
2 Kilner Bank Stand
3 South Stand
4 Future North Stand
5 Car park
6 Access road
7 River Colne
8 Golf driving range

4.6

relatively mundane, but still vital requirements related to other uses of the venue. For example, the provision of storage areas for retail or catering areas or of access routes for large vehicles delivering materials for other events. The multiple use of spaces in sports buildings is therefore a prime consideration in the masterplanning process, affecting as it does many of the most fundamental decisions concerning site layout and building geometry.

Our design for the Royal Selangor Turf Club in Malaysia (see case study in Part II) is just one such example. In order to maximise the stand's usage, yet minimise its operational complexities, it was planned as two parallel buildings, with racing facilities (such as seating and betting outlets) on the track side, and restaurants and other facilities along the entrance side. Between these two halves of the building was added an atrium, designed either to connect or to separate the two areas, depending on what may be required on any particular occasion. So, on event days, racegoers can cross the atrium in order to enjoy the full range of consumer facilities contained within the outer half. At other times the atrium link is blocked off so that the outer half may function independently as a general leisure facility for the local community, open seven days

a week and with its own self-contained service routes and access points. (Fig. 4.5)

But whatever the level of the building's sophistication, the likelihood is that at least some part of it will need to be used for other activities on non-event days, and that all such usage must be considered at the masterplan stage. If it is not, later changes or additions may well turn out to be complex and expensive, and perhaps even impossible.

Planning for the future

Sports complexes are seldom constructed in their entirety in a single phase. For reasons of finance, land availability or changing needs, a site may be developed piecemeal over a period of years or even decades. To avoid the work completed during the first phase of development conflicting with later additions it is therefore advisable to create, at least in outline, a comprehensive plan for the entire site's long-term development. Later phases can then be implemented if necessary by different committees, boards or even architects in the safe knowledge that what they are planning is less likely to create new problems in the future. This consideration of the future is one of the most important functions of masterplanning. (Fig. 4.6)

Spectator needs

The three previous chapters outlined our general strategy when approaching the initial stages of design. We now turn to the more specific needs of the three primary interest groups identified in Chapter 1, the spectators, owner/operators and participants (the so-called SOP). Starting with the most important interest group of all, we firmly believe that the best way to design for spectators is to look at the facility from their point of view, tracing their progress from the stadium's entrance gate, through to the public concourses and on to the viewing areas, highlighting at each stage the issues which affect their comfort, safety and well-being.

The queuing experience

No public assembly building, least of all a large stadium can ever hope to serve all its customers simultaneously. A spectator attending an event must inevitably stand in a series of queues; for entry at the stadium entrance, to be served at the bars, eating places or at the shop counter, to use the toilets and finally to make their exit. It follows that if their queuing experiences are boring or stressful then it is unlikely the spectator will wholeheartedly enjoy the event, stay as long as possible or, most importantly, want to come again. Queuing should therefore be made as congenial and discreet as possible. People's willingness to stand in a line is highly variable and depends on both physical and psychological influences. The physical factors are plain enough. The more comfortable and attractive the surroundings, the more

tolerant people in the queue are likely to be. But the psychological influences are not so obvious.

One of the chief factors likely to influence people's level of tolerance is the purpose for which they are queuing. If the queue is for tickets to a major event, individuals may be prepared to wait in line for an hour or more, knowing that their choice of event has been vindicated by the large numbers of other people also wanting tickets. In addition, they may encounter a spirit of kinship with their fellow enthusiasts. However, if the queue has a purely functional purpose, perhaps to gain entry to toilets within the venue, then individuals are more likely to become vexed and impatient after only a few minutes. A second factor is the nature of the queuing experience itself, a factor which can be illustrated by comparing a queue at, for example, an old-style football stadium with one at a theme park such as Disneyland. (Fig. 5.1)

In the case of a football match lasting 90 minutes, a 15-minute queuing time represents a queue-to-event ratio of only 1:6. Yet, clearly, people who are required to stand in poor conditions in bleak surroundings, exposed to the elements and with no distractions, will soon become bored or impatient. Worse, the duration of the queue in such circumstances might persuade those individuals who are less than committed that the experience is not worth repeating. In contrast, people attending Disneyland may have to queue for, say, 45 minutes for a ride lasting only 1.5 minutes. In this instance, the queue-to-event ratio is an apparently punishing 30:1. So how do Disneyland's operators manage to persuade their customers to undergo this queuing experience not once, but repeatedly during the course of a single day? The answer is, of course, that they attempt to transform the queuing experience into a 'pre-event', first, by ensuring that people are as physically comfortable as possible and, second, by enlivening the experience with interesting and attention-catching diversions designed to form a minor source of entertainment in themselves. Typical techniques include the following:

– The queue is routed around a twisting line of barriers so that people can more easily see others moving forward gradually, while at the same time giving them the impression that they are close to the entry points. This will mean that they are less inclined to jostle their way forward
– The queue is routed through a sequence of attractive, relevant spaces specifically designed to create an enjoyable atmosphere. Along the route, happenings are staged to serve as a warm-up to the main event; for example, brief appearances by clowns or other performers. In this way customers are kept entertained, while at the same time their sense of anticipation is enhanced as they queue
– While people are queuing they are provided with a continuous flow of information, for example, telling them how long they must still wait before reaching the entry point and what other rides or events are on offer for their later enjoyment. Whether people are awaiting a ride at Disneyland or a commuter train at a station, most individuals are far less likely to become irritable if they are kept informed of progress
– The design and routing of the queuing area is discreet rather than plainly visible to large numbers of patrons, who might otherwise be deterred from joining

Largely as a result of these relatively simple but effective techniques, a Disneyland crowd usually comes away from its 1.5 or 3 minute ride well satisfied, even though they might have spent most of the previous hour standing in line. But even at stadia where such techniques might not always be possible to implement, a few basic factors should always be considered.

For example, people queue more happily in spaces that are commodious, light and airy, and with surfaces finished in materials, textures and colours that are interesting and stimulating. The determination of widths and heights is important. Excessively large spaces are uneconomic, and can encourage queues to become wider and less manageable. On the other hand, excessively narrow spaces with low ceilings are unpleasant and even dangerous. To determine the appropriate

5.1 Twisting routed
queue form at
EuroDisney

5.1

dimensions and layouts of areas where people might be queuing (inside or outside the stadium), typically designers need to ask the following questions:

–   How many people will need to use the space at any given time?
–   At any given point along the route, are people more likely to be stationary, moving slowly or moving rapidly?
–   Are they likely to be purposeful or merely passing time?
–   Are they likely to be heading in a clear direction or milling around, uncertain of where to go?
–   In what frame of mind are people in queues likely to be – will they be eagerly anticipating an exciting event or merely waiting their turn for something routine?

As we have noted earlier from the Disneyland experience, people who are impatient, tired or bored need to be stimulated. This can be done by utilising a number of different methods:

–   Things to look at – such as display windows, wall posters, informational signs, advertisements and video screen displays. Some of these visual displays could provide information about the history of the venue or its resident team, or about current and future events. Others could be rented out as commercial display space. With a captive audience the latter can be a profitable proposition.

–   Things to listen to – such as recorded announcements, commercials and music, or even live music. For example, on the ground floor concourse of the North Bank Stand of Arsenal Football Club in London (see case study in Part II) a live band plays during the hour or so before each match, adding enormously to the festive atmosphere and to crowd enjoyment. Once the actual event has started, people in queues may also want to hear live coverage of the event so that they don't lose touch with what is happening.
–   Strategically located respites – to provide a break from the routines of walking and waiting. Again in London, halfway down the main exit stairs at Chelsea Football Club's North Stand (see case study in Part II) a lobby space has been provided leading directly to a reception and bar area, where people can stop off for a short rest, drink or snack until the conditions are quieter. This is the indoor equivalent of one of those strategically located resting places or cafes one sees along walking trails. (Fig. 5.2)

All the above possibilities should be explored, but there may be plenty of other techniques, which suit particular situations or types of spectator. For example, also at Arsenal Football Club, we decided to place mirrors directly on the walls next to the queuing areas for food and drink concessions. This was in the hope that people would jostle less if they could see themselves doing it. After a couple of seasons' use, it seems to be working.

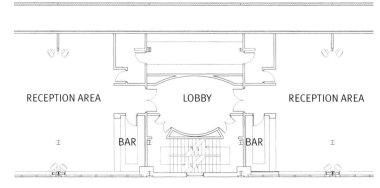

5.2 Lobby space leading to reception and bar areas at Chelsea Football Club

RECEPTION AREA   LOBBY   RECEPTION AREA

BAR   BAR

5.2

Spectator safety

As spectators move towards their seats (or back towards the exit after the event) they must not only be safe but they must also feel safe – no simple matter in large venues with stepped tiers, ramps and stairs, and possibly boisterous crowds. A number of key factors can assist in this aspect of the design of spectator circulation routes. First, the geometry of stadium structures should be sufficiently open and clear to allow spectators always to see where they are going, and to see alternative routes should the obvious path be blocked. Awareness of what lies ahead is vital to crowd safety, since experience has shown that the unknown can prompt anxiety and even panic among large numbers of people in confined situations. (Fig. 5.3)

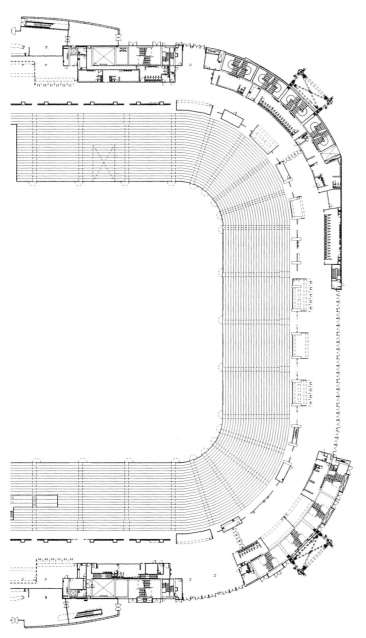

5.3 Plan showing clear open concourses (South side) at the Millennium Stadium, Cardiff

5.4 Directional signage in the concourses at Arsenal, North Stand

5.3

5.4

5.5 'Indoor streets' of
Stadium Australia,
Sydney offering a
range of concessions

5.5

Routes of labyrinthine complexity with closed views are therefore definitely to be avoided along circulation paths wherever possible. Sudden changes in surface level, in corridor width, or in lightness and darkness must be seen in advance so that when the crowd happens upon the change they are not caught by surprise. Provided they are properly designed, such changes in the circulation route are not necessarily bad, and in certain situations they can actually be beneficial. For instance, a change of level within the vomitory (that is, the entry point to the seating area of a stand) may help to dissipate any forward pushing movement into the seating area. It may also assist people in moving crowds to orient themselves by seeing over the heads of those in front.

This spatial clarity should be reinforced with an equally clear and visible signage system. For example, directional signs should ideally offer routes to no more than two alternative sections of the stadium. Once spectators have reached their appropriate section, the next sign may offer a further choice between two alternative blocks of seats within that section. The third sign may direct them to the correct row of seats. To reinforce this clarity, each part of the stadium might also feature a distinguishing colour, applied to some or all of the

elements in that area, such as the tickets for that area, the signs for that area and even the actual seats within that area. This allows the spectator to be guided almost without thinking. (Fig. 5.4)

Even in the best planned and most clearly signposted venue, some spectators will inevitably be indecisive about where they are going and, as a result, hesitate or change course, thus potentially obstructing the people behind. Or they may know exactly where they are going but decide suddenly to turn back, perhaps to go to the toilet at the last minute or to retrieve a forgotten item. Such sudden changes of movement and direction, even on the part of just one individual, can have serious consequences in crowded situations. For this reason, each circulation route should have strategically placed lay-bys, or quiet areas out of the main stream of traffic, where people can stop, think, wait for their friends to catch up or perhaps change course without obstructing the moving crowd. Lay-bys are particularly useful at those points where people enter or leave an area within the venue (which is where they tend to become most indecisive), and also at points near to exits, where the spatial widening helps to increase the flow capacity of the exit route just where it is most needed.

Spectator services

The majority of services provided for the largest percentage of spectators within a stadium are usually located along the main concourses (the Zone 2 referred to earlier). Such concourses are in effect 'indoor streets' with shops and outlets just as one would find in a typical high street, but with most of the queuing taking place within the street area itself. Clearly, the better these concourses are equipped and designed, the more revenue they are likely to yield. This is not always easy, if only because of the shallow building depth available in most stadium situations. But at least the use of illuminated advertising panels, themed signage and subtle lighting can help to give the impression of a street frontage. This impression can be further strengthened by designing each outlet with an inviting, open frontage, and making sure that the

less visually appealing spectator service areas, such as toilets, first aid rooms and maintenance areas are tucked away behind the public facade. (Fig. 5.5)

Catering facilities, which offer the owner/operator a significant income, will normally dominate the services provided on a stadium concourse. But their wares have to be imaginatively presented, varied and appropriately priced if spectators are to patronise them rather than any other rival fast food outlets, bars, cafes or restaurants which might exist in the streets and areas around the stadium perimeter. This almost certainly requires the involvement of professional expertise in planning and designing such outlets. However, the rewards make it worthwhile. The better the facilities and the more they appeal to different types of consumers (from those who want a hot dog to those who prefer a sit-down meal), the more likely spectators will

5.6

5.6 Restaurant at Stadium Australia, Sydney, providing banqueting facilities all year

be encouraged to arrive well before the event has started and stay on after its completion. This will not only significantly boost the venue's earning capacity but also relieve some of the pressure placed on the transportation system at the beginning and end of events (Fig. 5.6)

As one would expect, fast food and beverage outlets usually serve the highest percentage of spectators, often with a designed service rate of 20–30 per cent of the overall stadium's capacity being able to be served within a 15–20 minute period. However, a growing trend in recent years has been the provision of ever larger, formal dining areas. Typically these cater for between 5–10 per cent of the total audience, sitting down to dine at the same time. One example of a particularly generous provision is the Colonial Stadium, Melbourne (see case study in Part II), where we have designed for 6,500 diners in a stadium holding 52,000 seats overall.

Catering services at stadia are either managed directly by the owner/operators or franchised out to specialist caterers. Self-managed catering has the advantage of giving the stadium direct control of its business, and arguably a more flexible approach to serving its customers (many of whom may be regular fans). On the other hand franchised catering may have the advantage of being more professionally managed and perhaps generating upfront revenue earlier on in the venue's life. Choosing between self-management and franchising is thus one of the more difficult decisions an owner/operator has to make. Similarly, the owner/operator has to consider what other commercial outlets and concessions will be located within the stadium. These too can have a considerable bearing on the venue's income, particularly as the spend-per-head of most spectators at most venues is rarely high. The expenditure of an extra pound or dollar here and there over the course of a year's operation, spread among perhaps between 500,000 and a million or more spectators, can therefore have a significant impact on profitability. Among the numerous possibilities of commercial outlets at stadia are the following:

- A stadium shop selling a variety of gifts, sports goods, souvenirs and memorabilia
- A stadium museum and exhibition space for displays of trophies and other objects associated with the history of the sport and the venue
- Programme sales and information points distributed throughout the stadium, possibly augmented by individual vendors
- Betting outlets
- Amusement arcades and play areas
- Hire shops for binoculars, cushions and so on
- Ticket sales counters to tempt fans into buying tickets for future events before the excitement and euphoria induced by the current event has faded
- Customer information points and database terminals
- Health and fitness facilities

These facilities are in addition to other ones geared towards specific attendees, ranging from crèches for small children, soft waiting areas for parents (useful at venues staging rock concerts), telephone and ATM points, right up to fully equipped business centres. They can also include quality hotel accommodation and associated leisure facilities such as bowling alleys and golf driving ranges to encourage visitors to stay for more than just a few hours.

A key service upon which many a venue is judged is toilet facilities. Generally, spectators want toilets to be located as near as possible to their section of seats. They do not want to have to queue for long when they get there, and they have a right to expect a spotlessly clean, pleasant facility once inside. If they find otherwise then certainly less committed spectators will be deterred from further attendance, particularly women. However, satisfying these requirements can be extremely expensive, both in terms of the initial capital costs and the ongoing management required. The following notes therefore propose a realistic balance between the ideal and the practical. (Fig. 5.7)

Toilet numbers should be predetermined according to the overall capacity of the section to be served (rather than simply squeezed on to whatever space is left available after other facilities have been planned). To establish suitable numbers, expert guidance must be sought, taking into account local regulations and the fact that provision for females should be more generous than the minimums (because research shows that in general, females need twice as much time as males).

5.7 Plan showing good distribution of toilets at Stadium Australia, Sydney

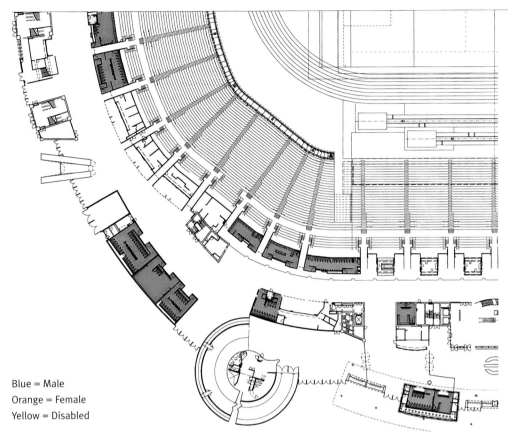

Blue = Male
Orange = Female
Yellow = Disabled

5.7

5.8 Typical layout of (a) a male toilet block and (b) a female toilet block (this example used at the WestpacTrust Stadium)

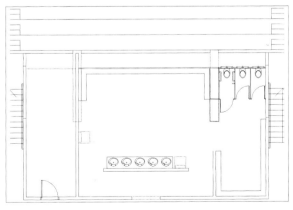

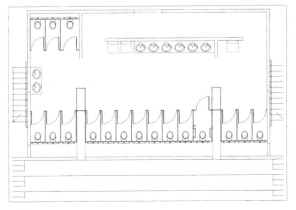

5.8a

5.8b

In addition to numbers, a decision should be made in advance concerning male-to-female ratios. A male-to-female ratio of 80:20 should suit most sports venues, but this will depend largely on the particular sports catered for, with, for instance, a higher ratio of males for football than for tennis. Where events such as pop concerts are also staged, a male to female ratio of 70:30 or even 50:50 might be more appropriate. Moreover, experience has shown that the more generous the provision for female spectators, the more likely they will attend on a regular basis. Because of these variables, and the high cost of providing toilets which may be used only infrequently, it may be sensible to include interchangeable sections which can be labelled 'male' or 'female' as required for particular events. Toilets should be planned to lead off public concourses, preferably on the same level as the concourse. If possible, for reasons of economy, they should be concentrated around a small number of drainage stacks. The toilets' internal layouts should encourage smooth traffic flow by allowing users to go in through one entrance and exit by another, preferably without having to open or close doors in the process. Careful consideration should be given to the provision of toilets for spectators with special needs, including those with disabilities, semi-ambulant or elderly people and young children. (Fig. 5.8a, 5.8b)

General viewing areas

From the public concourses spectators make their way to the viewing areas, of which there are likely to be two main types – public and private. While the design requirements of these categories differ in some respects, both must offer patrons clear viewing, in comfortable seats with suitable support services. Spectators' viewing standards essentially depend on three factors:

– Not being too far from the action (the viewing distance)
– Being able to see past the heads of people in front (the sightline)
– Not having the view impeded by obstructions (columns, beams, barriers or fences)

Regarding the viewing distance, for each individual sport there is a recognised maximum viewing distance, measured from pitch to seat. When looking at the plan of a stadium, the outer limit for viewing can therefore be shown as a notional 'envelope', within which, ideally, all seating should be located. Knowing that the floor space required is in the order of 0.5 square metres per spectator, the design team can then begin to fit the required number of seats into the limiting envelope. Clearly, the cheapest way to construct the seating geometry, and also the safest for crowd movements, is to limit the design to a single tier. However, for large numbers of spectators, or because of site restrictions, it may be necessary to consider two, three or even four tiers in certain situations. The stand geometry should concentrate seats in the best positions for the sports to be played at the venue. (Fig. 5.9)

5.9 Diagram showing maximum viewing distance 190 metres from the furthest corners of the pitch

5.10 Diagram showing sightline calculation

The maximum viewing distance should be no more than 190 metres from the furthest corners of the pitch (the optimum is 150 metres)

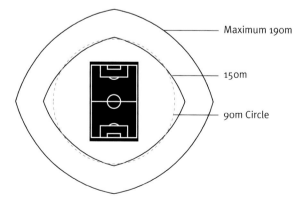

Maximum 190m

150m

90m Circle

5.9

The second design issue concerns sightlines, or the ability of spectators to see the track or playing area past the heads of those sitting in front. Their ability to do this – that is the quality of their sightlines – is measured by a variable called the 'C' value. This is defined by the height of a spectator's eye line above the eye of the spectator in front.

The achievement of good sightlines (i.e. high 'C' values) is no simple matter. For example, the recognised formula for calculating 'C' values, strictly speaking, requires that dimensional changes be made for each row of seats in each part of the stadium. Similarly, although the best way to achieve high 'C' values is to build steeply raking stands, typically between 35 and 42 degrees, in certain countries, such as Britain, safety requirements limit the rake to no more than 34 degrees (roughly the gradient of a normal stair). It is often necessary, therefore, to find a workable compromise between the two ideals of optimum sightlines and reasonable safety. In former times this was a task which required designers to undertake an immensely repetitive and laborious set of calculations. For our part, we have written our own computer programme to carry out the task in a fraction of the time and with pinpoint accuracy. (Fig. 5.10, 5.11)

The third requirement is to avoid spectators' views being impeded by obstructions such as columns, beams or other fixed obstructions. This is primarily achieved by using long-span or cantilevered forms of column-free roof construction, and by ensuring that there are no high barriers between the seats and the track or playing area (which in some situations requires a high degree of crowd management expertise in addition to careful design). The Reebok Stadium in Bolton (see case study in Part II) provides one illustration of how all these spectator viewing issues were resolved. First, the seating plan was based upon the optimum viewing distances for football of not more than 150 metres from the four corners of the pitch, and not more than 90 metres from the centre of the pitch. This limiting envelope resulted in the design of four stands shaped like the segments of an orange. Second, in order to give each spectator a high degree of comfort, it was decided to make each tread, that is, the concrete step upon which the seated spectator rests his or her feet, a depth of 800 mm. Despite this relatively generous depth, it was still possible to fit in the 30,000 seats required by the client. Third, the angle of rake was calculated by combining the tread depth of 800 mm with a minimum 'C' value

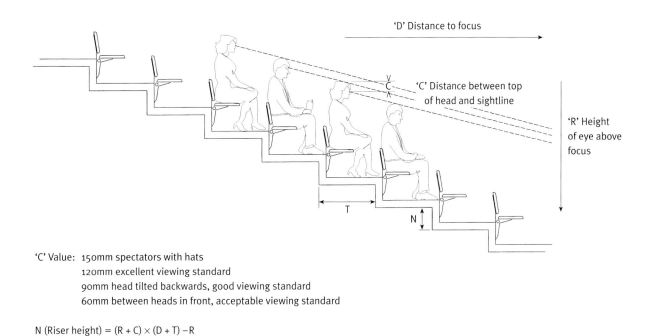

'C' Value: 150mm spectators with hats
            120mm excellent viewing standard
            90mm head tilted backwards, good viewing standard
            60mm between heads in front, acceptable viewing standard

N (Riser height) = $\dfrac{(R + C) \times (D + T) - R}{D}$

5.10

5.11 Diagram showing effect of various 'C' values on viewing standards

'C' value = 0 mm – inadequate view

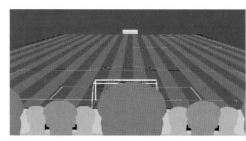

'C' value = 90 mm – typical for medium stadia

'C' value = 60 mm – typical for large stadia

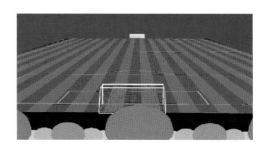

'C' value = 120 mm – typical for small stadia

5.11

of 90 mm. Finally, a roof form was developed providing a drip line shelter to all seats along the length of each stand, without any need for intermediate supports.

In addition to satisfying spectators' viewing standards, the seats themselves must be economic in both capital and lifetime costs. Experience has shown that the cheapest seats on offer may not always be the most durable or economic in the long term. As a result, up-to-date, informed research should be undertaken to decide which specification of seat is best in each particular situation. (Advice on this may be found in another publication, *Stadia: A Design and Development Guide*, Sheard and John 1997). Generally speaking, seats should be comfortable, safe (that is, not easily combustible and with no sharp edges), easy to keep clean and, if not riser-mounted, they must also be easy to clean around, a vital factor for owner/operators who need to maintain a tidy facility. We recommend to clients that the ideal minimum dimensions for comfort are seats between 475 mm and 500 mm wide, placed on treads measuring between 760 mm and 800 mm deep. Another safety and comfort factor concerns the number of seats per row, placed between aisles. In the UK the maximum number permissible is 28 seats per row, with other countries allowing up to 40. Our view is that between 24 and 32 seats per row is about right for most situations, and that, whilst local regulations may dictate other numbers, often there is little hard research to justify them.

There are some important safety and commercial reasons for stadia in the future offering more generous seat dimensions. A wider tread depth, for example, allows not only greater knee room for the seated spectator, but also more room for the spectator's personal effects, such as fast-food items, drinks or bags containing merchandise. The extra depth also makes it easier for people to walk along the row in normal and emergency conditions. Extra room might also be needed to allow for the growing range of accessories offered by owner/operators. These include seat-back pockets for venue brochures and programmes; sockets for audio-visual services, allowing spectators to see and hear action replays or call up statistics and information from the stadium database; communications services for ordering snacks, drinks and merchandise; holders for drinks and binoculars, and even personal heating or cooling systems. Also to be considered is the fact that, certainly in the Western world, people are generally growing larger as a result of improved health and better diets. The extent of floor area required to accommodate all these growing people and enhanced facilities is in the order of 0.5 square metres per person for sports of relatively short duration (where spectators are likely to remain in their seats during most of the event), increasing to around 1.0 square metres per person for those venues where people tend to be mobile during longer events, such as horse racing. As we emphasised earlier, the stadium of the future will increasingly have to compete with television viewing in terms of comfort, safety and the constant flow of audio-visual information and entertainment available. Designing spectator areas using minimum dimensions will almost certainly therefore prove to be a false economy in the long term.

Private viewing areas

Private viewing facilities have become common throughout the sporting world as a potentially rich source of income for the owner/operator. Such facilities,

whether they be private boxes, viewing lounges or individual club seats, have also become more and more luxurious and sophisticated, as owner/operators attempt to compete with other leisure and entertainment venues (including, as repeated above, the most popular entertainment venue of all, the TV room at home). In each stadium the type of private facilities on offer should be tailored closely to customer profiles and demand. Private boxes are potentially the most lucrative, with executive club enclosures and members' enclosures taking their place in the hierarchy of commercial provision. The main reason for this profitability is that these facilities can be 'sold' upfront, thus greatly enhancing the venue's financial viability by contributing to paying for the capital cost. (Fig. 5.12)

There are various approaches to their design, but one significant issue is their interface with the actual event. For example, a fixed glass screen between the playing field and the viewing area may offer patrons

5.12 View from a box at the WestpacTrust Stadium, Wellington

5.12

5.13 Isometric
drawing showing
conversion of private
boxes into function
rooms

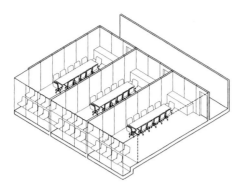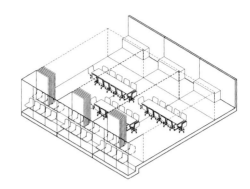

5.13

greater comfort, but it reduces their contact with the game, its sense of excitement and the prevailing atmosphere in the rest of the stadium. For this reason we have, for many years, designed boxes which provide the best of both worlds, by turning the glass screen into a glass sliding door, with seats linked to the box immediately in front. In that way, patrons can decide to watch from inside or outside, depending on the conditions outdoors. Whatever the design of the box or viewing lounge, in all cases kitchens, serveries and the lifts and corridors giving access to them, should be situated at the back of the stand so that catering staff can come and go without disturbing the occupants and their view of the event. Because of the general high quality and extensive servicing of these private areas it is always possible to design them so that they can be converted in whole or in part for other uses when the venue is not being used for its prime purpose. For example, individual boxes can become small meeting rooms, or even hotel rooms. By linking boxes or removing partitions and seats, a whole range of dining, conference or exhibition-style functions on non-event days can be made possible.

Divisions between spectators and participants

In the majority of cases barriers placed between spectator areas and playing areas are largely there to protect the players and the playing surface. Nevertheless, all too often the restrictive effect of such barriers on spectator viewing is ignored. Particularly at football stadia, where the threat of pitch invasions is deemed to be the greatest, the barriers can sometimes be so high – between 2.0 and 3.0 metres – that they restrict all viewing from the lower 10–15 rows of seats. This encourages spectators in these areas either to stand or to crowd up against the barrier for a better view, a highly unsatisfactory situation in every respect.

In recognition of this we have managed to avoid installing any such barriers since the early 1980s, by designing for moats to be used instead, or variations upon that idea when other forms of barrier were thought to be preferable.

Moats have the advantage of not obstructing spectators' views of the game. They are effective as barriers, and offer a useful circulation route around the pitch for officials, emergency services and the media (particularly photographers). Moats may also accommodate refreshment kiosks to which spectators descend by stairs, and they can act as collection areas into which refuse is swept between events for collection and removal. If not used for any of these functions but designed simply as a neutral space, they should still be wide enough to prevent spectators from leaping across. Equally, temporary means of bridging the moat must always be provided for spectators to cross in an emergency, and for pitch maintenance. (Fig. 5.14)

One disadvantage of moats is that they increase the distance between spectators and the game, typically by around 3.0 metres. However, this distance will be less noticeable in large stadia, where it represents a relatively small percentage increase on the average viewing distance. An alternative to moats is to raise the first row of seats to a height that will deter most spectators from jumping down onto the pitch. This geometry is popular in the USA and offers the advantage of accommodating large numbers of players and officials along the pitch perimeter without obstructing spectators' views. However, it also increases the height of the stand overall. In some situations neither a moat nor a raised first row might be necessary. (Fig. 5.15)

As experience has shown at many British football grounds since the implementation of the all-seated rule, it is also possible to have only the simplest low barrier between the spectator areas and the pitch. This method works provided spectators are warned as to the consequences of crossing the barrier without good cause, and the venue's crowd management team are trained to steward the perimeter effectively. Again, this is an issue which must be discussed early in the design stage, and on which an experienced stadium architect can offer meaningful advice.

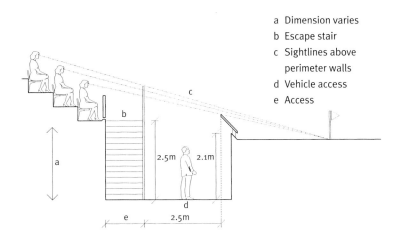

a Dimension varies
b Escape stair
c Sightlines above
  perimeter walls
d Vehicle access
e Access

5.14 Section of a
typical accessible moat

5.14

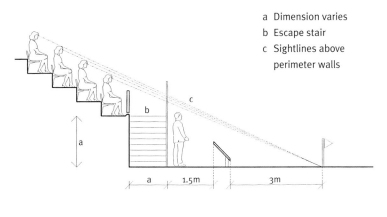

a Dimension varies
b Escape stair
c Sightlines above
  perimeter walls

5.15 Section showing
pitch separation by
raising the front
seating row

5.15

Owner/operator needs

The second of the three primary interest groups, the SOP, identified earlier, are the owner/operators, the people whose responsibility it is to manage the stadium and to ensure that events run smoothly (and, of course, at a profit). Generally offices and associated facilities are required for five groups:

– Permanent and temporary stadium management
– Stadium safety and security personnel (police and emergency services)
– Stewards brought in on match days (crowd control)
– The media
– Ground staff and maintenance personnel

In large stadia, particularly those catering for events at international level, separate and possibly extensive accommodation may be needed for each of these groups. As this can be costly to achieve, the possibility of different groups sharing certain facilities should always be investigated.

6.1 Plan showing club facilities at the Reebok Stadium, Bolton, West Stand

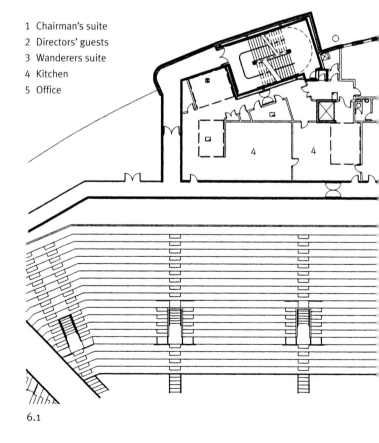

1 Chairman's suite
2 Directors' guests
3 Wanderers suite
4 Kitchen
5 Office

6.1

Management facilities

Facilities for the full-time management staff should be provided roughly in the centre of the main stand (usually the West Side). These will include offices, a boardroom (possibly with a bar for entertaining visitors) and perhaps a dedicated appeals room. Outside staff brought in to manage special events, such as pop concerts, may require additional rooms. For easy intercommunication, these should be adjacent to the permanent management facilities. The area set aside for the management staff ideally should also be directly accessible to:

–   Directors' and VIP hospitality rooms, viewing boxes and similar facilities
–   Team managers' and event officials' rooms
–   Media and press officers' rooms
–   A reserved area of car parking for officials and their guests

They should also have direct communication links with the stadium's safety control suite and, if possible, direct physical access also. (Fig. 6.1)

Safety and security personnel

All stadia nowadays require at least some form of stadium control suite from which safety and security personnel (including representatives of the emergency services, first aid operatives and, if appropriate, the police) can oversee the crowd management operation during events. These suites are usually glass-fronted rooms or cabins overlooking the pitch and spectator areas, although in some situations a separate or adjoining room fitted with closed-circuit television (CCTV) monitors may be deemed acceptable. Access to such areas should be strictly controlled. In larger stadia the control suite should adjoin a waiting/meeting room, a toilet and refreshment facilities. At stadia where police

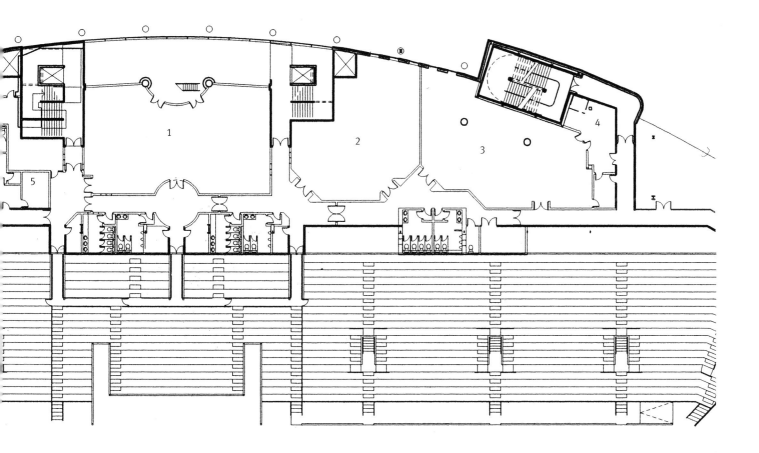

personnel form part of the security operation, consideration should be given to their needs, although in most cases, briefing and refreshment facilities can be shared or linked to those of the stewards. Where crowds may be unruly, consideration should also be given to the provision of one or two small detention rooms with toilets, or a large detention compound accommodating up to thirty people. (Fig. 6.2)

Owner/operators will usually require the provision of CCTV systems for security and crowd control. These systems should be complemented by a public address (PA) system, augmented by an appropriate external telecommunications system for public phone booths and the necessary external links for media needs.

Stadium stewards will require a briefing room, cloakroom and ideally their own small refreshment area. The ratio of stewards to spectators will vary from one venue to the next and needs to be researched for each project. It is likely to fall in the range of between 1:300 and 1:500. Very highly stewarded events which involve an additional quota of peer security personnel (that is, trained young people of similar age to the target audience) may well have much higher ratios of between 1:75 to 1:200. Access to the stewards' facilities should be strictly controlled.

Media facilities

As discussed earlier, the design of new stadia is inextricably tied to developments within the media, especially television. Whereas in the past events might have been covered by only three or four television cameras, nowadays the number can exceed 20, not including roaming camera operators. Equally, the demand for space from radio and newspaper reporters, and photographers, continues to rise. Indeed, for large events such as the Olympics and the FIFA World Cup, the media can take up a significant proportion of the seated accommodation normally available for ordinary spectators in the

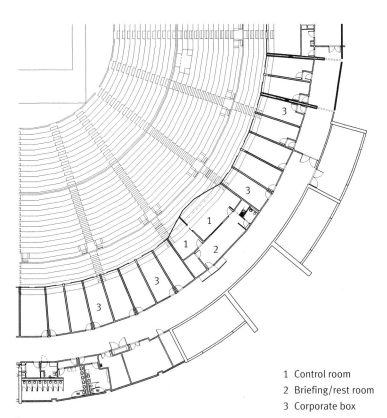

6.2 Plan showing the control suite with view over the pitch at the corner of the suite level at the Millennium Stadium, Cardiff

6.2

1 Control room
2 Briefing/rest room
3 Corporate box

6.3

main stand. But even the smallest stadium must now be designed to provide for the media. (Fig. 6.3)

Ideally media facilities should be provided as a complex or grouped set of rooms near the team dressing rooms, so that interviewers can readily meet players under strictly controlled conditions. At stadia where events are regularly televised, a designated area for external broadcasting vehicles, catering and toilet units, should be provided, which is easily accessible to the main media areas and, particularly at large events, securely fenced in with controlled access. In addition, owner/operators are increasingly being asked by the media to provide studios that overlook the playing area. Such facilities can be provided either by converting an executive box area whenever necessary, or, again, by ensuring that the studio forms an integral part of the design.

Television quality

Within the stadium, permanent and/or temporary platforms for television commentators and cameras will be required in various positions to suit the events being staged. In order to ensure that these positions are integral to the overall design and do not restrict the views of spectators, rather than being added as an afterthought, consultations with broadcasting companies should be held during the briefing stage. More than that, the actual quality of televised pictures is also an important design consideration. Our design philosophy is to provide for broadcast images which will be excellent in terms of their exposure, contrast, depth of field and so on, but also distinctive, enabling broadcasters to show the drama of the stadium, particularly from their main camera positions. To achieve this, the following considerations should form part of the design brief:

– Sufficient fixed camera positions suited to the event, plus provision for dynamic moving cameras (to allow close-ups, long shots, pitch- or trackside interviews and so on)
– Suitable lighting in strategic areas to enhance picture quality, for example around the players' tunnel and dug-outs, where close-ups and interviews may be required
– The use of translucent roofing materials to avoid complex shadow patterns
– The best possible field lighting, up to the required lux levels for colour television broadcasting
– Wherever possible, concentrate the spectators in areas covered by the general camera sweep, in order to discourage views of empty seating

We have conducted detailed discussions with various television companies to gather additional design intelligence, so that, for example, travelling cameras can be installed both at pitch level and along the underside of the roof, linked to microwave receivers. But, as stressed earlier, all these considerations must form part of the brief at the earliest possible stage, remembering always that although there may be up to 80,000 spectators present in the stadium for any given event, there may also be several millions watching from home.

Participants' needs

The last of the three primary interest groups, the SOP, is the participants, that is, the players, athletes and officials.

The activity area

The geometry, dimensions and markings of a sports pitch are prescribed for each individual sport by its governing body. (A general overview of these can be found in *Stadia: A Design and Development Guide*, Sheard and John 1997.) In addition to the basic dimensions, it is important to allow adequate safety and overrun space around the pitch. Our database stores the relevant dimensions and safety margins for all international sports. As suggested earlier, the key design issues affecting the participants in field sports are the type and quality of the playing surface.

Artificial surfaces offer the more cost-effective solution in the long term, because they require relatively little maintenance and allow intensive use and play in all weathers. However, for both rugby union and rugby league, for soccer, Australian Rules football, Gaelic football, hurling and cricket, artificial surfaces are neither desirable nor, in many cases, permitted by the sporting authorities. Even where such surfaces are permitted, for example in baseball and gridiron football, experience from the USA strongly suggests that the players prefer natural turf. Only in first-class hockey has the artificial pitch become widely accepted.

The installation and maintenance of a natural grass surface in a modern stadium is no longer a straightforward matter, however. The turf must not only provide a flawless surface for the participants but it must also appear to be flawless, both to the live and the remote audience. Furthermore, in those stadia used by more than one resident team, the standard of the surface must not be harmed by more intense usage. Finally, and most problematically in some situations, the turf must be able to coexist with tall or overhanging stadium roofs which tend to hinder growth by casting shadows or by inhibiting free air circulation at pitch level. In order to cope with such demanding conditions, research into new species of grass and into advanced planting technology has become ever more intense in recent years. The eventual aim is to find a type of turf and installation technique that will allow natural surfaces to be used in any situation, including stadia with closed or at least retractable roofs, and in environments more dependent upon artificial ventilation and artificial lighting. (Fig. 7.1)

Until that breakthrough, designers should aim to ensure that, wherever possible, stadia structures should allow for as much natural ventilation and exposure to solar radiation as possible within the design parameters of the project. In short, the growing environment must be absolutely right for the turf to prosper, a requirement which demands expert knowledge, particularly of species selection, substrate construction, feeding systems, irrigation and drainage networks and, if appropriate, subsurface warming systems.

7.1

7.1 The open corners at the Alfred McAlpine Stadium, Huddersfield permit good air circulation across the pitch, which is reinforced to withstand intensive use of two home teams

7.2 Corner mast floodlights at the Alfred McAlpine Stadium, Huddersfield

Floodlighting

Apart from the playing surface, a second major consideration for participants in many sports is the provision of artificial illumination, or floodlighting, as it is generally known. The aim of the installation should be:

–   To deliver a sufficiently high level of illumination on the playing surface. The recommended or minimum level varies from sport to sport and from one level of play to another, but is usually prescribed by the governing bodies or by television companies
–   To deliver even illumination across the field, with no excessive contrasts between lighter and darker areas. This is known as the 'uniformity ratio'
–   To avoid glare, that is, bright light sources shining into players' eyes. This requirement applies equally to spectators and to people in adjoining properties, who may be adversely affected by an 'overspill' of light

In small stadia floodlighting can often be mounted on high-level fittings installed along the side of the pitch. In larger venues a more common configuration is four

7.2

tall corner masts, each with light fittings mounted at a height not less than 0.4 times the distance on plan between the mast and the centre of the field. In very large stadia there may be light fittings mounted about 40 metres above ground, on masts or, often, along the leading edge of the stadium roof.

Achieving the required performance in a cost-efficient manner requires skill and experience, hence we always advise that specialists be consulted. (Fig. 7.2, 7.3)

Competitors' facilities

A basic requirement for all venues is to have changing rooms, baths, showers, toilets and all the associated medical, social and media facilities needed by the players who perform there. These rooms should be located with the following considerations in mind:

– They should offer direct and easy access to the pitch, preferably on the same level. If there is any risk of players being subject to crowd intimidation, the route between the changing rooms and the field should be protected

– There should be direct and easy access, again preferably on the same level, to the external service road used by team coaches and by ambulances, in case of serious injuries

– Private areas used by the players should be secure against unauthorised entry by members of the public or the media. Players need to feel completely safe and at ease

– Direct links should be provided with the media areas, via a lift if necessary, so that interviews and other media contacts can be easily arranged (Fig 7.4)

If the stadium has a resident team its members will want their own dedicated set of facilities, for their use only (and if there are two resident teams, preferably separate from their co-residents' facilities). However, it should be remembered that if teams of different sports were to share facilities, their different needs would need to be carefully researched. In addition to players' facilities the team managers must have separate offices and associated facilities, which in turn should be accessible both to the team changing rooms and the stadium management offices.

7.3 Roof mounted pitch lights at the Colonial Stadium, Melbourne

7.3

Officials' facilities

Every venue needs changing rooms, general facilities and perhaps some administrative space for officials, judges, umpires and referees. Like players' facilities these must have direct and easy access to the pitch, and, if there is any risk of crowd intrusion, then the route must be secure and protected. Officials' facilities should be designed to have strictly controlled access to the team changing rooms and to be secure against unauthorised entry by members of the public or the media. Again, requirements need to be individually researched for each project. For example, stadia increasingly have to provide for female as well as male match officials, and most sports have specific requirements for anti-doping facilities.

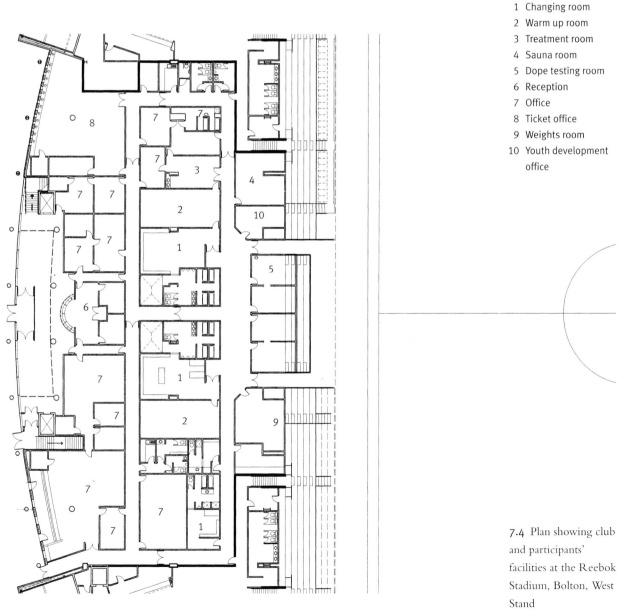

1 Changing room
2 Warm up room
3 Treatment room
4 Sauna room
5 Dope testing room
6 Reception
7 Office
8 Ticket office
9 Weights room
10 Youth development office

7.4 Plan showing club and participants' facilities at the Reebok Stadium, Bolton, West Stand

7.4

The environment

Environmentally responsible sports venues are unfortunately few and far between. But that is set to change, as Environmentally Sustainable Development (ESD) becomes an increasingly important factor in the design of all buildings. Indeed, the International Olympic Committee (IOC) are now insisting that sport-related facilities developed in their name are designed to show care and respect for the environment. This is not only in practical aspects such as the choice of materials, energy use and waste management, but also in terms of the buildings' visual impact and its relationship with its environs, roads and other transport links. Other leading sports governing bodies, and certainly planning and funding bodies, are sure to follow the IOC's lead.

Energy

One of the most important aspects an architect must consider is the amount of energy a building will use, since the less energy a building uses, the less fuel will be required. ESD requires that three main aims be met:
— To minimise the demand for energy
— To supply as much of the energy required as possible from renewable resources
— To meet the remaining energy demand with the efficient use of the cleanest possible non-renewable fuel
(Fig. 8.1)

In order to meet a stadium's needs with available renewable resources, energy usage should be based upon a detailed 'load profile' of the venue. This requires that the designer develop a clear understanding between the relationship of base energy loads and peak energy loads, particularly where the venue is to be multi-purpose. There will also be considerable differences in energy usage between event days and non-event days. Moreover, it is not only the cost of the energy which should concern designers and clients, since conventional energy sources are not currently priced to reflect their potential for environmental damage, for example, through the greenhouse effect, which is largely caused by CO_2 emissions. It is thus imperative that designers act responsibly to minimise emissions throughout the entire life cycle of their buildings, from their construction through to their demolition.

One significant way of ensuring this is to reduce the venue's dependence on mains electricity supplied from the national grid. For although electrical energy appears to be a 'clean' fuel, it has a significant environmental impact at its point of production. Heating water by gas, on the other hand, can produce around 70 per cent less CO_2 emissions than electricity. Even better, solar water heating, supplemented by a gas back up, can achieve a 90 per cent reduction or more in some parts of the world. Certainly self-generation of energy using photovoltaic cells, that is, the conversion of sunlight into electricity, is becoming increasingly viable. (Fig. 8.2)

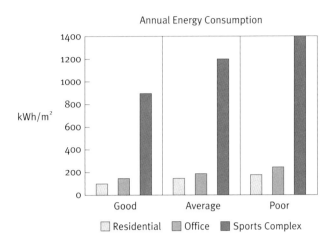

8.1

8.1 Graph illustrating comparative energy use in various building types and how low energy design and load management are essential for cost effective running

8.2 Graph illustrating optimised load management for energy use in a typical sports building

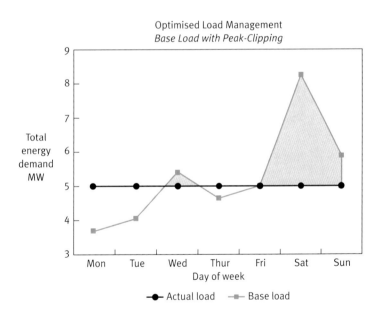

A 3.5 MW hydro power plant supplies the peak demand and reduces CHP plant from 8.5 to 5 MW

A 5 MW CHP base load facility supplies the everyday requirements

8.2

Other methods of reducing a venue's dependence on non-renewable energy sources are wind fans, the recycling of waste energy from plant systems and the use of combined heat and power (CHP). All are possible at sports venues. The energy consumed in providing artificial cooling systems and air-conditioning at sports venues can also be significant. Consideration should therefore be given to the use of natural ventilation, using 'stack' effect ventilators, supplemented by extract fans. This is particularly possible in tropical zones, where good air movement and the removal of hot air can be facilitated by the use of thermal chimneys throughout the structure. A good example of this approach is the Royal Selangor Turf Club grandstand in Kuala Lumpur, Malaysia (see case study in Part II), where the central atrium acts as a large 'chimney' for the warmed air which induces through-ventilation in the spaces leading off this central atrium core. (Fig. 8.3)

8.3 Environmental
control strategy for the
Blue Wings Stadium,
Suwon

WINTER – ENVIRONMENTAL CONTROL STRATEGY – WEST SECTION

Diurnal temperature range
Max 8 deg C
Min −5 deg C

Penetration of low altitude
winter sun can contribute to
space heating in atrium/street

Insulated roof to atrium/street
reduces heat losses and
assists buffering of internal
conditioned spaces

Openings on gable walls kept
closed to minimise air
infiltration from the external
environment

Reduced ventilation
through openings to
minimise heat loss
in atrium

Pre-heated air from atrium
supplied to occupied areas

Dec 21st at
15:00 : 18 deg

Plenum for access, service and
maintenance, (1–2 times a year)

Pre-heating of ventilation air
through ground pipes before
delivery into atrium

Atrium/street

Air conditioning zones

Ground temperature — 12–14 deg C

8.3

A further method of avoiding artificial cooling or heating systems is to position glazing so that there is minimum solar radiation build-up within internal spaces, perhaps supplemented at certain times of the day by the careful use of awnings. Insulation from both heat and cold is another important means of reducing energy usage, although it must be borne in mind that conditions for watching sport and many other events do not need to be the same as for sitting quietly in an office or at home. A typical temperature range for an office building may be 20–22 degrees Centigrade, whereas an acceptable temperature range for watching an event may be between 18–26 degrees Centigrade. It is also important to remember that air movement itself can reduce perceived temperature to quite a large degree. Indeed, ventilation rates of around five air changes per hour, with a typical speed of 0.23 metres per second, can reduce the temperature by around 1 to 1.5 degrees Centigrade. In temperate climates some form of heating will be required in many of the ancillary areas. Even so, taking the thermal mass of the structure itself into account can still reduce energy use. This thermal mass, together with the secondary heat gain from both the spectators and all the various appliances used within the venue, must be calculated, as

these can have quite an effect on the extent of heating required. In the same way as the extent of external fenestration and its orientation is a major factor in cooling, so it is with heating.

Pollution

There are essentially three types of pollution associated with buildings: air, noise and light. Air pollution, the emission of foul odours or vibrations does not usually stem from sports venues to any appreciable degree (although they do from the adjoining car parking areas, which necessitates the careful positioning of natural or artificial barriers). It is also rare for sports facilities to suffer from air or noise pollution from external sources, unless they are located close to sewage works (as was the case with a racecourse in Singapore), or to airports or busy roads. Rather, it is more common for people living within the immediate environs of a stadium to be disturbed by noise from the actual event, particularly from loud public address systems and from rock concerts. When planning a sports facility therefore, particularly one designed for concert use, an assessment must be made as to whether anticipated noise emissions will constitute a nuisance factor for the neighbourhood, and, if so, what methods of reducing the noise can be incorporated within the design. These methods might be quite simple; for example, shifting the main structure to another part of the site, or placing other structures or buildings to act as noise barriers between the venue and the nearest houses. A more complex solution is to provide the venue with a retractable roof, as was the choice at the Millennium Stadium in Cardiff (see case study in Part II), where there are a number of residential properties nearby.

Light pollution is another problem often associated with sports venues that use floodlighting. Artificial lighting can disturb nearby residents in a number of ways, through scattered lighting, or spillage, or, in the case of small sources of lights with a high intensity, through glare. If suitable lamps are selected, projection equipment carefully adjusted and anti-glare devices used, the negative impact of sports ground lighting can be reduced to an acceptable level, provided there is sufficient distance between the facility and sensitive locations. However, in urban environments where an existing venue is to be redeveloped, computer modelling for light spillage, glare and other factors should be undertaken.

Landscape

In order to preserve or even enhance natural habitats, it is our belief that fundamental restrictions should apply to dealing with green-field sites. In addition to a general exercising of economy in our claims on the land, we should be especially careful to protect rare and sensitive habitats. As the founder of the modern Olympics, Baron Pierre De Coubertin, once wrote:

The first thing to be taken into consideration when staging a sports festival is the scenery. Before actors appear, the scenery strikes the eyes of the spectator. When the contestants appear, the spectator immediately is confronted with their mode of fitting in with environment, landscape and setting and the harmony of their performances with these. Sometimes, a wealth of material means was expended for arrangement and setting which, however, did not always prove

successful, whereas, on similar occasions, surprising effects were achieved with modest means and expenses. Before making any arrangements one should not be guided by the ideal of beauty alone, which often is beyond our reach, but by eurhythmy, that is proportion, regular measure and grace in any detail in concert with the whole.

Thus design in the broadest sense must seek to balance, integrate and reconcile all the elements of enjoyment, some of which are listed below:

– People – by helping them to find their way, to move freely, seek shade, shelter, water, food and to remember their way around
– Architecture – by creating a symbiotic relationship between the built environment and the landscape
– Art and culture – by incorporating elements of beauty, expressing culture in three dimensions
– Location – by using indigenous plants, reinforcing character, conserving heritage features, retaining trees and linking with the sport precinct
– Sustainability – by conserving and re-using natural resources, low maintenance, non-polluting outputs and longevity of plant material

Sports venues can offer a further benefit. Often the only sites available for their development in urban areas are what we call 'brown-field' sites – that is, abandoned former industrial areas, often on land that is polluted and heavily contaminated. Thus the decontamination of that land for a stadium can offer ecological benefits. Huddersfield (see case study in Part II) is just such an example.

Apart from the natural environment, new sports venues can also improve the man-made environment, particularly when used as a catalyst for urban renewal schemes. Two good examples of this approach are the Millennium Stadium in Cardiff and the Colonial Stadium in Melbourne (see case studies in Part II). Each of these venues forms the focus of new urban life in areas of the cities which had been left behind while other districts were developed. (Fig. 8.4)

8.4

8.4 The Millennium
Stadium, Cardiff,
aimed at becoming a
catalyst for urban
renewal

Transport

Finally, designers and planners have a fundamental
responsibility for ensuring that as many spectators as
possible are encouraged to travel to and from the venue
by public transport, while those who do choose to drive
are encouraged by incentive schemes to fill every seat in
their vehicle. In the 1960s and 1970s the United States
started the trend for stadia located well away from centres of population and accessible only by private car.
One such stadium ended up with space for no fewer
than 31,000 cars around its perimeter, almost enough

for one car per two spectators. Fortunately, that trend has now been reversed. Stadia are moving back into the cities, or to the edge of cities, where public transport networks may already be established and available to serve the venue. Many major stadia now plan on the basis that up to 60 to 80 per cent of all spectators will travel by public transport, thus negating the need to cover vast areas of land with tarmac for car parking and reducing congestion on event days.

Sport and responsibility

The environment of our planet is the air we breathe. It is of fundamental importance to all mankind. But as professionals whose task it is to build upon that natural inheritance, architects have a greater responsibility than most to ensure that we do not create one environment at the expense of the other. Sports architects, whose work is supposed to celebrate people's natural gifts as athletes and performers, are not exempt from that responsibility. The highest levels of sporting endeavour are moments in time founded upon years of meticulous preparation and cultivation. Thus, as designers, our primary duty is to support and protect those moments, and to give them as fine a stage as they surely deserve. Elite sport cannot survive in a hostile environment, any more than spectator numbers can survive mediocrity. The greatest achievements in sport differ from mediocrity by a fraction of a per cent or a hundredth of a second. Paramount to providing an environment where sport can reach the highest level is the need to ensure that the provision of facilities is of the highest technical standard. Athletes endure the hard work of training for many years. When the time comes, possibly for their once-in-a-lifetime moment of achievement, they must be ready. For them, the feeling of the moment must be right. The stage must be set. Our stage. Our responsibility.

Case Studies **Part II**

Alfred McAlpine Stadium

Football and rugby stadium

Project data	Consultants	Chronology	Project information	Economic information
Location:	*Structural engineer:*	*Design:*	*Site area:*	*Main building cost:*
Huddersfield, England	*YRM Anthony Hunt,*	*October 1991*	*51 acres*	*£14,500,000 Phase 1,*
Owner:	*Modus*	*Documentation:*	*Total parking spaces:*	*£8,500,000 Phase 2*
Kirklees Stadium Dev.	*Services engineer:*	*June 1992*	*1,200 cars and 8 coaches*	*External works:*
Ltd	*RHB Partnership*	*Construction:*	*Total number of seats:*	*£2,140,000*
Main contractor:	*Quantity surveyor:*	*August 1992*	*24,700*	
Alfred McAlpine	*Franklin + Andrews*	*Opening date:*	*Total building area:*	
Building		*November 1993*	*24,200 square metres*	

Background

Founded in 1908, Huddersfield Town Football Club became one of England's foremost clubs during the 1920s and 1930s, achieving three consecutive League Championships, finishing as runners-up three times, and reaching no fewer than five FA Cup Finals (winning once in 1922). But by the 1970s the club's fortunes had declined sharply and its old stadium on Leeds Road (opened in 1908) had deteriorated into a shabby, unsafe and loss-making venue, attracting fewer than 8,000 spectators to the club's matches in the Football League's Third Division. If both the club and its stadium were to have any chance of survival, let alone progress, clearly radical action was sorely needed.

Fortunately, the club chairman during the early 1990s, Graham Leslie, was a man of vision and was able to inspire John Harman, leader of the local Kirklees Metropolitan Council, to join him. Together they took a leap into the future by forging a bold partnership between the football club, their neighbours, Huddersfield Rugby League Football Club, and the local council to form a new company, Kirklees Stadium Development Ltd. (Huddersfield, it should be noted, was the birthplace of rugby league, for it was in the George Hotel, about a mile from Leeds Road, that the final split had taken place between rugby league and rugby union in 1895.) The aim of this new company was to plan, develop, own and manage a commercially viable, multi-use venue – for soccer, rugby and other sports, social and community events – which would benefit all three owners.

The brief

Having been noticed by the Football Club and by Kirklees Council for our part in drawing up a 'A Stadium for the Nineties', a concept design unveiled at a stadium exhibition in 1991, we went on to win a limited competition and were appointed as architects that same year by the Kirklees Stadium Development company. After considerable research into the football club's existing site at Leeds Road, the client proposed a wholly new venue on a site vacated by industry some years earlier, a few hundred metres away, across the road. The concept we developed with the design team (the client being very much a part of this team) was to integrate commercial facilities within the progressive curving form of the building, thereby offering financial benefits to both clubs and the council for years to come (despite the warnings of several leading financial

1.1 A model of the Alfred McAlpine Stadium as it was envisaged in the early 1990s and completed in the late 1990s

1.1

consultants who had forecast that this would not be possible). From the Council's point of view it was additionally important that the venue should become a centre of community activities, open to local people for as many days of the year as possible. This was particularly relevant since Huddersfield's town centre lies within 10 minutes' walking distance of the site. A brief, a 'wish list', in effect, was then developed by the team, including facilities which had never before been associated with a lower division football or rugby club. The list included the following:

– 25,000 capacity all-seater stadium
– 26 executive boxes
– Bars and restaurants
– 500-seat banqueting hall
– Commercial offices and hotel
– Suitability as a pop-concert venue
– 30-bay floodlit golf driving range
– Multi-screen cinema
– Good disabled facilities
– Health and fitness club
– Parking for up to 2,000 cars

The brief required that the stadium and its social and commercial facilities could be used either together or separately as the occasion demanded. The design also had to allow for the development to be built in phases, dependent on funds becoming available for various elements. Also, the highest standards possible had to prevail throughout. As lead consultants, we developed an initial sketch of curving shapes in plan, section and elevation into an outline design demonstrating that it would be possible and practical to accommodate everything the client wanted on the site, yet avoiding those areas contaminated by the previous dumping of industrial waste. At this stage a new chief executive, Paul Fletcher, took on Graham Leslie's vision and soon adopted a catch phrase he had heard in an epic American film about baseball, *Field of Dreams*. The words 'Build it and they will come' summed up the spirit of positive thinking which pervaded every aspect of the development, even during the very difficult times, of which there were many. The total capital cost of the scheme was estimated at around £20 million in 1991. An initial financial package of £15 million was gradually assembled, consisting of the following elements:

1.2

1.3

1.2 The Lawrence Batley or Riverside Stand, showing the dramatic and perhaps daring contrast of colours and materials. A first for British football

1.3 The dramatic junction of floodlight tower, trusses and finger supports from below

Commercial sources:
Sale of the existing football ground: £5,000,000
Commercial and private investment: £3,750,000

Grants:
Football Trust: £2,500,000
Kirklees Metropolitan Council: £2,000,000
Foundation for Sports and the Arts: £1,000,000
Urban Development Grant: £750,000

Although grants from the Football Trust formed a familiar element of most football-related stadium developments in the immediate aftermath of the 1989 Hillsborough disaster, at that time it was still unusual for local councils or other bodies to fund any stadium developments which involved professional football or rugby clubs. In this respect, the Kirklees development team broke new ground and encouraged other clubs to raise their expectations.

Design concept

The design proposed a 75 × 120 metre pitch, large enough for football and rugby (including safety margins), with stands on all four sides and an adjoining hotel, retail and commercial block, separated from the sports facility by means of a glazed atrium. This arrangement would allow the stadium and the commercial facilities to function either together or separately as required, with the offices, hotel and retail areas accessible from the 'town' side as a completely independent building. For the project to be a commercially viable enterprise, a minimum core of these facilities had to be built immediately, with the rest following later in a phased programme. The masterplan envisaged the initial phases as follows:

–   Phase 1: Riverside Stand, 8,500 seats, 26 private viewing suites, guest lounges, conference and banqueting suite, club administration offices, car parking, golf driving range, plant and maintenance areas, plus Kilner Bank Stand, 7,800 seats
–   Phase 2: South Stand, 4,200 seats
–   Phase 3: North Stand, 4,200 seats
–   Phase 4: Hotel, commercial offices, shops, museums, crèche, multiplex cinema and other facilities envisaged in the brief

For economic reasons the original concept of two buildings separated by an atrium was eventually superseded by a design linking the two elements, so that the banqueting and conference areas could be built at the same time as the Riverside Stand. At this stage it was envisaged that the commercial facilities would follow later, although the basic principle of a sports venue and a commercial/community complex sharing the same site remained firm. Soon after construction began on the first phase, approval was given to include the second phase as well. This meant that the two phases of development were completed at the same time under the same building contract.

As part of the first phase, the banks of the Colne River, which flows alongside the venue, were to be remodelled and landscaped to offer leisure amenities for the local community and be accessible to the general public. Our brief was to provide 25,000 spectator seats and, in line with the marketing plan, to provide superior quality rather than low prices as the key to success. Thus the brief set standards that were well above the

1.4 Detail of how the roof of the Lawrence Batley Stand floats over the main elevation at the grandstand

1.4

levels generally prevailing in football stadia during the early 1990s, as follows:

- All seats had to be under cover
- No seats could be further than 90 metres from the centre of the pitch
- No seats to be further than 150 metres from the furthest corner of the pitch
- No spectator should have a 'C' value of less than 90 mm
- No view of the pitch should be obstructed by a column
- Tread depths were to be a minimum of 800 mm

At the time these were standards no other comparable stadium in Britain could match. (For example, most new stands were built with tread depths of between 660 and 760 mm. A depth of 800 mm was then unheard of in a football context.) Using the above standards, and aided by our dedicated stadium design software, we worked towards a stadium based around a plan of four stands shaped like orange-segments. These satisfied all the viewing criteria and also concentrated as many seats as possible close to the centre line, where experience shows that most spectators prefer to be. In section, the computer had then to calculate variable stepping heights combined with the 800 mm tread

1.5

1.5 Panoramic view from New Panasonic Stand (North Stand) capturing the play and atmosphere of the completed stadium bowl

1.6 The long tapered curved truss supporting the roof became known as the 'banana' truss. There is a bunch of four in total

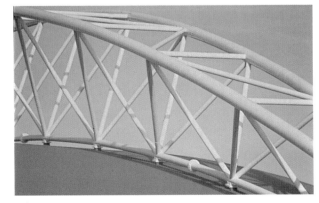

1.6

depths. These calculations resulted in angles of rake no greater than the maximum allowable under English building regulations of 34 degrees, and ensured 'C' values of not less than the agreed 90 mm minimum.

Three-dimensional view modelling was particularly important to ensure that views under the forward sloping and curving roofs were possible and to calculate the cut-off points, particularly important for spectators viewing high balls during games of football and rugby. The escape time for spectators was calculated to be within 8 minutes from all parts of the venue. To cover the stands a roof form was developed in conjunction with Steve Morley, a structural engineer then working with YRM Anthony Hunt Associates (who had also worked with us on the 'Stadium for the Nineties' concept design).

The forms chosen provide 90 degree shelter over the front row of seats along the entire length of each stand, with no need for intermediate supports. Each curved profiled metal roof plane is supported from a 135 metre (long side) 'banana' truss of triangulated tubular steel providing both structural efficiency and a landmark image important to the visual identity of the new venue. At 78 tonnes per truss these structures are also far more lightweight than the conventional cantilevered solutions found at many other modern stadia. Nor do they require such a heavy rear structure to counterbalance the cantilever. In addition, the loads of these trusses meet the ground in the four corners of the venue, thereby minimising the amount of disturbance necessary to the poor quality ground. Structurally the main frame generally consists of steel, employing tubular sections for the main roof trusses and simple 'I' sections elsewhere. The tubular roof trusses are painted white. The stand roofs are in profiled steel sheeting with blue upper surfaces and white undersides, resting on white cellform steel beams. All steppings are in pre-cast concrete, with the main floors in pre-cast concrete planks with an *in situ* topping.

As a centre designed to serve the local community the stadium has to be accessible to disabled people. Accordingly, the Riverside Stand has space for wheelchair users along its front row, plus special seats for the ambulant disabled, the blind and those with hearing difficulties elsewhere. Additional space for wheelchair users is provided in front of the Kilner Bank Stand, at a high level in that stand's corner, and at high level areas in the South Stand. Overall, the venue is able to accommodate up to 200 people in wheelchairs, with associated facilities, including toilets, distributed throughout the stadium.

Public food kiosks are located on each of the concourses. Level 2 of the Riverside Stand accommodates two snack bars and two fast food concessions to serve the lower spectator tier, with Level 4 accommodating four fast food concessions. These concessions were designed to serve a third of all the spectators at half-time. The central kitchen, located on Levels 2 and 3 of the Riverside Stand, is designed to serve up to 700 hot meals in the stand's three main guest areas. These are:

— 26 hospitality suites on Level 3, made up of 24 suites holding up to 10 people, plus two holding up to 20 people. Each suite is served by hot trolleys and waitress service. Each offers clear views of the pitch and is fitted with television sets, dining tables and servery units. The suites have been let at annual rentals ranging in 1994–5 from £3,000–7,000 for rugby matches only, £5,000––11,000 for football matches only, and £7,700–17,000 for rugby and football combined. All have since been consistently sold out, thus demonstrating the contribution private facilities can make to stadium revenues even before taking into account the monies spent by these patrons on food, drink and other services. In addition, each suite can be interconnected to provide greater flexibility for letting for functions during non-event days
— The banquet and conference area, also on Level 3, which can accommodate 450 guests
— The guest rooms for press, players and sponsors on Level 2, which can accommodate up to 150 guests or be subdivided into three separate function rooms

The total number of toilet facilities in the stadium is divided on the basis of a ratio of males to females of 80:20 on concourses, and 50:50 in hospitality areas.

1.7 The leisure pool in the North Stand with light from adjacent swimming pool through translucent glazing

1.7

Operation

Since its opening the stadium has met its client's intention of becoming a landmark venue, attracting sustained international publicity and winning a number of design awards. The most significant award was the 'Building of the Year' from the Royal Institute of British Architects, in 1995, the first time this honour has been given to a sport building. Since its opening, spectator attendance has doubled that of previous years, and Huddersfield Town have maintained their position in a higher division of the Football League. Huddersfield Rugby League Club have also been promoted and have greatly increased attendance, from a very low base at their previous ground.

Perhaps the most encouraging aspect of the two clubs' tenure at the stadium has been the success of their sharing arrangement. Before the stadium opened many observers in both football and rugby league were sceptical that the pitch could take the extra wear and tear. However, the high-quality natural turf has proved capable of accommodating around 80 matches a year. To ensure a robust surface, the pitch construction features advanced drainage and under-soil heating systems, and has subsequently also benefited from a new synthetic turf reinforcing system being tested on the pitch. Another fear was that the two clubs would be unable to share facilities harmoniously while maintaining their separate identities. For this reason, we were careful to locate the administration areas of each club at opposite ends of the main stand, each being provided with their own entrances. In fact there have been few problems.

A number of observers were also sceptical about the chances of a relatively small Yorkshire town being able to attract non-sporting events. Once again, however, the doubters were proved wrong. Paul Fletcher's first coup was to sign up the American rock band REM for a concert in 1994. When tickets sold out within a few hours, a second night was organised, and this too was a 35,000 capacity sell-out. Since then the stadium has hosted a number of concerts, from brass bands to Brian Adams, Beautiful South and the Eagles. The venue has also lived up to the Council's dreams of holding a range of regular community events, including school sports carnivals. Another pioneering aspect of the stadium, in the British context at least, was the fact that the main contractor Alfred McAlpine, was sufficiently impressed with the project to purchase the 'naming rights' for a reported sum of £2 million over the first 10 years of operation.

Final phases

In 1997 HOK LOBB proceeded with Phase 3, the construction of the North Stand, thereby completing the bowl and including some of the facilities not included in the two original phases. As a result of a few design amendments, the North Stand accommodates a further 4,700 seated spectators (500 more than originally planned), but to the same high standards as the three existing stands. The North Stand also includes a stepped restaurant area, 16 private hospitality boxes and a central restaurant. On its ground level the stand also accommodates a swimming pool, dance studio, health and fitness centre and all associated changing and service areas. On the second level it contains commercial offices which have now been let to the Leisure Services Department of Kirklees Council. The stand has also been specifically designed to accommodate concerts, with large vehicle access at both sides, a retractable area of seats to allow for stage placement, and an increased height of arch truss to allow for a full stage set and rigging.

In conclusion, the Alfred McAlpine Stadium is a dramatic building whose strong curves and colours stand out starkly against the surrounding wooded slopes and the grey tones of most of Huddersfield's townscape. As well as providing a new home and new horizons for the town's two leading sports clubs, as intended by the local authority it has become a genuine and much appreciated focal point of activity for the town and its surrounding areas. Its innovative design and imaginative funding package have also encouraged other British sports clubs, towns and cities to aim higher in their efforts to replace ageing facilities.

1.8 Clear open reception area with glazed cafe bar and views into the 25 metre swimming pool beyond

1.8

Site plan

1 Business and leisure
  complex
2 Cinema
3 Golf driving range
4 Car park
5 River Colne

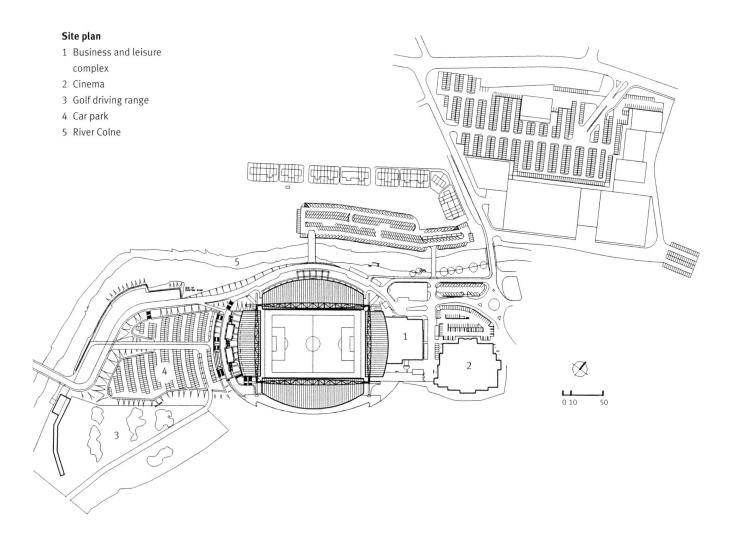

West elevation

Bowl plan

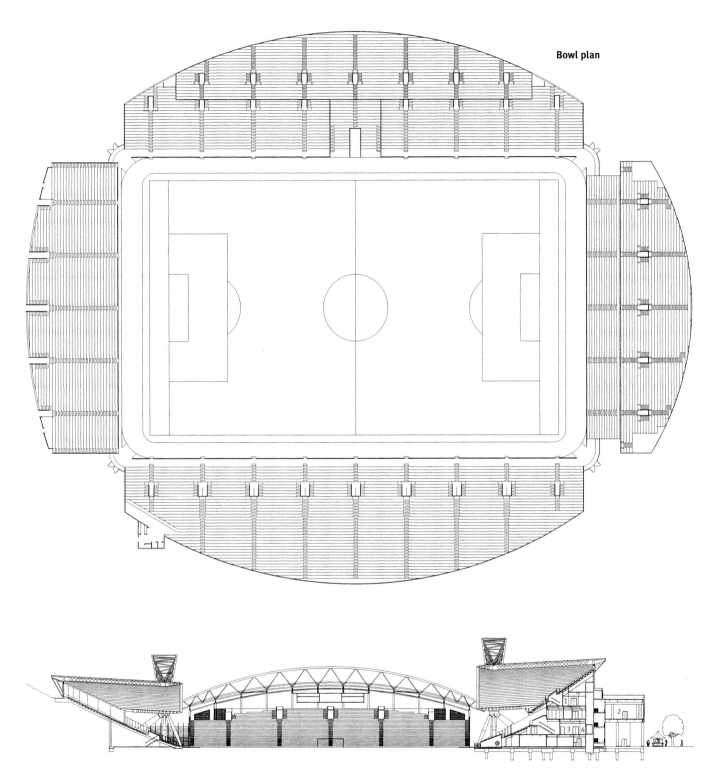

East-west section
1 Box
2 Banquet/conference
  suite
3 Office
4 Reception

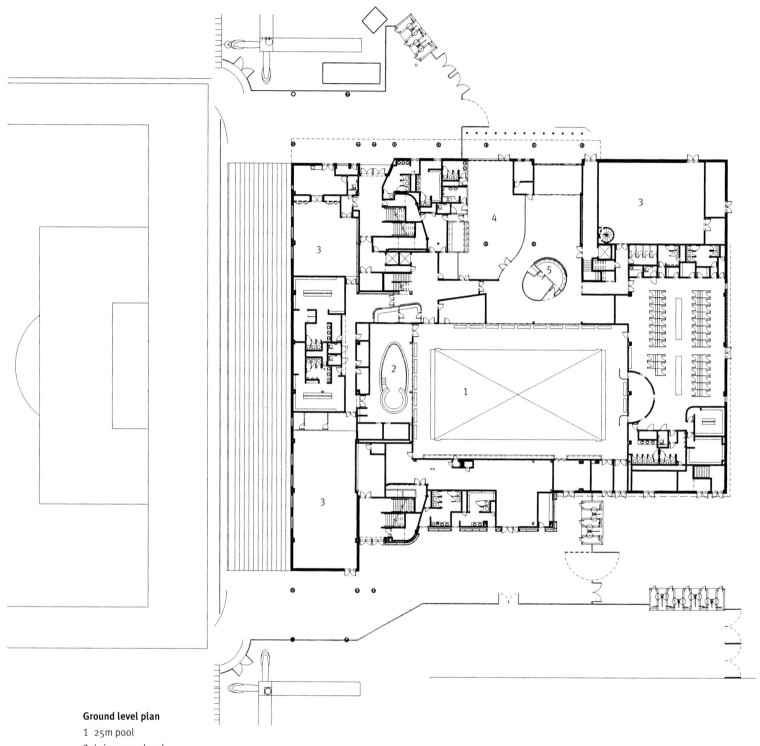

Ground level plan

1 25m pool
2 Leisure pool and
   Jacuzzi
3 Exercise studio
4 Cafe/bar
5 Reception

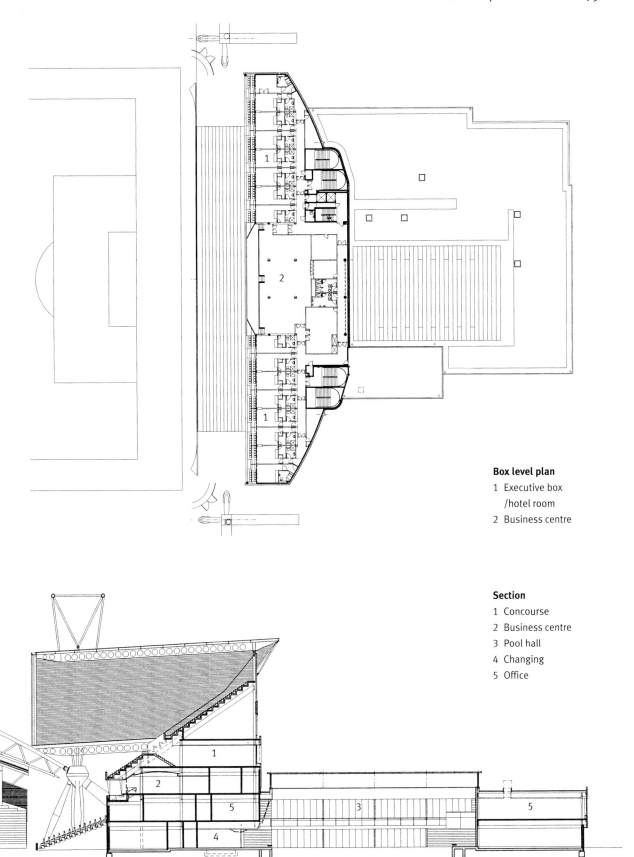

Box level plan
1 Executive box
   /hotel room
2 Business centre

Section
1 Concourse
2 Business centre
3 Pool hall
4 Changing
5 Office

Royal Selangor Turf Club

Racecourse and equine centre

Project data	Consultants	Chronology	Project information	Economic information
Location:	*Structural engineer:*	*Design:*	*Site area: 256 acres*	*Main building cost:*
Sungei Besi, Malaysia	*Tahir Wong*	*December 1989*	*Total parking spaces:*	*M $150,000,000*
Owner:	*Services engineer:*	*Documentation:*	*5,000 cars, 10 coaches*	*External works:*
Royal Selangor Turf Club	*E.R. Nair*	*March 1990*	*Total number of seats:*	*M $50,000,000*
Main contractor:	*Quantity surveyor:*	*Construction:*	*6,000, 10,000 standing*	
Sato Kogyo Construction	*KPK*	*June 1990*	*Total building area:*	
	Project manager:	*Opening date:*	*60,000 square metres*	
	WTW Consultan	*July 1993*		

Background

The Royal Selangor Turf Club was founded in 1895 and remained on its original site in central Kuala Lumpur for more than 90 years. In 1988 the committee finally decided that it was time to move to a less congested location. However, finding a suitable site at an affordable cost is no easy matter for racecourse developers, owing to the significant area of land they require; that is, around 200–300 acres, yet still reasonably close to a centre of population, and served by well developed transport and service infrastructures. Most sites that satisfy all these requirements are usually too expensive, while cheaper sites are often of such low quality that considerable improvement costs must be added to the costs of land purchase. A compromise must therefore be sought between the cost of land and the cost of improvements.

Adopting this approach, the Selangor committee turned their attention to a disused tin mine at Sungei Besi, around 16 km south of Kuala Lumpur and adjacent to a new motorway and railway line, along which would be built a new international airport. After an invited limited competition, in January 1989 we were chosen from among four international firms with expertise in racecourse design to work on the Selangor project, in association with the local firm of T.R. Hamzah and Yeang.

The brief

Our first task was to lead the design team through a process of analysis and research. In other sports this is not usually a lengthy matter. However, only one or two entirely new racecourses are built in the world every ten years or so and therefore, unlike stadia, there is less consensus on design guidelines than might be supposed. This is also partly because racecourse committees tend to be more conservative in their approach, in contrast to the rapid pace of technological progress. Thus the design team could take little for granted and had to embark upon an unusually lengthy and detailed investigation, between early 1989 and 1993.

During this analysis three key issues were identified as being of fundamental importance to the client. The existing racecourse had a loyal core of ageing, male Chinese gamblers, which the Selangor committee was keen to retain. But these patrons spent little money other than at the betting window. The committee felt it important, therefore, for the new racecourse to attract a wider range of customers of all age groups to a wider range of facilities. Consequently the client required the

2.1 A design was
developed which
divided the race
viewing and betting
side of the venue from
the food and beverage
areas. This dividing
space was designed as
an open atrium for
vertical circulation
throughout the
building

2.1

venue to be developed, as a multi-use complex with trading days not restricted to racing days.

At the same time they were adamant that the quality of the racing facility itself was of primary importance and should not be compromised in any way. The design team had meanwhile discovered that the initial site identified could not accommodate the dimensions of the required track and viewing facilities. An additional area of land was therefore purchased. However, this extra land was relatively low-grade. Decades of mining had left polluted soil, barren soil heaps and open pits filled with noxious materials. The low cost of the land's purchase had to be counter-balanced by the cost of significant environmental improvement works.

In addition to the quality of the land, racetracks require a relatively level topography. Yet the former tin mine formed part of a hill covered in dense foliage and surrounded on half of its perimeter by large areas of water. This hill had therefore to be completely remodelled, resulting in a total balanced cut and fill of 5 million cubic metres, plus significant landfill on one side.

Construction

Owing to the diverse range of buildings and infrastructure constructed on the large site, the project managers divided the works into a number of different packages, the main one being the construction of the grandstand. Before any building work could be started, however, as mentioned above, a large earth-moving programme was required. This contract included the filling in of several areas of 'slime', which was either pumped out or filled.

The project costs were continually monitored against the predetermined budgets, throughout the course of the construction programme. This was particularly important because of the diverse nature of many of the projects in hand. As well as the more traditional building works, these ranged from laying the new grass track to reclaiming parts of the adjoining lake areas. A sub-committee of the racecourse was established to meet with the design team on a regular basis and to make decisions on issues which arose from time to time. This system worked in everyone's interest and meant that there were no surprises which could affect later packages of work.

Spectator facilities

The main viewing areas are located on the south side of the track, to ensure that spectators do not have to face the sun. The grandstand is designed in three distinct sections. These are:

–   The racegoers' facilities; that is, public and private viewing areas, and directly related support facilities located on the track side. These include an extensive tote hall at ground level. Above that there are three viewing tiers. In our original concept, this track side area serves the track's primary use

- Catering and leisure areas are located on the entrance side, ensuring that they are independently accessible to the public, even when there are no races being held. The facilities on this side include food and beverage concessions, plus several restaurants that operate seven days a week. A 'racing theatre' is designed into the grandstand at ground level along with a range of event spaces where a variety of secondary attractions can be staged. These facilities have helped to change the venue's public image from simply that of a racecourse to the more general ambience of a leisure centre, where non-gamblers are more comfortable and whole families feel welcome. The secondary spaces can be quite radically rearranged and refitted over time without compromising the primary elements

The two parts of the building are located on either side of a central atrium, thereby allowing both areas to be linked or separated as required. The latest information technology is used throughout. Racing fans can brief themselves on forthcoming races and place bets from their seats using state-of-the-art equipment, while patrons throughout the building are kept fully informed and encouraged to explore the track's other facilities.

Equine facilities

In recent years there has been significant progress in the design of tracks in order to provide a better running surface for modern, thoroughbred racehorses, while at the same time reducing the likelihood of horse wastage. As a result, the design team evolved a track based on a series of concentric tracks for racing and training, carefully banked or super-elevated at the ends.

The stables are divided into two groups; one for the resident horses and one for visiting horses. The resident enclave is situated to the end of the track, with direct access to a tunnel under the track, providing access to the infield training areas. The visiting stable is

located at the opposite end of the track. Both areas are securely fenced in for equine safety, with access via three controlled entry points, one providing access to the racetrack and two giving access to the perimeter service road.

One important aspect of the site planning was that no horses arriving at the racecourse would ever have to cross a road, a critical element that determined the various circulation systems on the site. Each of the resident and visiting equine enclaves is designed as a series of trainers' modules, arranged in clusters. Each cluster contains twenty horse stalls and support spaces surrounding a central courtyard, with the outer rim of each cluster providing security for the horses, most of which are extremely valuable. To minimise heat stress, the modules are designed for good cross-ventilation and heat dispersal. Each trainer is also free to provide air-conditioning to his stalls, with all servicing provided from the outside, again to avoid infringing the strict security barriers. Shared training facilities are arranged round the above modules, and the entire area enclosed within a second secure barrier.

The well equipped equine clinic, veterinary and quarantine areas are all situated between the visiting and resident stables areas, on the northern side of the site. This area also accommodates resting areas and straight training gallops, making the new Royal Selangor Turf Club a major equine centre of excellence.

Design concept

Selangor was an unusually large project, requiring a bold design to ensure cohesion across a large site accommodating many disparate functions. Being the biggest and most used of all buildings, the grandstand provided the dominant theme, which was then carried through to the other twenty-six separate buildings on the site, ranging from electrical sub-stations to feed stores. The visual integration of all these structures was a key factor in achieving a total entertainment package for visitors, both paying and participating.

The viewing area of the main grandstand has an extensive cantilevered roof for solar shading and rain

2.2

2.3

2.2 Roof coverage has been carefully designed for sun protection in the tropical climate of Kuala Lumpur. The roof provides shade to spectators in front of the building which is a popular place for watching horse racing

2.3 Large betting halls at ground level reduce the need of most spectators to visit the upper levels and extensive food courts provide all the support these spectators require

shelter. The curve of this roof is reproduced over each of the other parts of the building, cascading from the apex over the atrium and almost down to ground level at the entrance. The changes of plane between the overlapping roofs ventilate the spaces below, with the tall atrium space acting as a stack effect ventilator which draws air from every level of the building and allows this rising warm air to escape at the top, well above the spectators. The building beneath these overlapping roofs is a highly serviced framework, designed to allow for continuous adaptation to changing circumstances. Most of the framework is filled in, but, except for the fixed viewing areas, all other elements can be radically rearranged or refitted should this ever be necessary. Some areas have been left open for future infill, but in the meantime are used to provide spare capacity and air volume to crowded areas.

The central atrium forms the main circulation space and is designed to be as clear and legible as possible, so that visitors can always see where they are going and need minimal signage to direct them – a valuable safety factor. Circulation routes of different kinds are kept rigorously separate. In this way, food and beverages can be delivered, prepared and circulated to the kitchens and serveries at all levels without crossing customer routes. Similarly, staff handling cash in the various betting outlets can circulate to all sales positions without leaving secure routes or mingling with other services. This is made possible by the provision, underneath the atrium, of a spine of service tunnels running the length of the building, connecting the central plant and service areas with a series of vertical cores. The lifts and ducts of the latter then provide access to every level of the building at key locations.

Conclusion

As mentioned earlier, we undertook a great deal of research during the early stages of the project, even though we had designed many racecourse projects before this commission. We felt this research was necessary because of the unique nature of all racecourse projects, and were rewarded for our efforts by helping to evolve a solid and effective design. The result was that, after nearly four years of work from the first design sketches to the final planting of the palm trees, the equestrian centre that emerged proved to be popular both with the management and the public alike. The track has proved to be consistent, fast and, most importantly, safe for the horses, thus making it popular with owners and trainers too.

When we made our first visit to the site in late 1989 the area surrounding the site of the new racecourse lay totally undeveloped. Now, several years later, the racecourse lies within a high technology service corridor designated by the Malaysian Prime Minister. This corridor stretches between Kuala Lumpur's new airport and the city centre, and is the focus of considerable commercial, retail and leisure development. The developments around the racecourse have, in turn, brought in a whole range of new patrons to the racecourse and its related leisure facilities, and thus, as hoped by the client, have diversified its patron base considerably.

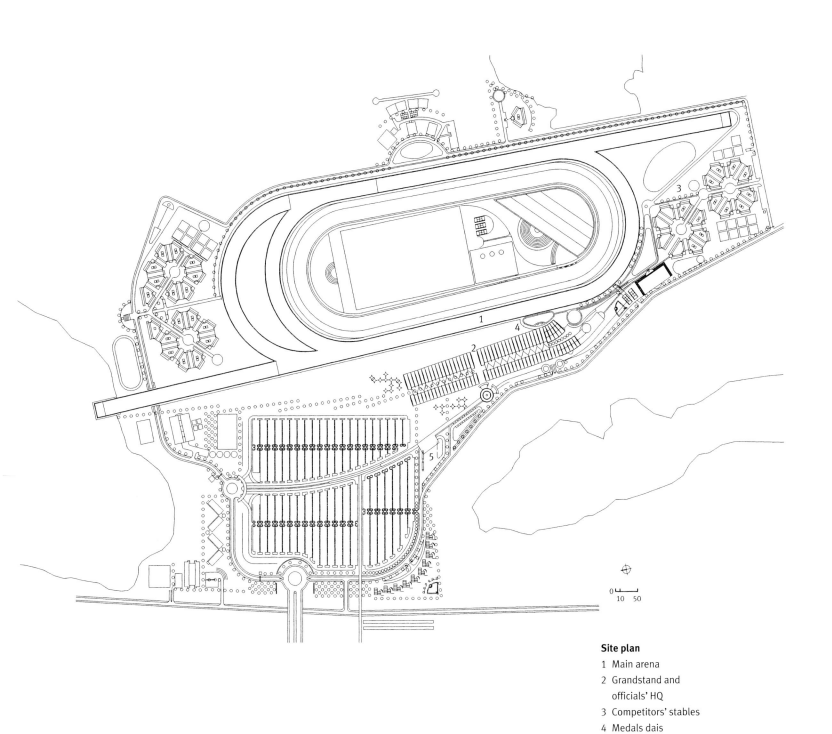

Site plan
1 Main arena
2 Grandstand and
  officials' HQ
3 Competitors' stables
4 Medals dais
5 Bus station

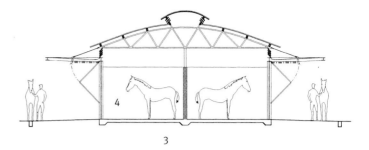

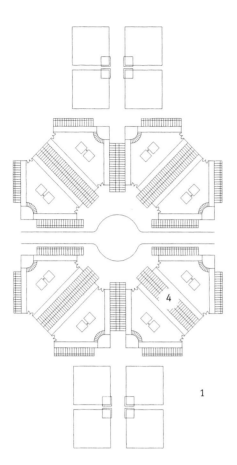

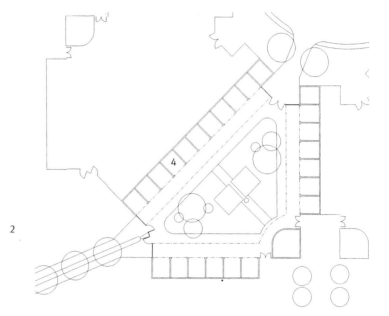

Stables modules

1 Stable module layout
2 Plan of typical stable
 module
3 Typical section
4 Horse stall

Section

1 Betting hall
2 Chairman's box/VIP
 level
3 Annual members
4 Day members
5 Sculpture court

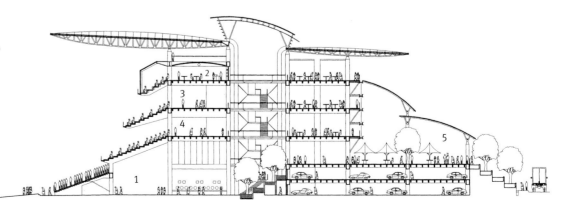

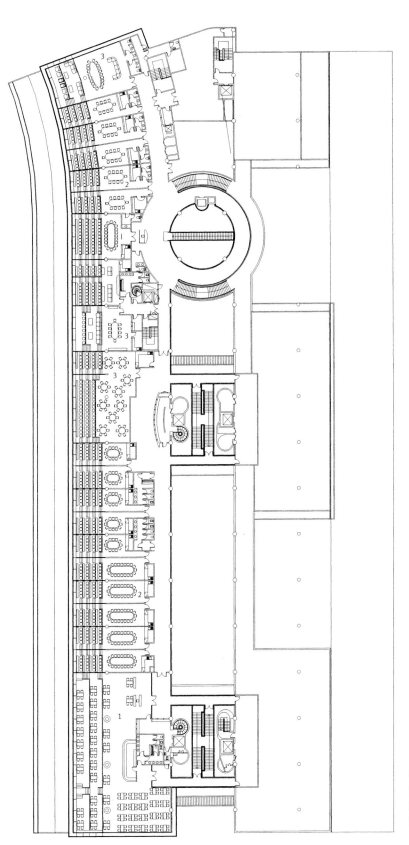

Box level plan

1   Stepped restaurant
2   Corporate boxes
3   Chairman's guests

Stadium Australia

Stadium and sports precinct

Project data	Consultants	Chronology	Project information	Economic information
Location:	*Structural engineer:*	*Design:*	*Site area:*	*Main building cost:*
Homebush Bay, Sydney	*Modus Consulting*	*March 1995*	*39.5 acres*	*A$463,000,000*
Owner:	*Engineers, Sinclair*	*Documentation:*	*Total parking spaces:*	*External works (precinct):*
Stadium Australia Trust	*Knight Merz*	*October 1996*	*200 cars, 60 coaches*	*A$20,000,000*
Main contractor:	*Services engineer:*	*Construction:*	*Total number of seats:*	
Multiplex Construction	*Sinclair Knight Merz*	*November 1996*	*110,000*	
	Quantity surveyor:	*Opening date:*	*Total building area:*	
	WT Partnership	*March 1999*	*100,000 square metres*	
		Olympic opening:		
		September 2000		

Case Study

3

Background

Sport is exceptionally popular in Australia. One-third of all Australians participate in active sport, 74 per cent attend sporting events, and an even greater percentage watch sport on television. The success of Australian teams around the world is well noted, as is, increasingly, the crucial role played by the Australian Institute for Sports. The country has already staged one Olympiad, at Melbourne in 1956. More recently after a well managed and enthusiastic campaign, in 1994 Sydney was selected as the host city for the twenty-seventh Olympiad. The site chosen for the main stadium is a former cattle-holding yard in Homebush Bay, west of the city centre. Tenders were invited by the New South Wales Government for a 80,000 seat stadium. The winning bid came from our team, Australia Stadium 2000, a consortium consisting of Multiplex Construction and Hambros Australia Ltd, with HOK LOBB as architects in conjunction with the local architects Bligh Voller.

The brief

The client required a stadium that would provide a benchmark standard for the twenty-first century. It had to be a powerful icon for the millennial Olympic Games; to offer the highest possible standard of facilities for both participants and spectators both during the Games and for subsequent sporting use. It was also to serve Sydney as a long-lasting major cultural and civic centre after the Games were over. Extensive design requirements were set by the OCA (Olympic Co-ordinating Authority) and SOCOG (Sydney Organising Committee for the Olympic Games) and included the following:

- A capacity of 80,000 seats during the Olympics
- Suitability for all Olympic games but with the ability to convert the stadium to suit major football codes thereafter
- External concourses designed to function as grand, civic spaces
- Integrated landscape features and artworks

Finance

The main finance for the stadium was based upon public participation through a fully underwritten listed vehicle on the Australian Stock Exchange, funding raised by the Australia Stadium 2000 Trust, and a long-term debt facility to fund construction and ensure the

3.1

stadium's viability at minimal cost to the taxpayer. In addition, one of the fundamental principles agreed by the project team during the early, pre-submission stages of the project was that their bid had to offer the clients not only an impressive stadium but also an effective and attractive means of helping to fund its construction. Thus it was decided to base the submission upon the simple principle of providing more seats than the 80,000 required in the brief. These extra seats could then be sold at a premium, in order to assist in the financing of the stadium. After a great deal of analysis

3.1 The temporary seats at each end of the bowl that will be removed after the Olympic Games can be clearly seen

3.2 Each side of the
stadium has a main
entrance with escalator
access to the upper
levels for a range of
spectators

3.2

the team decided to design a stadium with 110,000 seats. These extra 30,000 seats could then be sold for A$10,000 each, thereby raising A$300 million towards the costs.

Design concept

According to our analysis of stadium development (as outlined in Part I), the Olympic Stadium for Sydney would, without doubt, be a 'fourth generation' stadium. It was to be a multi-functional facility where sport is the focus, but not the full story, where people of all types and ages would be attracted to its eating and drinking places and shops, and where a range of cultural and entertainment activities would be centred around the sporting fixtures.

In addition to the requirements of the main brief, which was itself a demanding one, we set three further goals, all achievable through excellence in design:

–   First, as a focus of international attention during the millennial Olympics, the stadium would have

to inspire immediate recognition, unifying people's mental image of the Olympics with those already firmly implanted by familiar images of the city of Sydney

–   Second, as a functional sports facility, the stadium facilities should offer maximum pleasure and convenience to both spectators and participants. This was to be a stadium full of happy crowds, with athletes sufficiently inspired by their surroundings and motivated by the excellent conditions to set world records

–   Third, as a valued part of the sporting and cultural life of Sydney for decades to come, the design called for built-in durability, adaptability and an iconic status like the internationally renowned Harbour Bridge and Opera House

Masterplan and circulation

The stadium is sited in a Sydney suburb, close to the geographic centre of the city's conurbation. The sensitive integration of a large and complex venue into the

3.3 On club level,
comfortable seating is
provided allowing
spectators a more
relaxed enjoyment of
food and beverage
away from the main
circulation

3.3

surrounding suburban grain was therefore one of the major challenges for the masterplanning team. All forms of access were intensively studied by a range of consultants under the direction of the OCA, with the clear objective of making arrival at, and circulation within the site as convenient as possible. For spectators, site circulation is, as a result, concentrated upon the Olympic Boulevard that runs through the centre of the site, from one end to the other with the stadium located approximately in the centre. The legibility of this main route and various destination points along its length is particularly important. On arrival, and during subsequent perambulation around the site, the four large ramp towers of the stadium act as landmarks, or points of reference, so that visitors always know where they are. Circulation paths are designed to be highly visible and easy to understand, without visitors needing to consult maps.

Spectators will enter the building at a location that is close to their final destination on plan, and, once in their seats, they will find all major facilities on the same level with no need to make long journeys.

Vertical circulation is via either the four spiral ramp towers or two central circulation cores located within each of the East and West Stands. These circulation cores contain banks of escalators and lifts to provide convenient access to upper levels. The four ramp towers offer different routes for the public: by using a steeper line of ascent taking an inside route up the spiral, or via an outer line of ascent at an easier gradient of 1:20 which is suitable for wheelchair access. In addition, the central core of each of these four ramp towers serves two practical functions; first, as vertical service routes (not for public use), and, second, as the main exhaust ducts for the substantial passive ventilation system which naturally ventilates the public concourses.

Particularly important for such a high-profile event as the Olympics is the need to ensure that, for security, convenience and efficiency, the circulation routes used by spectators, participants and service personnel are designed never to cross each other. All services are therefore concentrated in the stadium's basement. Also contained within the basement is a loop

3·4

3.4 Temporary lighting masts adjoining the temporary seating tiers at each end of the 110,000 seat bowl

3.5 Revenue derived from banqueting facilities in stadia has become a significant income stream for new venues

3·5

road which circumnavigates the stadium, provides direct vehicular service access to the four spiral ramps, to the track and field level, and to all levels of the stadium when the public are not present. Service lifts within each of the four corners of the building complete the service access.

Spectator facilities

There are three main spectator groups in the stadium – general admission, members and corporate hospitality, although the membership group actually consists of two groups, platinum and gold members. There are also opportunities for public admissions to upgrade to open box seating and there is a range of different viewing qualities in the general group of corporate hospitality, including stepped restaurants. In the stadium's Olympic mode there are four tiers in the two side stands and two tiers in the two end stands. In post-Olympic mode, the upper tiers of both the northern and southern end stands will be removed, thus reducing the number of seats by approximately 30,000.

In spite of the unusually large capacity of the Olympic mode stadium, 80,000 to 90,000 being the typical limit of most large modern stadia, the maximum distance between any spectator and the farthest parts of the playing field remains at the recommended maximum of 190 metres. Sightline calculations had to be assessed for both Olympic mode and post-Olympic mode, a process that tested our computer software to the limit. This was because in Olympic mode the sightlines had to be calculated for optimum viewing of both the track and field. Yet in post-Olympic mode, the entire lower tier moves forward to enclose the rectangular playing field, thereby imposing quite different parameters for viewing. Despite this, there could be no compromise in the quality of sightlines.

The design therefore aimed to achieve a minimum 'C' value of 60 mm in both modes, that is:

–   In Olympic mode, based upon a focal point either to the outer lane of the running track or jumps, whichever is the closest
–   In post-Olympic mode, based upon a focal point to the edge of the rectangular playing field

It should be noted that a 'C' value of 60 mm is the minimum, and that the vast majority of spectators will enjoy a far higher standard of view. In both modes, the maximum angle of rake in the upper tiers is 34 degrees. Seat widths are generally 500 mm, with a generous tread width of 800 mm.

Toilets are evenly distributed on the basis of one WC per 600 male spectators, one hand basin per 300, and one urinal per 70. For females there is one WC and one basin per 35 female spectators. The male-to-female toilet ratio for the venue is 70:30 for general admission spectators and 60:40 for members and corporate hospitality areas (resulting in an average male-to-female split of 67:33).

For all types of spectator, the overall intention is for as much as possible of the entertainment cycle to be catered for within the site. This means providing a range of facilities which encourage visitors to arrive at the venue earlier rather than eat and drink at home or in nearby pubs and to remain there longer, so as to ease peak time congestion and, in the process, increase the operator's revenues. As regards catering, the total number of covers in the stadium for seated dining is 5,000, distributed among a range of locations throughout the facility. For the general public, in order to reduce the need for multiple queuing, the most popular food and beverage outlets are strategically located and distributed around the main concourse areas. Those concourses are also wide enough for people to gather comfortably, and to allow space for the provision of various forms of entertainment, such as live bands and other performers. Security, a major concern at any mass venue, will depend on discreet 'management' techniques, rather than heavy handed 'control' measures, relying as much on clear signage and electronic surveillance as on obtrusive physical barriers.

Participants

All athletes and event officials will have first-class changing facilities and other support accommodation, combined with playing surfaces to the best current world standards. The grass infield will have a reinforced sand profile, with computer-controlled irrigation and

3.6 Since the playing area is orientated on a north–south axis the main facades face due East and West and, in the harsh Australian sunshine, shade protection is necessary. The panels are perforated to provide shading but allow views out of the building

3.7 Two trusses, which span 296 metres, provide support for the roof and present the option of panels being inserted in the future so that the entire stadium can be enclosed if it is ever required

3.6

fertilising regimes. The athletics track will have a synthetic surface to International Amateur Athletics Federation (IAAF) standards.

Media and communications

As discussed earlier, it is our belief that the digital revolution will generate an almost insatiable demand for sports coverage in years to come, particularly as a proliferation of cable and satellite television channels seek to fill their schedules with popular and easily produced programmes for international viewing audiences. With this in mind, Stadium Australia has been designed to operate almost as a giant television studio, with broadcast picture quality given the highest possible priority. This requires implementation of the criteria listed earlier (Part I, Chapter 6). Briefly, these are: flexibility of camera positions (including several interview locations with the stadium as backdrop); stadium lighting to suit TV cameras (including the provision of translucent roof sections); and well equipped media facilities, including in-house studios and processing suites, with separate circulation routes from other users.

Structure

The main stadium structure is based on rigid frames without bracing planes, in order to maximise flexibility and adaptability in use. Shorter construction times and reasonable construction costs have been achieved by exploiting the use of *in situ* concrete, pre-cast concrete and steel, to best effect. The rear sections of the North and South Stands will be removed after the Olympic Games, and the lower tiers moved inwards to achieve a tighter configuration for football games. These tiers can then be moved outwards to make space for other sports, such as Australian Rules football, or even the re-installation of an athletics track.

Since our design for Stadium Australia first became public, there has been a great deal of comment, not least about the derivation of the chosen form of roof structure. Some have likened the form to a commercial potato chip, which the hyperbolic paraboloid shape certainly resembles. But as far as we were concerned, there is no doubt that when we started generating the early sketches in our London office, we actually had the Australian slouch hat or 'akubra' more in mind. The roof covers the spectators as the hat covers the man.

The two side roofs are formed by curved triangular trusses, spanning the 296 metre length of the spectator accommodation on each side (each truss is capable of covering four jumbo jets side by side). From the edge of these trusses a roof plane curved in two directions is supported. This hyperbolic paraboloid roof form derives partly from a rational approach to covering the seating bowl, and partly to the creation of a visually impressive shape. There are also functional advantages. Such a form is easily constructed, as all the structural lines of the diagrid are straight, while the low front edge makes for effective weather protection, offers good acoustics and good access of sunlight to the playing surface, and provides an ideal mount for floodlighting. Each roof has a maximum span in the centre of 70 metres, reaching 43 metres at the highest point along the front edge, and 58 metres at the highest point along the outer edge. The basic roof

3.7

structure is steel, covered by polycarbonate triple-skin sheeting set in a support frame network that mirrors the structural diagrid below. This cladding's translucency helps to promote pitch growth, while offering better quality television pictures than is the case with opaque roofs.

The roofs were built up in phases. In Olympic mode each side roof will shelter 32,300 seats behind the drip line. After the stadium is converted to post-Olympic mode, the roof will be extended in modular fashion to cover the spectator areas at each end. Finally, the roof structure has been designed to allow for the addition of two retractable sections, in order to allow for the complete covering of the event arena, should that be desired in later years. Such a planned approach means that costs are incurred only as and when new sections of roofing are required, rather than all at once. At the same time, after each phase of the construction programme, the roof structures are designed to look complete.

Services and ESD

Services are designed to current 'best practice' standards, but with a margin for flexibility so that upgrading will be possible as technology advances in new directions. In addition, because the stadium's layout is modular and zoned, each sector has easy access for servicing, for temporary adjustment to different loading, and for future upgrading. All communication and data provisions within the building have also been designed with the future in mind. In line with the brief the whole design is based upon the principle of Environmentally Sustainable Development. The selection of constructional materials is based on an analysis of scientific evidence, rather than subjective opinion. Environmental control systems will make maximum use of passive heating and cooling, natural ventilation and natural lighting. Electricity and hot water will be produced in an energy-efficient manner by gas co-generation. Plant waste will be composted, waste

3.8 The elegant curve of the perimeter truss will only be completed after the Olympics when the true form of the stadium roof will be evident

3.8

water recycled and a subterranean aquifer will detain and store storm-water run-off for irrigation.

Conclusion

There is little doubt that Stadium Australia will be seen by a larger percentage of the world's television viewing population than any previous Olympic venue. The stadium's 110,000 capacity also means that it will be the largest venue ever to have staged the Games (the previous largest being the Los Angeles Coliseum in 1984, which reputedly held 101,000). But its place in history will hopefully not be confined to statistical records. Stadium Australia's overall design responds to different scales, that of pedestrians and that of its urban context, in a form which is expressed as a series of elements, each clearly articulated in response to function.

The fabric of the building is detailed as a series of layers, with the curve of the main roof trusses acting as a transition between the complex geometrical differences of the upper tier and the roof. The cladding behind the four ramps is subdued and modular, to act as a backdrop to these dramatic ramp towers. The external floodlighting of the building also expresses the structural sculpture of the ramps. Sunshades lining the banquet rooms are a visible statement of the environmentally sensitive design and are detailed as lightweight skeletal structures to contrast with the solid mass of the structure behind. Floating canopies at the entries provide a human scale to the base of the stadium, which is 'tactile and grained' in finish, while the main entry and rising escalator shafts are glazed and transparent, enticing people into the building.

Interiors are boldly conceived and will reinforce the unique character and experience of this Olympic stadium throughout its life, with neutral backgrounds highlighted by bold colours and rich materials and specific areas additionally highlighted by an integrated lighting scheme. Thus it is hoped that Stadium Australia will set new aesthetic and functional standards for buildings of this type, while at the same time creating a fitting stage for all that the Olympic Games represent, and becoming another icon of Sydney's and Australia's international image.

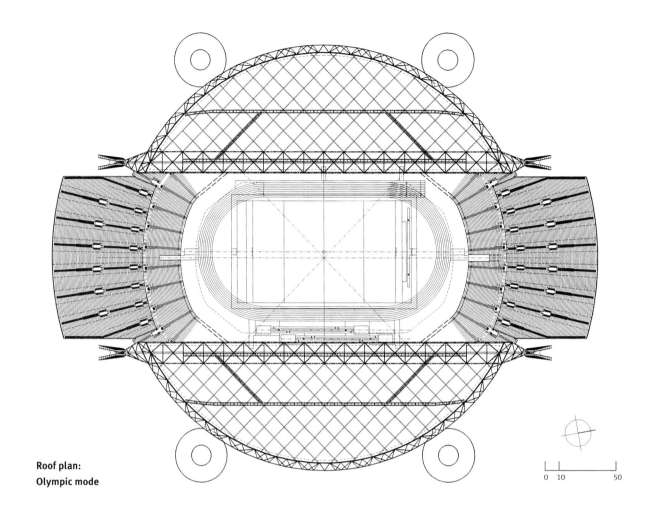

Roof plan:
Olympic mode

0 10   50

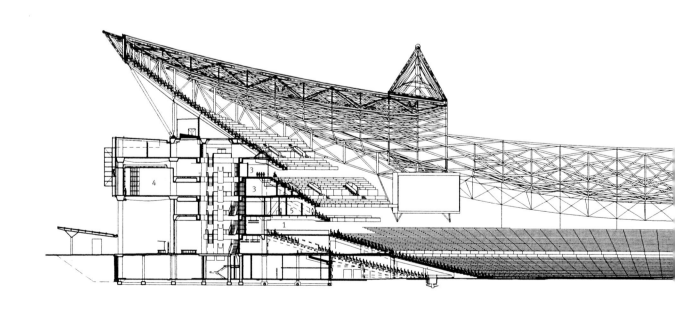

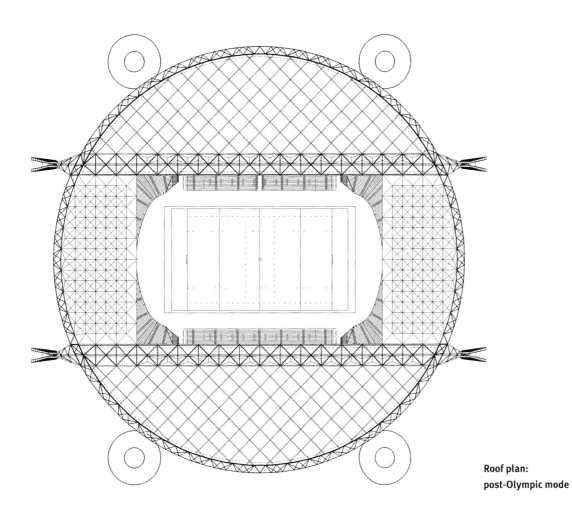

Roof plan:
post-Olympic mode

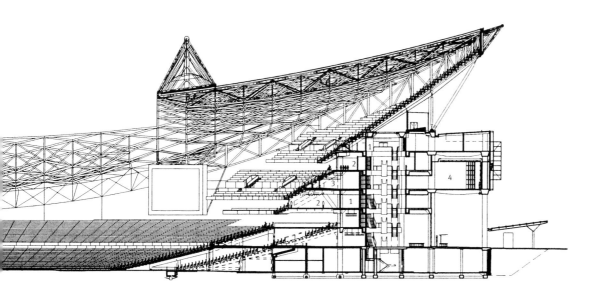

Section
1 Concourse
2 Private suite
3 Members' area
4 Banquet room
5 Radio
   communications box

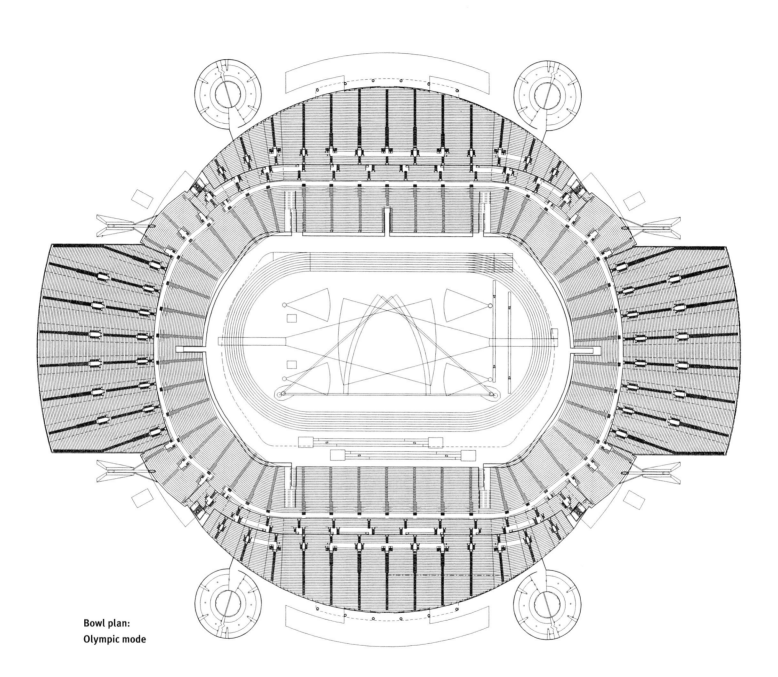

Bowl plan:
Olympic mode

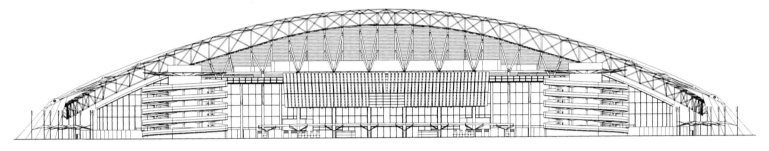

Post-Olympic elevation, east–west

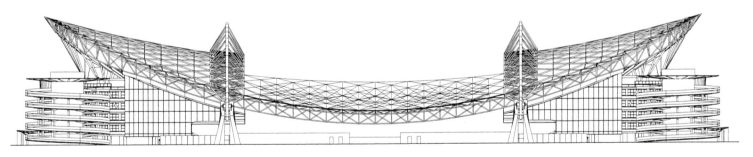

Post-Olympic elevation, north–south

Cheltenham Racecourse

Masterplan and implementation

Project data	Consultants	Chronology	Project information	Economic information
Location:	*Structural engineer:*	*Design:*	*Site area:*	*Main building cost:*
Cheltenham, England	*Jan Bobrowski and P*	*April 1977*	*370 acres*	*£1,400,000 – Phase 1*
Owner:	*Services engineer:*	*Construction:*	*Total parking spaces:*	*£10,000,000 – Phase 7*
Cheltenham Racecourse	*Rosser & Russell,*	*April 1978*	*5,000 cars, 500 coaches*	
Main contractor:	*John Bradley Associates,*	*February 1997*	*Total number of seats:*	
Taylor Woodrow	*Hoare Lea & Partners*		*3,500, 17,000 standing*	
James Longley & Co.,	*Quantity surveyor:*		*Total building area:*	
John Mowlem	*Davis Langdon Everest*		*8,250 square metres*	

Case Study

4

Background

The racecourse was originally set out in the natural amphitheatre that is Prestbury Park, just outside Cheltenham, in 1902. Prior to that, racing had been staged at a number of locations in the area, most notably on the top of Cleeve Hill, which nowadays forms a beautiful backdrop to today's national hunt racing. Until the 1970s the course's stock of buildings had been developed, as is common in British sport, in an ad hoc manner, to form a collection of stands ranging from two to four storeys, with a variety of viewing sections and constructed in a range of different materials and designs.

Our involvement began on a small scale in 1974, when we were commissioned to design a banqueting facility, to be grafted onto the existing 1950s weigh-room and members' entrance. The new building to consist of an open plan banqueting space, an open bar area, complete with full kitchen facilities, ventilation and heating systems signalled Cheltenham Racecourse's first attempts to market the venue for non-racing activities, beyond the usual programme of sixteen race days per year. The banqueting facility was sufficiently successful for us to be commissioned to prepare an overall masterplan for the site in 1977. This was intended to establish a framework for the future redevelopment of the racecourse. (A second masterplan would follow in 1991.)

Masterplan One (1977–94)

Development of the brief for this first masterplan evolved over a period of time. Several parties contributed, leading to agreement on the following key issues:

- The masterplan should develop a strategy for the redevelopment of the racecourse, to take place over a fifty-year period
- The first phase of the masterplan would be the construction of a new members' grandstand
- All new spectator facilities would provide a high standard of both seated and standing accommodation, designed to modern standards of safety and to create an ambience of fun and entertainment
- Bars, restaurants and entertainment suites, which offer direct views of the racecourse, should be designed for adaptation for non-raceday activities
- Kitchen and food distribution systems should offer the best quality service

4.1

4.1 The striking night-time image of the Tattersalls Grandstand is captured from the 'running rail'

- There should be improvements to all operational facilities, such as the racing integrity areas provided for the judge, stewards and photo-finish equipment, as well to areas for the media (including an improvement to various television camera positions)
- Back of house handling activities inside the grandstand, and the circulation network around the racecourse, should all be rationalised
- Opportunities for development should be set out, ensuring that each one can be completed in viable phases, and constructed within the eleven-month period which falls between the staging of Cheltenham's most lucrative programme of events, the annual National Hunt Festival

Members' Stand – design concept

The first phase of the five-storey grandstand was completed for the 1979 season and accommodated around 3,000 spectators, plus a number of private hospitality boxes. From the central spine of pre-cast concrete 'H' frames, the steppings slope down towards the course, providing seats on the upper tiers and standing terraces on the lower. Cantilevering over these steppings are the

4.2 From the main car park the barrel vault of the entrance takes the visitor in carpeted comfort directly into the main grandstand

4.2

hospitality viewing balconies and the concrete framed roof. The roof is formed of pre-cast concrete parabolic shells only 80 mm thick, spanning between pre-cast, pre-tensioned roof beams set at 7.2 metre intervals. Each beam, measuring over 20 metres long, was cast in a single piece, and shaped like an inverted 'T' to incorporate the main rainwater drainage gutters.

Implementing Masterplan One

The completion of the Members' Stand proved to be a modest beginning for what would become an ongoing redevelopment programme. Further phases of the masterplan followed, some of which were revenue earning, such as new private boxes or restaurants, plus others including new stables and toilet areas which yielded no income but greatly improved the racecourse's overall provision for participants and spectators alike. However, the project team agreed to adopt a development strategy which, whenever possible, ensured that any phase of construction involving non-revenue facilities would be followed by at least two projects which would enhance the course's operational income.

Between 1979 and 1994 seven phases of development were undertaken. Each was completed both within the allocated time programme and the agreed budget. As a consequence, the masterplan was implemented in barely fifteen years rather than the originally proposed time-scale of fifty years. This rapid progress was largely possible thanks to the growing financial success of the racecourse itself, combined with funding assistance from the Betting Levy Board.

Masterplan Two (1994)

In 1994 it was recognised that a new masterplan for the racecourse was required, one that would be even more ambitious in its scope than the original, drawn up in 1977. During that period the project team, consisting of the lead consultants and the client, had learnt not to underestimate Cheltenham's potential and popularity, nor the positive effects new developments could have on its revenue-earning potential. A new brief was therefore developed and agreed upon by all parties, with the following objectives:

–   To build on the strategies established in Masterplan One
–   To move the boundary of the building area outwards, away from the track, in order to release more space for development and circulation
–   To continue improvements to the entrance areas, so as to enhance the meeting and greeting of racegoers and create a new main entrance with direct access to the grandstand and non-racing activities

- To form strong visual axis and strong visual reference points across the site in order to simplify circulation routes
- To provide a greater variety of entertainment spaces
- To provide more covered areas specifically for general racegoers, including the provision of a large video screen, showing Parade Ring activity
- To physically segregate the horse management circulation routes from those of racegoers, while at the same time allowing visual contact wherever possible
- To enhance the range of viewing options available to spectators, and include innovative forms of viewing and entertainment

Implementing Masterplan Two

The first phase of work to initiate the second masterplan was a non revenue-earning section of building which included the redevelopment of the existing offices and the creation of a new entrance and car parking area for members. It also encompassed a new pre-parade ring, horse-walk, paddock entrance and other ancillary areas completed for the 1995 National Hunt Festival meeting. The previous scattered office accommodation was brought under one roof, in approximately 800 square metres of modern commercial space, designed around a central courtyard. Below this entrance level, new service and storage areas have been created for the restaurants above.

The new car park comprises 340 spaces, divided by sloping banks of planting. A paved walkway now leads people to a new entrance, where VIP parking and set-down points have been created. This entrance provides access to the new offices and a 'gallery' connection, linked to an existing restaurant area. The circulation routes for horses, leading between the stables

4.3

4.3 The complete racing experience inside the Panoramic Restaurant: watching the race, five-star food and beverage service, and placing a bet, all without leaving your table

4.4 The stepped table layout of the Panoramic Restaurant provides diners with an uninterrupted view of the racing and the dramatic 'panorama' of Cleeve Hill through the raking suspended glazing

4.4

and the pre-parade ring, has been segregated from the public by forming a lower level equine circulation route, with vehicle and pedestrian bridges above. The new pre-parade ring and saddling boxes have improved stepped viewing facilities and offer unimpeded access for the horses to and from the parade ring. Close to this new feature a paddock entrance has been created to form a meeting and access point to the grounds from the car park, thereby helping to define the axis between the paddock ring and the tented village.

The second phase of work on Masterplan Two started in March 1996, immediately after the Gold Cup, Cheltenham's main race meeting which forms part of the annual Festival and was completed in time for the following year's event. This phase involved the construction of a new grandstand, first called the Gold Card Stand but now known as the Tattersalls Stand. This building replaced two old grandstands, which lay immediately opposite the new entrance (completed during the previous phase) and consist of five floors of accommodation. Although an entirely new construction the stand is effectively an extension of the new Members' Stand, completed in 1979.

On the lowest level is a bookmaker and tote area, with bars and the main public toilets. Above this, on level two, is a large Irish theme bar and on level three are restaurants accommodating 850 annual members. The new entrance and lobby of the adjacent grandstand (begun during the previous phase) connects directly into level three of the new stand, thereby linking the office and extensive back of house catering areas with the main viewing areas.

On the two top levels there are further private boxes, on the same level as those in the earlier stand, and at the very top is a restaurant, first known as the Gold Card Restaurant, now known as the 'Panoramic'

because of the spectacular views it offers across the racecourse and to Cleeve Hill in the distance. Indeed, it could be said that it provides one of the best views from any racecourse facility in the world. The restaurant accommodates 300 covers and is stepped, so that each table of four has a clear view of the racing. Mobile tote betting and television monitors on each table allow diners to place their bets without leaving their seats.

Conclusion

The redevelopment of Cheltenham over the last twenty years has been a huge success. It has been implemented in a consistently enlightened manner by the racecourse board, and has introduced a whole new range of facilities to the racing public. The result is that Cheltenham is now regarded as one of the most progressive and, possibly as a result, one of the most profitable racecourses in Britain. If there is one lesson to be drawn from this success story, therefore, it is that any project team drawing up a sports facilities masterplan should never underestimate the venue's earning potential, or its drawing power, if only the mix of new facilities is right.

Cheltenham will no doubt go on to complete their second masterplan, which includes an indoor betting and entertainment hall, and a grandstand which will span across the track, to link the main grandstand areas with the infield. Once complete the result will be one of the finest racecourse facilities in the world. It will also be proof that although British racecourses do not, historically, generate the same enormous level of revenue as their counterparts in Asia, they can compete favourably on the world stage through sensible, long-term planning, when combined with vision and imagination.

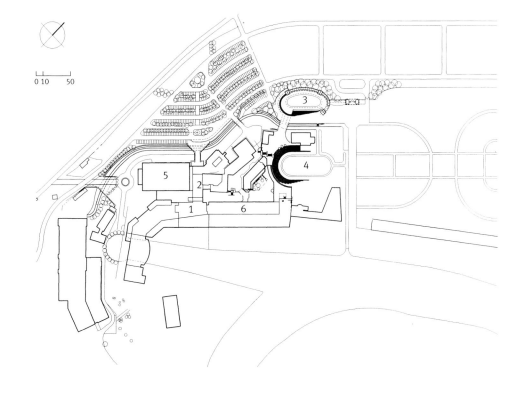

Site plan
1 New Tattersalls stand
2 New Tattersalls entry
  bridge
3 New pre-parade ring
4 Existing parade ring
5 Proposed covered
  Tattersalls concourse
6 Existing main
  grandstand

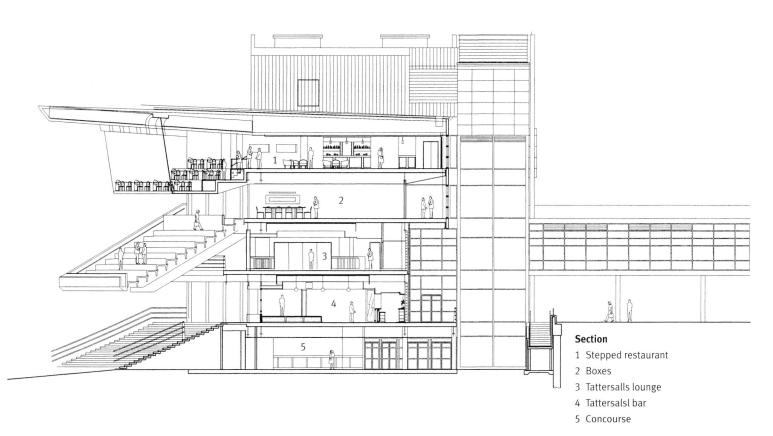

Section
1 Stepped restaurant
2 Boxes
3 Tattersalls lounge
4 Tattersalsl bar
5 Concourse

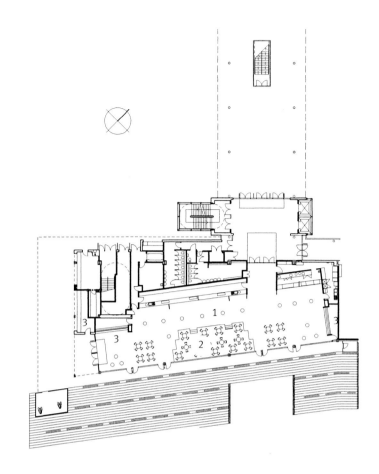

Level 2 plan

1 Tattersalls bar
2 Podium
3 Betting

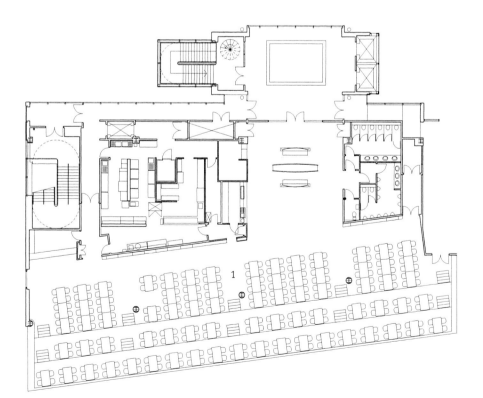

Restaurant level plan

1 Stepped restaurant

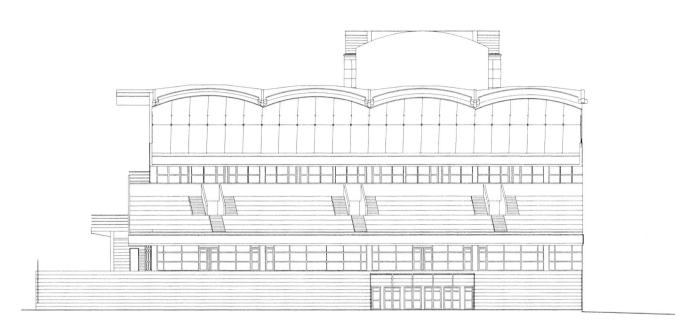

Front elevation (east)

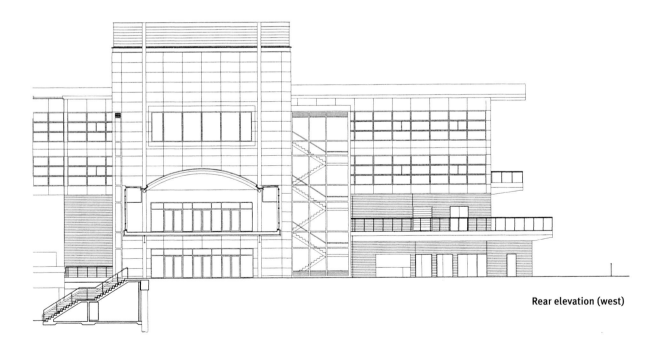

Rear elevation (west)

Silverstone Circuit

Grand Prix masterplan

Project data	Consultants	Chronology	Project information	Economic information
Location:	*Structural engineer:*	*Design:*	*Site area:*	*Total construction cost:*
Silverstone, England	*John Parkhouse*	*July 1988*	*275 acres*	*£5,000,000 (estimate)*
Owner:	*Associates*	*Submission:*	*Total parking spaces:*	
Silverstone Circuits Ltd	*Quantity surveyor:*	*September 1988*	*20,560 cars*	
	Davis Langdon Everest		*Total number of seats:*	
			10,000	

Background

Silverstone, the venue for the annual British Grand Prix, is nearly 5 miles south of Towcester, Northamptonshire, and is Britain's principal motor racing circuit. The venue has grown piecemeal over many decades and in 1988 we were commissioned to do a Masterplan Feasibility Study, to investigate a range of possibilities for the rational development of the site.

The brief

It quickly became clear to the design team that the Silverstone site was not planned efficiently, was under-used, and could be made considerably more efficient and therefore profitable by a number of carefully judged strategic planning measures. These were deemed to be the following:

- The main vehicular entrance to the grounds needed to offer a far more visible and emblematic image for arriving motorists
- A number of the other entrances needed repositioning and improving, as they were clearly failing to work to full capacity or, in some cases, were creating bottlenecks

- Several of the car parking areas, and the internal site roads connecting them, needed to be more efficiently planned

The masterplan

The integration of vehicular, pedestrian, service and official circulation networks on a site as large and diverse as a Grand Prix circuit is unusually demanding. It is important for anyone coming to the venue to feel a sense of arrival, irrespective of the point at which they enter the grounds. It was therefore decided that the main entrance known as V8, currently used all year round, because of its good links with the administrative offices and track, should be made more effective. It should be set back from the highway for maximum visibility, be given a strong design theme, and the access road from it, into the grounds, should be re-planned and simplified to form a major axis. Secondary facilities would be concentrated along this axis and a formal entrance square would be created to give visitors an impressive introduction to the site.

Other entrances around the site perimeter would be re-planned or moved so that each gate leads more clearly to a particular parking area, and all entrance gates should be given the same characteristic design theme (though at a lower hierarchical level than the main entrance), again to emphasise the Silverstone identity. Selective enlargement and reshaping of individual car parks was planned to increase parking capacity and to allow a more effective routing of circulation roads. In addition, pedestrian routes leading from the car parks to the actual track viewing areas would be upgraded, and ideally covered. This would mean that these people routes would become a visually dominant link to a new grandstand tower that would form a focal point for arriving visitors.

The masterplan also proposed, as part of the client's brief, several new grandstands at selected locations along the track, each to have its own local character and price level, but designed to convey one recognisable cohesive image for the entire site. The main (and highest-priced) viewing area would be alongside the Woodcote and pit straight. Other viewing locations could be developed at the Copse, Beckett and Stowe corners to give visitors alternative focal points for viewing the race.

Design concept

To assist with the analysis of what each viewing location required we developed a modular approach to the design of the proposed grandstands. The concept was for the stands to be constructed in interchangeable sections which could be easily assembled, added to or moved around, according to need. Modular sections would incorporate concourses, gangways, vomitories and stairways, with regularised dimensions calculated to ensure safe escape times for all spectators. Each grandstand was to be made up of some of the following elements:

- A trackside run-off area, barrier and safety zone
- Five types of spectator accommodation overlooking the track, as follows: public standing areas; public seating areas; private boxes (with seating either inside the box or on a balcony); restaurant areas (either on level one or a stepped viewing basis); club rooms
- Behind the spectator areas but attached to them there were to be private and public circulation

areas, food and beverage concessions, toilet facilities, trade stand areas and retail or merchandising outlets
- Two service zones were possible, with one beneath the front seating tier to service trackside functions, and a ground duct to the rear of the stand to service the external trade retail areas

By establishing this flexible model we could examine the effect of various sightline and other optional standards to arrive at the best solution for each of the locations being considered. This approach would also allow for future developments to take place at the circuit.

Because spectators at motor-sport events tend to leave their seats and wander around the stand more freely than at many other sports, the standard tread widths of the seating modules was set at a reasonable minimum of 800 mm. Alternative angles of rake were calculated, aimed at giving all spectators a 'C' value of either 120 mm, 90 mm or 75 mm. These values, it will be noted, are generally higher than those provided for other sports, because the sheer speed of the action makes it crucial for spectators to have a clear view. Alternative plans for bay layouts were also produced for each level of the pavilion, to illustrate the flexibility of the model and to test the effect of each layout on the number of seats and other facilities.

The track side elevation was also developed, with zones for advertising hoardings, while the service road elevation made allowance for the presence of video screens (showing images of the race, information about lap positions and times, plus all the usual advertising).

At the time of the initial brief, attendance for one day at Silverstone numbered around 95,000 people. More recently this has grown to 120,000, of which some 12,000 visitors require sit-down hot meals to be served (largely in marquee tents). This is in addition to the selling of innumerable casual snacks and drinks throughout the day. In response to this high demand, we devised a strategy for the proposed catering operation, based on five levels of service, from the lowest and simplest vendor and fast food outlet, at the bottom of the range, to reserved-table restaurant at the top.

The proposals also provided suggestions as to how, in addition to, yet without compromising Silverstone's core business of motor racing, other revenue-earning activities could be added to the site, thus enhancing its year-round profitability. The masterplan therefore allocated areas for the following non-racing facilities:

—   A hotel built close to the track could be used for corporate hospitality on main race days, and for race teams and visitors to Silverstone on other days
—   A market for office space was identified, particularly for companies directly related to the motor sport industry
—   The site's existing rudimentary business park could be expanded and upgraded to provide high-tech accommodation and workshops for businesses in the motor sport industry

—   An exhibition area might simply be a covered space for temporary exhibitions, or the nucleus for a museum or for permanent exhibitions

Conclusion

The masterplan was primarily a planning and logistics exercise. Over the years certain aspects of it have been put into effect. The Silverstone project remains a good example of how to masterplan a large and complex site, and contains several thought-provoking ideas which could clearly assist in the improvement of most major sites which have been developed *ad hoc* over a period of time. Above all, the masterplan demonstrates that the first task of the designer is always to identify the problems, and only then to design the solutions

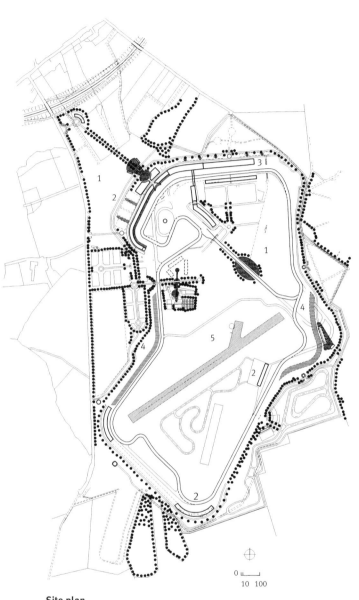

Site plan

1 Public concourse
2 Existing buildings
3 Proposed buildings
4 Improved spectator
  mounding
5 Runway

5.1

5.1 The inherent
complexity of
planning a vast site for
a huge event once a
year with minimal
fixed facilities has been
rationalised to improve

revenue generation
and sense of place and
orientation

WestpacTrust Stadium

Cricket and rugby stadium

Project data	Consultants	Chronology	Project information	Economic information
Location:	*Structural engineer:*	*Design:*	*Site area:*	*Main building cost:*
Wellington, New	*Holmes Consulting*	*April 1996*	*16.8 acres*	*NZ$96,000,000*
Zealand	*Services engineer:*	*Documentation:*	*Total parking spaces:*	*External works:*
Owner:	*Beca Carter Hollings*	*May 1997*	*700 cars, 135 coaches*	*NZ$12,000,000*
Regional Stadium Trust	*Quantity surveyor:*	*Construction:*	*Total number of seats:*	
Main contractor:	*Russell Drysdale &*	*February 1998*	*34,500*	
Fletcher Construction	*Thomas*	*Opening date:*	*Total building area:*	
	Project manager:	*January 2000*	*26,970 square metres*	
	Beca Carter Hollings			

Case Study

6

Background

Discussions concerning a new regional stadium for Wellington first arose in 1994. The intention was to replace the now dilapidated rugby ground, Athletic Park, with New Zealand's first, purpose-built multi-use venue for both rugby and cricket. Moreover, the new stadium would have to compare favourably with some of the more modern venues appearing in Australia. In 1995 we were approached by the Stadium Trust to undertake a review of a feasibility study and design already completed by the local firm of architects, Warren & Mahoney. This review completely reassessed the design and the proposed facilities, taking into account the need to incorporate all the latest design and safety developments. The review also established design parameters, which would ensure that the stadium should meet the Trust's aspirations.

As a result of this review our Australian office was appointed to work in association with Warren & Mahoney, to provide architectural services for the project which had been named the WestpacTrust Stadium after the main sponsor, Westpac Banking Corporation. Schematic designs for the stadium were begun in April 1996 and completed by October. These drawings then formed the basis for the Development Consent, submitted

the following December. Consent was received in April 1997 and consequently the consultants were asked to proceed, in May 1997, with the preparation of the documentation drawings and the first stage of tenders to appoint a main contractor.

The brief

The Trust required a world-class venue that would cater for the main sporting codes of Rugby Union and cricket and, at the same time, provide a stadium capable of hosting concerts and other international events, such as a Commonwealth Games. To comply with this last requirement the stadium had to be designed so that it could be reconfigured to facilitate the incorporation of a temporary (international standard) athletics track and field. The initial designs set the stadium's capacity at 34,500.

The venue was also to cater for the corporate sector through the inclusion of sixty-four corporate boxes, located at a vantage point able to offer raised, unobstructed views for both resident sports. A club membership scheme was also proposed for a silver service dining suite for up to 1,000 people on the corporate/club level, offering views into the arena with an adjoining seating area. Catering and back-of-house

6.1 The bowl has been designed as tightly as possibe to allow for both cricket and rugby to be played without having to resort to relatively expensive moving tiers and stands

6.1

facilities were also to provide a good level of service to the public, corporate boxes, stadium members, and players' areas. During the development of the brief the stadium's main concourse was conceived as a gallery space which would provide Wellington with a seven-day-a-week entertainment, cultural and exhibition facility serving the community. Also required in the stadium were facilities directly related to the two main sporting codes. These included a Sports Medicine Centre for the University, a Sporting Museum, and a Sports Centre of Excellence.

The site

The site selected for the new stadium was adjacent to the city's central business district, comprising reclaimed land that had been used for railway goods yards serving the port of Wellington. In terms of its location, the site was ideal, not only because of its close proximity to the city centre but also because it was next to the main transport interchanges that serve the city. It was also hoped that the stadium's development would stimulate other developments within this former industrial area. The site was not without its problems, however. Wellington is located on a major geological fault and is prone to earthquakes. These have the potential to cause liquefaction of the sort of fill material which had been used to reclaim the site. To prevent the likelihood of

liquefaction, therefore, prior to construction the ground had to be vibro-compacted. This is a process that requires piled steel tubes to be vibrated, in order to promote local settlement. Graded hardcore is then poured down the centre of the tube and compacted. After this the tubes are removed leaving behind a series of stone piers which provide added stability in the event of an earthquake. The stadium building was then piled independently and supported on approximately 400 reinforced concrete, 12 metre piles.

In terms of its accessibility, the site is effectively land-locked on three sides, with all vehicular and pedestrian access gained via a plaza linking the venue with the main railway station, which lies just to the south. Underneath this plaza is a railway track providing access to the harbour and container port. As the site is so accessible to all forms of transport, the client was keen to encourage its future patrons to make the maximum use of public transport. Car parking on the site is therefore deliberately limited to just 700 cars, on two levels predominantly beneath the pedestrian plaza. However, a number of other car parks in the centre of Wellington are within walking distance of the site, a benefit of its close proximity to the Central Business District (CBD).

To encourage the use of public transport, people arriving by train will be able to walk straight from the platform to the stadium plaza, a distance of less than 300 metres. For bus and coach travellers the local bus

6.2

6.2 Situated on old
railway land close to
the city centre the
stadium has been
designed as a single-
tier bowl with an
upper level of
corporate and
hospitality suites
around its perimeter

terminal will be relocated, and a new parking site built for 135 coaches, to give similarly short and direct pedestrian connections to the plaza. These provisions will be strengthened by various management strategies. For example, shuttle buses will run to the CBD's parking areas, while ticketing arrangements will allow people to book a stadium seat, buy a coach or train ticket, and reserve accommodation and meals in a single transaction. It is hoped that by adopting such measures, up to half the spectators will arrive by public transport.

Design concept

In order to provide a pitch area able to cater for both rugby and cricket, including an international standard five block-cricket wicket and field, the stadium was planned as a large oval-shaped, fully enclosed amphitheatre. A traditional cricket pavilion was incorporated into the overall plan, to provide the usual cricket VIP, members' and players' facilities. The design was thus one of the first modern cricket venues to be devised as a complete entity from the outset, rather than be developed in the piecemeal fashion common in other cricket venues. The base level of seats for cricket will be 34,500. However, at a later date, a further eight retractable rows of seats can be added in order to increase the capacity to 40,000, and also to close the gaps which arise when the rectangular rugby pitch is positioned in the centre of the cricket field.

The building is envisaged as a series of planes and tight skin surfaces, enclosing the accommodation and providing a dramatic sculptural form following the bowl plan. Reflective silver cladding forms the tight skin surface, creating a continuous disc punctuated by areas of glazing, which identify various points of entry. The close fit skin starts above the recessed ground floor accommodation, to create a floating plane or surface that hovers above the main public concourse. This sculptural quality is further emphasised by the insertion of a continuous strip of glazing around the top of the cladding, so that the roof structure above appears as a continuous, floating horizontal disc.

The client's additional accommodation requirements are housed on the south side of the building, enclosed within a curving form, which effectively peels away from the main stadium. This section of the build-

ing marks the entrance and lounge areas, and is enclosed by the tight skin cladding utilised elsewhere. This element of the building is defined by a glazed roof-light, which delineates a vertical canyon containing escalators and entry voids. The glazing to the entrance is designed as a back projection screen, offering an electronic advertising board for forthcoming events, visible from the external plaza. The floodlight towers form the only external expression of the structure of the building and are designed as mast forms, thus echoing the yachts which sail the waters of Wellington Harbour. These masts rise to a height of 53 metres and act as beacons for the building on the edge of the city.

Accommodation within the venue is provided on five levels. Level 1 is the main service and administration floor. It houses the major food preparation areas; offices and board rooms for the various sports organisations using the building as their headquarters; and changing and warm-up rooms for players. Sports participants will walk straight from their coaches into these areas, free from contact with the public. Both players and service vehicles will also be able to move from this level directly onto the playing field. The only parts accessible to the general public will be a sports science centre offering postgraduate teaching for 200 students a year, plus research and medical facilities, and a full-sized commercial gymnasium.

A service road circumnavigates the perimeter of the accommodation at this level, providing access to all the facilities as well as to the pitch, via four wide vomitories. These openings and the service road are designed to accommodate the type of large vehicles used by concert promoters and event organisers. This provision will ensure that Wellington will have a venue capable of hosting the range of concert tours and shows which have, to date, not visited the city owing to the absence of an appropriate venue.

The main service and back-of-house accommodation is located on the south side of the stadium, nearest the entry ramp. Another ramp is located on the northern side of the stadium accessing the main public concourse above. This ramp is designed to accommodate vehicular traffic used to service the concourse. It also provides emergency egress from level 2. Goods and passenger lift cores are situated on the south and north sides of the stadium, to provide vertical access to all levels.

Level 2 is the main public floor. This opens off the paved pedestrian plaza fronting the stadium, from where all spectators will enter via the thirty-two turnstile entrances and VIP gates. Due to the constraints of the site, turnstiles and gates are located in four separate groups, each offering access to specific seating zones inside. The internal concourse on level 2 is an enclosed, 13 metre wide, double height gallery space, with a rich variety of public facilities arranged around the perimeter. It is envisaged that this gallery will be open seven days a week and will contain food and beverage concessions, plus various other entertainment and cultural facilities for wider public use. The concourse is also intended to provide linear exhibition space suitable for large-scale exhibitions, trade shows and product launches on non-match days. The main entry area pro-

vides facilities for the Sports Hall of Fame and the entrance to VIP and member areas. Escalators cross the lobby area in a top-lit vertical circulation canyon, making the delineation between the viewing bowl and the additional depth of accommodation required for the lounges on the upper levels.

Level 3 contains a variety of lounges on the south side of the stadium, located in the Cricket Pavilion. These lounges provide accommodation for cricket VIP use, cricket players and cricket members. These facilities will also be rented out during the rugby season to provide try-line lounges for corporate and members' use. Cricket players and officials will be able to sit here during matches. To enter the field, players will walk down a gangway placed amid the spectator areas in the traditional manner. Access to the players' changing rooms, located on level 1, is via a secure route. Kitchens, bars and toilet facilities are provided on this

6.3 A roof has been positioned to give partial cover to the spectators providing a sense of enclosure but sufficiently open to still enjoy the outdoor atmosphere

6.4 A dramatic bowl which has proved popular with spectators

6.3

6.4

level to serve the lounges and ensure that the level is self-contained.

Level 4 forms the second level of accommodation of the Cricket Pavilion and, on the west and north sides of the stadium, contains media facilities for television, radio and the written press. This level is situated at the top of the seating bowl and gives a good elevated viewing position. A stadium members' lounge is also located on this level, in the southwest corner. To satisfy the requirements of televised cricket, three master camera positions, a television control suite and commenting booths are located on the south, north and west sides of the bowl. The facilities on the west side provide the

media and commentary facilities for rugby, with positions for sixty reporters adjacent to the television and radio facilities. An event control room and police observation rooms are also located on the north side of this level, providing clear and unobstructed views of the seating bowl.

Level 5 is the main corporate and members' floor, accessed from the lower concourse by lifts and escalators. This level provides space for 3,000 spectators, or around 8 per cent of the total capacity. Accommodation is split on this level between private corporate boxes, lounges and all the related back-of-house facilities required to make this level entirely self-contained. The sixty-four boxes accommodate between 15 and 30 occupants. Each box has its own food serving facilities, a toilet and a glazed frontage to the field, with three rows of seats outside providing patrons with the option of watching from inside or outside the box. A 1,000-seat members' lounge overlooks the field from the southwest corner and provides silver service dining to all members. In fact it will be the largest dining facility in Wellington. Another lounge accommodating 380 people is also located on the southeast corner, providing a corporate facility suitable for viewing rugby or cricket. Three rows of seats are located in front of the lounge, with direct access to the seats from the dining areas. All of the facilities on this level can be used on match or non-match days.

6.5

6.5 Vertical circulation is used as an exciting part of the event experience

Spectator facilities

The total of 31,500 public seats and 3,000 corporate/member seats are divided between the main, single tier of the bowl, and the corporate tier cantilevered above. The single tier is made up of thirty-two rows of seats, designed in section as a parabolic curve. This is to achieve sightlines with a minimum 'C' value of 60 mm to the cricket focal point, which is 1 metre above the field perimeter. The seat widths are a minimum of 500 mm, and are located in blocks with an average of twenty-eight seats per row, although this number varies from between 24 and 34 seats as a result of the oval format of the bowl. The tread width is 800 mm, sufficiently generous to facilitate easy access to the seats from the vomitories and aisles. The corporate and members' seats on level 5 are arranged in three rows, forming a continuous second tier. Roof coverage to the drip line is provided for approximately 75 per cent of the public seating, and 100 per cent of the corporate/members' seating. Of the overall capacity, 1 per cent is allocated to spectators with disabilities, half of which is for people in wheelchairs, and the other half for enhanced amenity seating.

Public toilets on the main public concourse are tucked in behind the raking tier, to take advantage of the reduced head height. There are a total of twenty-two blocks, comprising thirteen female and nine male blocks, with an additional nine unisex facilities for spectators with disabilities. A male-to-female toilet ratio of 70:30 has been adopted for the public areas, and a ratio of 60:40 for the corporate and members' areas.

Escape time is calculated at around 8 minutes from any seat to either the entry plaza on the south side or to the nearby railway yards to the north. These areas have been designed as 'permanent safe zones' in the strategic stadium zoning plan (or Zone 4, as explained in Part I, Chapter 4). Due to the fact that the stadium has only a single access point and that the enclosed concourse forms the only access to the emergency egress gates, the concourse area is designed as a secure fire route. Fire suppression and isolation design is applied to all fire risk areas, to minimise the potential hazards at source, while ventilation of the concourse is also carefully designed to remove the potential for smoke build-up in the escape routes and stairs. In accordance with accepted practice, the pitch is designed as an area of 'temporary safety' in the event of an emergency, even though this additional safety area has not been included in the safe exit calculations.

Participant facilities

The oval stadium encloses a 132 × 70 metre playing field, suitable for a five-wicket cricket block, a rugby field, a soccer field, or with the addition of a temporary raised running surface and field an athletics track, should Wellington's bid for a Commonwealth Games be successful. The most advanced turf technology is planned for the playing surface, consisting of a reinforced sand profile with a top layer of 750 mm of sand laid on a comprehensive irrigation and drainage system to encourage a healthy root system, strong growth and rapid recovery for all-year use. The field has a crown of 700 mm at the centre, not for drainage purposes but to improve views to the centre of the cricket block.

In order to meet the different viewing standards required for rugby and cricket, the cricket oval has been designed to be as small as is technically possible. The western and eastern sides of the stadium provide the preferred seating areas for rugby, while the southern and northern segments are likely to be preferred by cricket spectators. Should a running track be required, viewing standards for athletics should not be compromised, as the track and field will be raised above the normal level (although to make room for the track the first few rows of seating will have to be built over).

The 53 metre tall floodlight towers will enable the staging of night matches, including televised night cricket. The height of the towers is to allow very tight focusing of the light beam, with minimal spillage into neighbouring properties. It is calculated that residents nearby will experience about the same illumination level from overspill as from ordinary street lighting. Using the same 'friendly neighbour' philosophy, the stadium's public address system will use numerous speakers situated as close as possible to the spectators, rather than relying on traditional banks of speakers. This should ensure that spectators hear good quality sound at a reasonable volume, without disturbing neighbouring residents.

Conclusion

The WestpacTrust Stadium opened in early 2000 and provides the New Zealand capital with a modern world-class stadium, indeed the first such stadium in the country. The enclosed amphitheatre will provide a suitably intense atmosphere for the sport most cherished by New Zealanders, that is, Rugby Union. But it will also serve as a wonderful arena for cricket. In order to cater satisfactorily for both sports within one venue, the design team has had to take into account differing field requirements, viewing criteria and support facilities. Although representing a considerable challenge, it has been solved through a sensitive and original design approach. These unusual functional requirements, together with the constraints of the site, have resulted in a unique venue with a distinctive sculptural form, a stadium which will provide Wellington with a landmark building at a reasonable cost, for use all year round.

6.6 A strong oval form sits comfortably with the existing architecture of the dock and the city; the stadium has been awarded the 2000 NZIA (New Zealand Institute of Architects) Resene National Award for Architecture

6.6

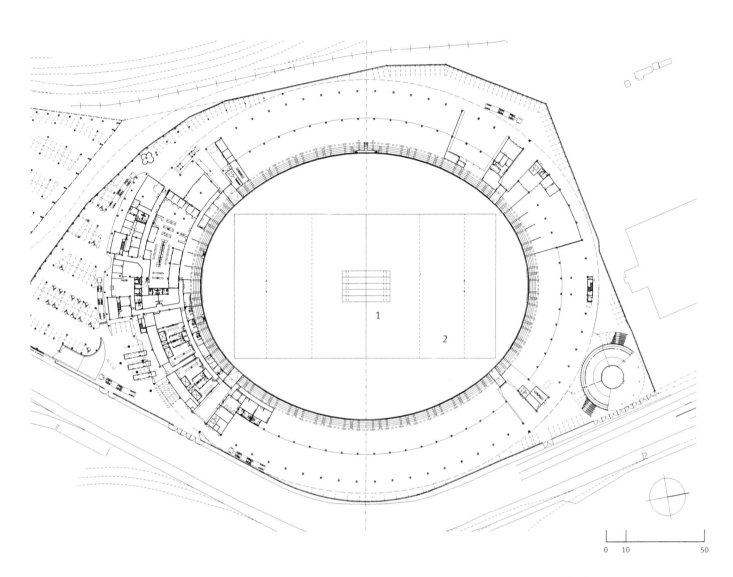

Site plan
1 Cricket wickets
2 Rugby pitch

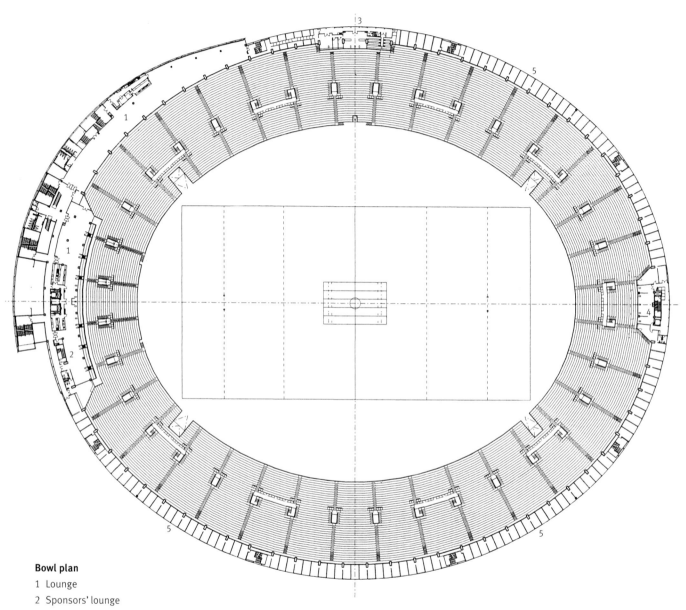

Bowl plan

1 Lounge
2 Sponsors' lounge
3 Press/production
4 Cricket media
5 Void

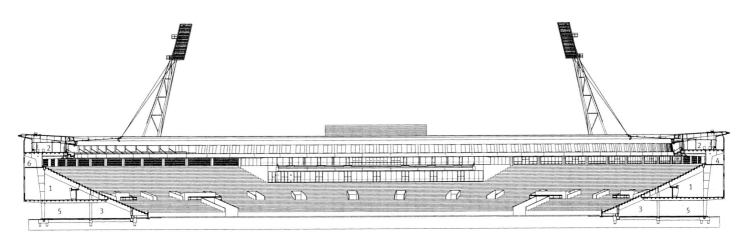

Section

1 Concourse
2 Box
3 Future tenancy
4 Media box
5 Outside broadcast
6 Possible future fit-out

Foster's Oval

Cricket ground redevelopment

Project data	Consultants	Chronology	Project information	Economic information
Location:	*Structural engineer:*	*Design:*	*Site area:*	*Main building cost:*
London, England	*Jan Bobrowski and P*	*April 1991*	*10 acres*	*£4,500,000*
Owner:	*Services engineer:*	*Documentation:*	*Total parking spaces:*	*External works:*
Surrey County Cricket	*James Longley T.S.D.*	*February 1992*	*200 cars*	*£150,000*
Club	*Quantity surveyor:*	*Construction:*	*Total number of seats:*	
Main contractor:	*Cook & Butler*	*September 1992*	*28,500*	
James Longley & Co		*Opening date:*	*Total building area:*	
		1 April 1995	*6,000 square metres*	

Case Study

7

Background

The Oval is the south London home of Surrey County Cricket Club and, together with Lord's (in north London), is one of the capital's two major test match venues. It is also one of the world's great cricket grounds, with a history going back 150 years. A range of mixed development has taken place at the ground during those years, but there was seldom any cohesive, long-term planning. As a result, by the 1990s the Oval had fallen behind the times in many respects, and behind many of its counterparts in international cricket. Among the main problems were:

– Many of its seats were too far from the sporting action and had unsatisfactory 'C' values
– The main pavilion needed modernisation
– The ground no longer satisfied current safety requirements
– Many of its facilities were substandard
– There was a lack of corporate hospitality facilities
– Non-sporting uses of the ground were minimal
– Television broadcast and media facilities were generally out of date
– Members' facilities compared unfavourably with those found at other similar venues

Before redevelopment could begin, however, two main factors had to be considered. First, any improvement works would have to be programmed over a ten-year period, for affordability. Yet sufficient improvements would have to be completed by early 1999 if the ground were to be deemed suitable as a venue for the Cricket World Cup. Second, because Surrey CCC is a lessee of much of the property, the Club has always had to seek consent for improvements from its landlord, the Duchy of Cornwall. Surrey could have tried to purchase the freehold, but such an approach was unlikely to succeed, if only because the Duchy already had other ideas for the redevelopment of its part of the ground. So the only other practical option was to put forward an attractive development plan that would yield substantial benefits to both parties, by increasing the capital value of that part of the land owned by the Duchy.

A masterplan was therefore commissioned from HOK LOBB in early 1995, to form the basis of a development scheme that would enhance the cricketing activities of the club, but also maximise the commercial potential of the site to suit both the club and the Duchy. In addition to eradicating the Oval's main problems, we were also asked to look into ways of linking the ground's facilities more closely to the needs of the local community.

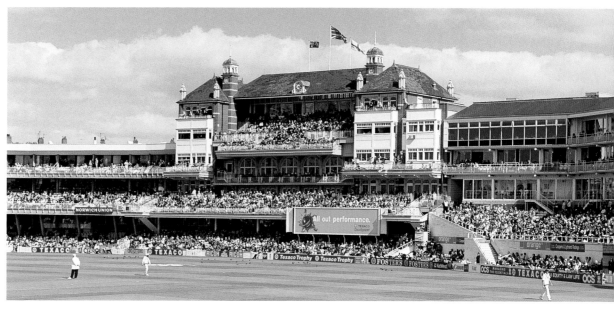

7.1 From the pitch the three seating balconies of the redeveloped building align with the three levels of new accommodation. Architectural references were taken from the original Pavilion to create a composition where new and old are barely distinguishable

7.1

The brief

In addition to requesting the complete redevelopment of the outdated members' pavilion, the client requested the following specific improvements to the ground:

- The capacity was to be expanded from 15,000 to not less than 25,000, organising the seats into smaller, more manageable areas that would aid stewarding and allow better crowd management at big matches
- Spectators were to be brought nearer to the game. This would require a reduction of the playing area, which was in any case one of the largest playing fields anywhere in the world. But any changes should not compromise the requirements of first-class cricket
- The pitch was to be redesigned to accommodate other sports, especially during the winter, and to be suitable for staging entertainment such as concerts
- Conformity with current health and safety requirements was to be ensured
- Areas suitable for commercial uses such as shops, a museum, conference facilities and car parking were to be maximised, though without compromising cricketing requirements

- Lawns and gardens were to be provided for spectators as picnic and relaxation areas, and to provide areas where practice nets could be set up
- The main entrance to the venue was to be made more inviting, spacious and safe

Design concept

In analysing the situation we identified the following key factors. The site is very compact and in a confined urban setting. All improvements would therefore have to be achieved by a careful re-ordering of existing spaces, while showing a special sensitivity to the needs of neighbouring residents and properties. The playing area centred around test wicket number 14 (there were 22 in total). This wicket should therefore form the starting point for setting out both the playing field and spectator tiers. On the eastern side of the site there was only limited scope for improvement to the redeveloped Members' Pavilion, the Bedser Stand and the Laker Stand. If the Laker Stand were moved forward, the existing office facility could be expanded, and if its rake were increased, spectator sightlines would be improved.

On the northern side of the site, the Lock Stand is too far from the action. Redevelopment should therefore allow improved viewing standards, while releasing

7.2 The six-level structure topped by reclaimed roof tiles and the original clock and cupolas reinstates the symbolic dominance of the Members' Pavilion over the adjacent stands

7.3 Painted mild steel and hardwood rail constructed in a style picking up details from the original balustrade

7.2

valuable circulation space to the rear. The Peter May enclosure was deemed to be outdated and in need of total replacement. While on the western and southern sides of the site, the Vauxhall Chalets and other areas were outdated and were restricting perimeter circulation.

We subsequently proposed that the better use of the land occupied by these stands and the Peter May enclosure, combined with a reduction of the playing area, offered the greatest opportunity for redeveloping the ground. The resultant masterplan therefore proposed the following:

– Release space by moving the practice nets to within the playing area
– Reduce the number of first-class wickets from 22 to 16
– Retain six wickets at the two ends, for community cricket use
– Establish a new field boundary, to be defined by a 75 yard radius centred upon the test pitch

7.3

The masterplan further proposed that new seating on three sides of the ground be set out from the centre of the playing area, and be arranged mainly as a single tier, rising from ground level. This would allow for easier stewarding and emergency provision, as well as providing easier access to the large concourse facilities provided below the stands. This solution had the added advantage of being less costly to implement. Also, because the new seating tiers would not be too high, they would not impact unduly on the neighbouring properties surrounding the site.

There would, meanwhile, be greater scope for taller seating tiers at the Vauxhall end of the ground. This is a location which offers good views of the pitch, and where the impact on neighbouring housing would be less problematic. For safety and convenience the design also allows for a wide circulation concourse at ground level. This would circle the ground and provide easy circulation to all parts of the site, eliminating the existing pinch points.

It is intended that public transport would remain the primary means of access to the Oval. On-site parking would therefore be strictly limited, while talks began with British Rail, London Underground and London Buses to discuss improved links between the set down points and the cricket ground entrances.

By utilising the site more efficiently our masterplan allows for the new spectator stands to achieve a possible overall capacity of 28,500 (from the original 16,399 seats). This new capacity is based on a higher seating standard, with minimum tread widths of 840 mm, and seat widths of 460 mm in the public tiers. Larger seats would be provided in the banqueting and corporate areas. The seating rake provides a 'C' value of not less than 60 mm in all the new tiers. The new stands would remain unroofed, however, because rain will generally stop play at cricket matches, during which time spectators can use the facilities offered in the newly extended covered concourses. To encourage healthy grass growth, the restricted height of the northern and southern tiers would allow air movement across the ground to ensure even drying, while the low southern boundary would ensure an open, sunny aspect.

Conclusion

The redevelopment of the Members' Stand, or Pavilion, has been completed, and is regarded as a major success for Surrey. Indeed, despite its modernisation, the conservation of many of the building's original Victorian details has meant that many spectators have hardly noticed the fact that it has been almost totally rebuilt, its roof replaced, and two additional floors incorporated into its fabric. At the same time, the redesign has re-established the prominence of the Pavilion, always a key element of any cricket ground, while providing some of the best facilities for members, players and media representatives to be found in any cricket pavilion in the world.

Otherwise, the masterplanning exercise for the ground as a whole is still in the development phase, applications having been made to the local planning authority for consultation and further consideration.

7.4 New pre-cast reconstituted stone framing and sash windows of the new committee room, blending with existing details

7.4

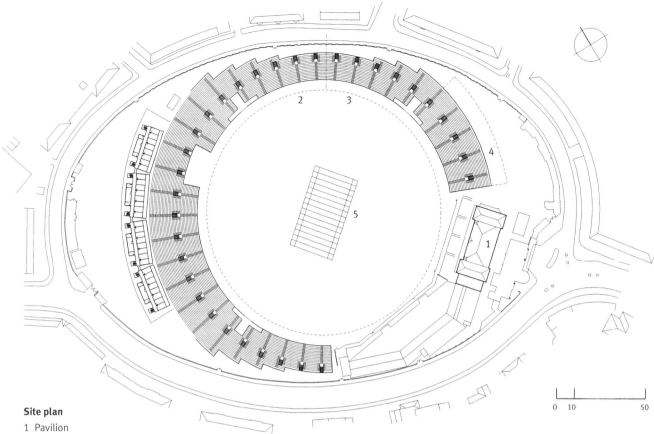

Site plan

1 Pavilion
2 Vauxhall end
3 Lock-Laker end
4 Proposed hospitality
5 Wickets

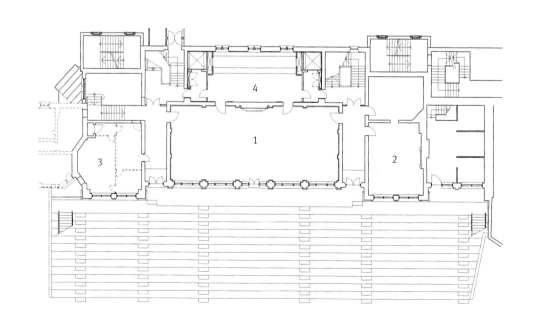

First floor level

1 Long room
2 Members' rooms
3 Hospitality
4 Bar

Front elevation

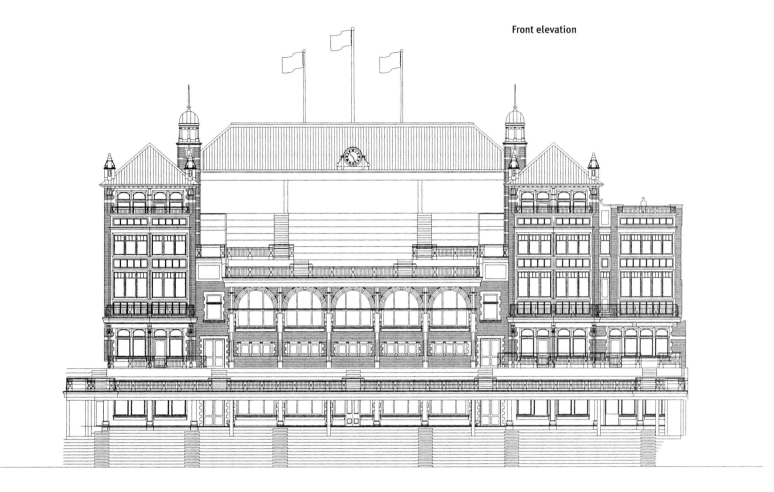

Rear elevation

Section

1 Long room
2 Bar
3 Restaurant
4 Cinema/TV
5 Refreshments

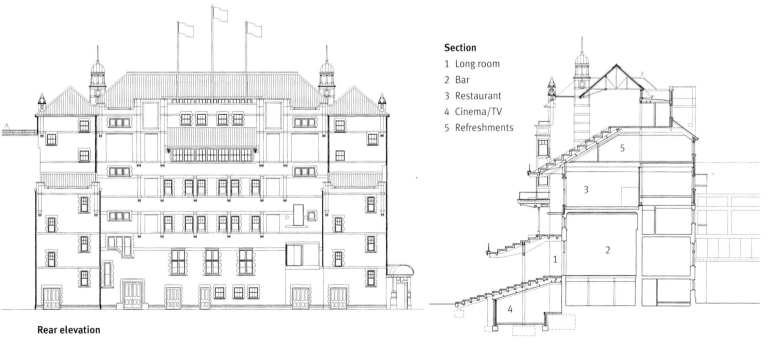

Arsenal Football Club

North Bank Stand

Project data	Consultants	Chronology	Project information	Economic information
Location:	*Structural engineer:*	*Design:*	*Site area:*	*Main building cost:*
Highbury, London	Jan Bobrowski and P	May 1991	8.23 acres	£16,500,000
Owner:	*Services engineer:*	*Documentation:*	*Total parking spaces:*	*External works*
Arsenal Football Club	Building Services Design	February 1992	40 cars	£500,000
Main contractor:	*Quantity surveyor:*	*Construction:*	*Total number of seats:*	
Norwest Holst Const.	Dearle & Henderson	May 1992	12,400 North Stand	
	Project manager:	*Opening date:*	*Total building area:*	
	Dearle & Henderson	August 1993	4,200 square metres	

Background

Arsenal Football Club was formed (though not under that name) in 1886 and moved to its current ground in north London in 1913. Development of the site was unimpressive until the appointment in 1925 of a new manager, Herbert Chapman. Chapman, a man of exceptional vision and energy, started redeveloping the ground in 1931 and within five years raised it to the status of Britain's most prestigious football venue. Whereas all stadia until then had been the work of engineers, most notably Archibald Leitch, Chapman commissioned the respected architect Claude Waterlow Ferrier to design the 1932 West Stand. Ferrier died in 1935 and it fell to his partner, William Binnie, to undertake Chapman's next commission – the 1936 East Stand.

These buildings represented the pinnacle of British stadium design in the 1930s. These were not mere sheds but handsome works of architecture which strove to provide visitors with the finest possible facilities. The 1932 West Stand, at £45,000 the most expensive football stand to date, was described at the time as 'the most architecturally advanced grandstand ever seen in this country' and the 1936 East Stand provided a standard of facilities so superior that visiting players were rumoured to be intimidated by its marble floors and heated dressing rooms. But by the late 1980s these once-great facilities had become outdated, shabby and seriously inadequate in terms of current viewing and safety standards.

In 1991 the club therefore proceeded with development of a scheme for a new North Stand that would provide top-quality accommodation for just under 12,500 spectators in an all-seated stadium – the latter being a requirement of the Taylor Report (Home Office 1990b). When the design was made public its bulkiness and general mediocrity evoked an outburst of protest from local residents and the Royal Art Commission, and the quality of viewing from some of the 12,750 seats was inadequate. In November 1991 the scheme was rejected by Islington Council's planning committee and Arsenal was given six weeks to come up with something better. The club then sought design and build bids, and the winning bid came from Norwest Holst with a design from HOK LOBB. Five weeks later the design outlined below was presented and accepted by all concerned.

The brief

The client required a stand that would accommodate as near to 12,500 spectators as possible under cover, in

8.1

comfortable seats, and with every seat enjoying clear sightlines. It needed to satisfy current safety standards and revive the earlier club tradition of good architecture and superior internal ambience that had very nearly become lost. It also needed to respect the urban context and not loom excessively over surrounding residential streets.

With regard to physical planning we evolved a new structural concept that would allow the height of the stand to seem less obtrusive from ground level while still accommodating nearly 12,500 seats at angles of rake that would offer good sightlines from all viewing positions. With regard to financial planning, the cost of refitting the East and West Stands to bring them in line with the

8.1 West turnstile pavilions with cylindrical staircase towers beyond. The goalpost roof structure, placed centrally between the front and rear of the stand on two posts, minimises the apparent depth of structure at the roof perimeter

8.2 Elliptical opening to the Museum and Bondholders' Restaurant on level 2 above the main public concourse

8.3 From the pitch the North Bank Stand is a strong statement with the 4,200 capacity upper tier cantilevering 17.5 metres over the lower tier

8.4 The main bar on the main ground level concourse. The good quality of finishes can be clearly seen throughout the stand

8.2

8.3

8.4

safety standards of the Taylor Report (Home Office 1990b), plus constructing a new North Stand, was estimated at £22 million. Within this, the total cost of the new North Stand itself would be about £16 million.

Design concept

To fit 68 steeply raking rows of seats under a roof whose height would not seem excessive when viewed from ground level required an inventive structural concept. The roof structure consists of a 103 metre long goalpost roof truss spanning the entire length of the stand and a series of 16.5 metre balanced cantilevers projecting on either side of this central truss, carrying the profiled roofing sheets. The latter are transparent at the rear of the stand, allowing daylight to flood in.

Because the central truss is positioned well away from the facade it is partly hidden from people looking up from ground level thus solving the earlier problem of an excessively obtrusive roof height. The roof structure is quite separate from that of the rest of the stand, and, being a balanced cantilever with all major stresses resolved it is notably light, using only 330 tonnes of steel. The two end columns, fabricated from the largest universal steel section available with plates welded across the toes, are surprisingly slender and allow for the truss they carry to move through expansion over the top of one and fixed by the other.

The upper tier of seats consists of a 17.5 metre propped cantilever off the rear circulation and service cores. This allows a 21 metre deep upper tier, seating 4,000 spectators, with no need for view-obstructing columns below. The massive overturning moment of this cantilever is resisted by two rows of columns at the back of the stand without hindering views. The primary structural element is the series of tapered steel plate girders which are a maximum depth of 1.2 metres and maximum width of 400 mm. They are supported horizontally by the large girder visible from the lower tier, the latter spanning between the stiff shear cores that surround the staircases at the rear of the building.

The stand consists of five levels, four for spectator use and the top level housing services, plant and equipment. The aim on all spectator levels was to create an environment conducive to maximum customer enjoyment and satisfaction. Level 1 has the main public concourse which houses video arcades, seven fast-food counters, the Gunner's Bar (which caters for spectators who wish to meet in a pub atmosphere at the stadium rather than a local pub), a fast service bar, confectionery counter, customer care desk, travel and ticket office, betting shop, souvenir shop, wash room, CCTV monitors and a football games room containing state-of-the-art electronic football games. The concourse is a bright, friendly area with uplighters illuminating an undulating enamelled ceiling and an oval opening in the ceiling above through which people on level 2 can look down on the fun below. It has been designed to woo customers away from the many rival attractions available to them in a modern metropolis and encourage them to come early, stay late, and spend their money on enjoyable activities while in the venue. A live rock band plays on a specially prepared stage at every match, creating a party atmosphere.

Level 2 is devoted to bondholders' facilities. It houses a museum, and the Bondholders' Restaurant, which is decorated with club memorabilia to give the club atmosphere. On match days the entire floor is reserved for bondholders only. The restaurant capacity was limited to 200 covers by fire brigade recommendations, which is less than ideal, but the operators aim to serve up to 400 bondholders every match day with the help of an efficient booking system. Level 3 which serves the back of the lower tier and level 4 which serves the back of the upper tier are identical. Each has four snack bars, fast-service bar and toilets.

Two food outlets remain open after each match to encourage visitors to stay, and it is stadium policy that all food and drink must be priced no higher than the competition in the high street. Toilets are provided on levels 1, 3 and 4. Total provision for the 12,400 spectators is based on a male:female ratio of 80:20 and the ratio of urinals to fans is 1:75 compared with a UK average of 1:200.

The upper tier seats 4,200 spectators in twenty-four rows and the lower tier 8,200 spectators in forty-four rows. 'C' values in the upper tier are 85 or better, in the lower tiers 60 or better. We used our sightline-generation computer programmes as described earlier to give the seating tiers a slightly hyperbolic paraboloid dished shape to ensure the best achievable sightlines. It was the first time that computer images of the view from the new seats were used to sell the seats. The new North Stand is designed to high standards of safety and convenience and its 12,400 spectators are served by seven vomitories and thirteen staircases, eight of which serve both upper and lower tiers, while exit time is less than 7 minutes. The opportunity was also taken to re-plan the ground entrance areas, and six turnstiles now allow the Arsenal ground to be filled in less than an hour as 40,000 spectators file through the turnstiles at a rate of 110 a minute.

The construction of the North Stand was completed in 15 months. Several measures were taken to minimise the noise nuisance to neighbours in this residential area, including an auger piling method with continuous vibration monitoring and pre-assembly of large sections of the building to confine site operations within restricted hours. The main truss, for instance, was pre-fabricated in sections which were then bolted together on site and lifted into position.

Conclusion

Since its opening in August 1993 the North Bank Stand has been acclaimed particularly for the quality of its internal environment. The ground floor concourse exemplifies the alluring consumer facility that has been required in the late twentieth century if customers are to be attracted away from rival entertainments and spend their time (and money) in a sports stadium instead. The club regards the new stand as a worthy successor to the 1930s buildings, which were seen as the best of their time.

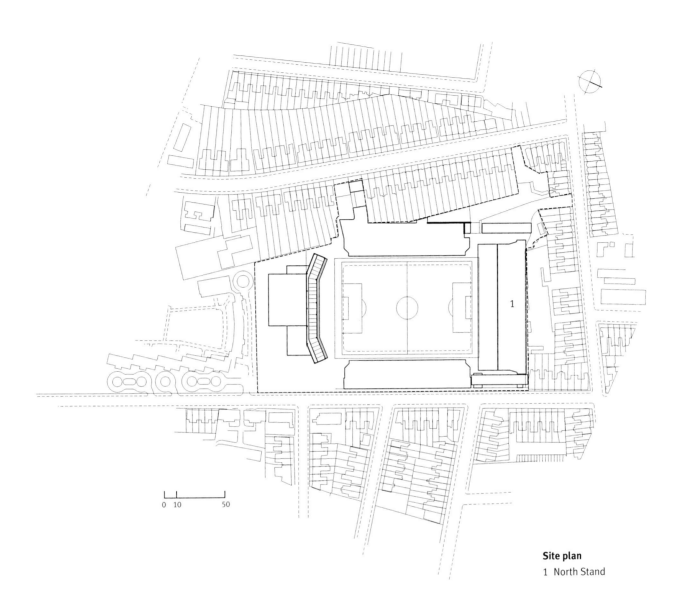

Site plan
1 North Stand

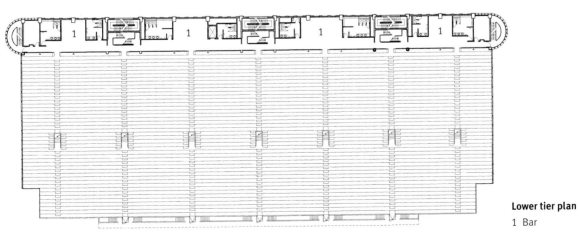

Lower tier plan
1 Bar

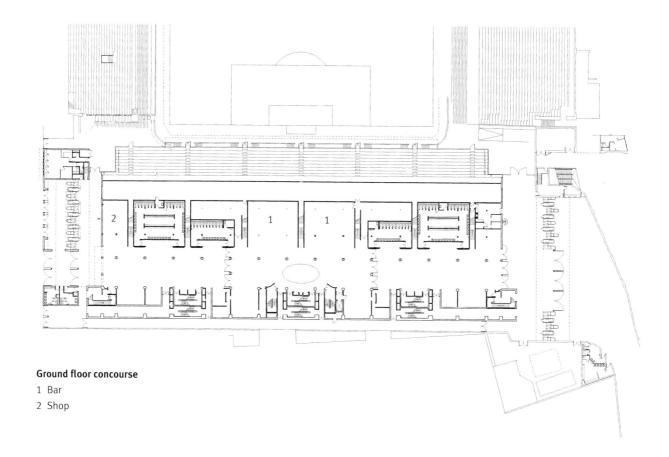

Ground floor concourse

1 Bar

2 Shop

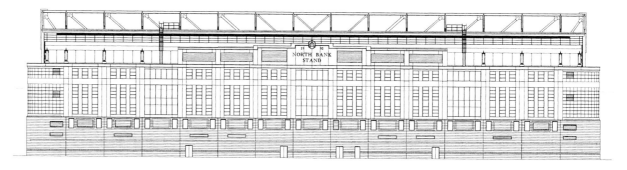

North elevation

Section
1 Concourse
2 Concession
3 Museum

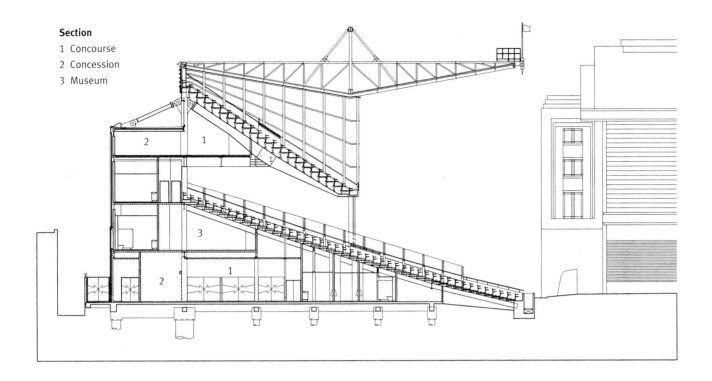

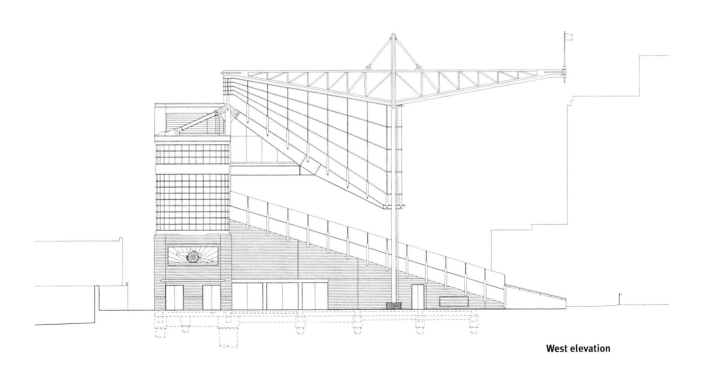

West elevation

Chelsea Football Club

Matthew Harding Stand

Project data	Consultants	Chronology	Project information	Economic information
Location:	*Structural engineer:*	*Design:*	*Site area:*	*Main building cost:*
Chelsea, London	*Modus*	*November 1993*	*11.5 acres*	*£9,000,000*
Owner:	*Services engineer:*	*Documentation:*	*Total parking spaces:*	*External works:*
Chelsea Football Club	*Roger Fuller and P*	*December 1993*	*100 cars*	*£1,000,000*
Main contractor:	*Quantity surveyor:*	*Construction:*	*Total number of seats:*	
Tellings Hill Construction	*Hand Dear and Cox*	*December 1993*	*8,500*	
	Project manager:	*Opening date:*	*Total building area:*	
	Kiley Associates	*December 1994*	*4,000 square metres*	

Background

Stamford Bridge, on the Fulham Road in west London, is one of the most historic and unusually situated sports venues in the UK. Formerly an athletics ground, a football stadium was created by speculators on the site in 1905 by surrounding the track on three sides by earthen banks, creating an overall capacity said to be in the region of 95,000 spectators. The stadium's developers then formed a football club, Chelsea, to play there. But despite its status and convenient inner London location, the venue slipped into gradual decline during the post-war years, blighted by its extended viewing distances around the now disused track, and its increasingly congested road and pedestrian access. The site is an awkward one, tightly squeezed between the narrow Fulham Road, two railway lines and a mix of residential and commercial properties. In 1972 Chelsea began a bold redevelopment programme, starting with the construction of a dramatic, three-tier East Stand seating over 10,000 spectators. This was intended as the first phase of a scheme which would ultimately enclose the ground with seating accommodation for 60,000 spectators. But then came the Safety of Sports Grounds Act of 1975 and a series of acute financial problems at the Club, largely induced by the East Stand's construction,

leading to the shelving of the remaining phases of the development plan. By the 1980s the ground had entered a state of limbo. In contrast with the new stand's concrete and steel walkways, bars, restaurants and plush new executive boxes were the crumbling, exposed terraces, decaying, archaic offices and a general mood of despair. And all this was set on a few acres of highly valuable, inner London land which, inevitably, attracted plenty of interest from property speculators.

Having finally secured the site from outside interests, in the early 1990s Chelsea initiated a new masterplan for the stadium. Drawn up by another firm of architects, the scheme consisted of a tightly squeezed, two-tier bowl seating 40,000, retaining the 1972 East Stand and surrounding two other sides with a hotel and residential development. Approval for the design team to proceed with the first phase of this masterplan, the redevelopment of the North Stand, was given in 1994. However, some way into the detailed design and documentation process, problems with the design came to light. We were then asked to look into these problems, and were subsequently commissioned to complete the design and documentation process so that construction could start as planned, and the new stand be open for the following season – a very tight programme indeed.

9.1

9.1 A limited site area was used to create a two-tier design using an ingenious roof structure developed by the engineer Steve Morley

9.2 The stand was designed to be continued around the grounds to complete a future stadium capacity of 40,000 spectators

9.3 A range of food and beverage facilities were planned into the fabric of the stand for the spectators on match day

9.4 A number of the support areas including a restaurant and banqueting spaces were designed for use all year round

9.2

The brief

The new North Stand, which was to replace a curved bank of open terracing, was to have a capacity of 8,500 on two tiers, with all seats under a translucent roof. There were to be good quality food and beverage outlets on each of the two public concourse levels, plus a separate functions level containing 'Drakes', a bar, restaurant and night club which would remain open during the week. Extensive kitchens already existed in the East Stand and so these were to be extended, enhanced and linked to the North Stand's new facilities.

Design concept

The two-tier stand contains public concourse facilities on levels 1 and 3 including toilets, food and beverage concessions and other support facilities. Level 2 contains the function areas, including 'Drakes', to which independent access is provided from ground level. A service zone stretches the full length of the stand above level 4 and at key areas around the stand.

The form of the stand was influenced largely by an ingenious roof design developed by the structural engineer, Steve Morley, of Modus Engineers, in response to the site's and the masterplan's specific constraints.

Essentially, in order to fund the masterplan and secure the club's future, the design called for an adjoining hotel, leisure and residential development. However, to accommodate these developments meant that there would be precious little room available behind the south and west sides of the venue for space-consuming roof structures (as are necessary when building large cantilevered roofs). Column supported roofs, which take up no external space, were out of the question, as these would restrict viewing, while goalpost-supported roofs would have resulted in columns in each corner, a serious drawback when planning a bowl-like stadium on such a tight site.

In fact there was less of a space constraint behind the north end. But it was rightly agreed that the structure of the new North Stand should be the same as for the two later South and West Stands to provide visual unanimity. Steve Morley devised a highly innovative method of constructing a column-free roof with no supporting elements protruding beyond the rear wall of the stand using the angled corners to provide lateral support. The space available measured approximately 23 metres between the rear of the stand and its front edge, facing the pitch, into which 8,500 seats had to be accommodated, under a column-free roof. The solution, never before used in a stadium, adopted the principles of catenary trusses suspended from tubular towers and angled around the sides of the stand on plan. This not only achieved the desired effect but it used very little steel, was lightweight, and was very pleasing aesthetically. It was this remarkable solution which firmly established the image of the North Stand.

Conclusion

The project was completed on time to a very tight programme, thus demonstrating what can be achieved under difficult circumstances if the team is focused and experienced in this type of facility development. The tight budgetary constraints placed on the project at its beginning were eased to some extent when a long-time Chelsea supporter and wealthy businessman became an investor and shareholder in the club. Tragically, however, as he was returning from a Chelsea match in Lancashire, he was killed in a helicopter crash. As a result, the North Stand now bears his name.

9.3

9.4

144

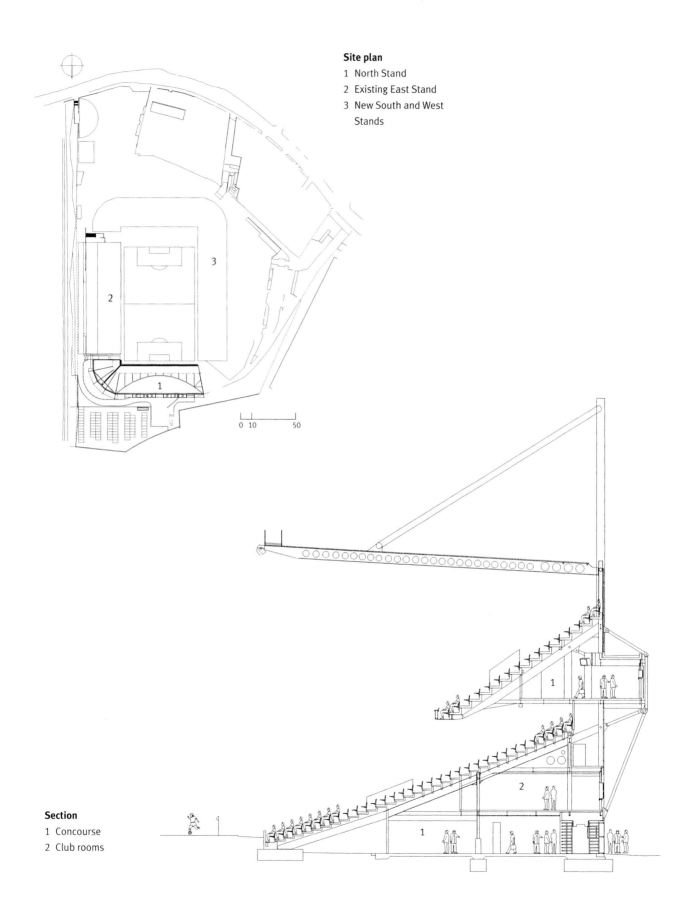

Site plan
1 North Stand
2 Existing East Stand
3 New South and West
  Stands

0 10   50

Section
1 Concourse
2 Club rooms

Lower concourse plan
1 Bar
2 Food concession

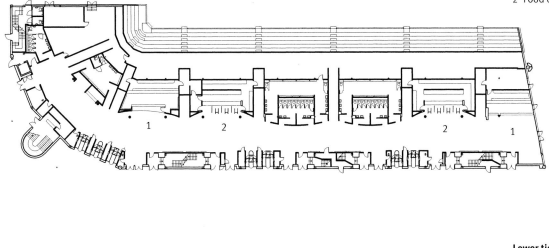

Lower tier plan

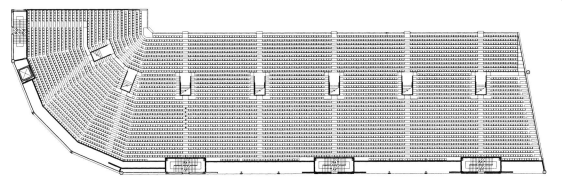

North elevation

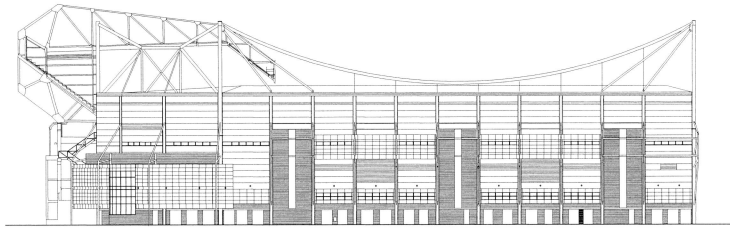

Colonial Stadium

Multi-purpose stadium

Project data	Consultants	Chronology	Project information	Economic information
Location:	*Structural engineer:*	*Design:*	*Site area:*	*Main building cost:*
Docklands, Melbourne	*Modus & Connell*	*June 1996*	*7.4 acres*	*A$229,700,000*
Owner:	*Wagner*	*Documentation:*	*Total parking spaces:*	
Melbourne Park Trust	*Services engineer:*	*April 1997*	*900 cars*	
Main contractor:	*Connell Wagner*	*Construction:*	*Total number of seats:*	
Baulderstone Hornibrook	*Quantity surveyor:*	*September 1997*	*52,000*	
	WT Partnership	*Opening date:*	*Total building area:*	
	Project manager:	*September 1999*	*104,000 square metres*	
	Office of Major Projects			

Background

Colonial Stadium forms an integral part of a radical renewal and transformation programme for Melbourne's railway and docklands area. The scale of the project reflects the city's ambitions to become a prosperous international city, anchored in the Asian Pacific Rim. The 220 hectares of the docklands area has been divided into seven precincts. These are Business Park, Technology Park, West End, Batman's Hill, Victoria Harbour, Yarra Waters and Stadium Park. The plan is for each of the precincts to evolve its own distinctive character and activities, but at the same time for them to form collectively an integrated, pleasant riverside setting for the people of Melbourne. In this respect it is worth noting that the extent of the docklands redevelopment site exceeds the area of the city's existing central business district.

The Stadium Park precinct lies at the centre of the docklands. This is a deliberate attempt by Melbourne to emulate the examples set by such North American cities as Boston, Baltimore, Vancouver and Toronto, each of which has revitalised a redundant inner city area by an urban renewal scheme centred upon a new stadium. Provided the stadium is operated as a high-quality, multi-functional venue, drawing visitors throughout the week, such a stadium, it is now recognised, can act as a genuine magnet for entertainment, retail and business interests, and even secondary housing developments. Melbourne's plan is for the 10-year development programme to be market driven, requiring no government funding, so that the project has the best possible chance of long-term sustainability.

The brief

The central requirements for the project were that the stadium had to seat 52,000 spectators and, furthermore, be suitable for the staging of international standard rugby union, rugby league, soccer and Australian Rules football. With its close proximity to the city centre the venue had to be suitable for the staging of entertainment events, such as shows and pop concerts. It would also have to form a long-term centrepiece for the redeveloped area, with a design life of fifty years. Functionality, services, finishes and fit-out had to meet international best practice standards, yet at the same time be provided at a cost consistent with commercial viability and within the available budget.

Fortunately, as the site lies close to the central business district, an excellent infrastructure is already in

10.1

place. One metro station and twelve tram routes will thus serve Stadium Park. There are also abundant car parks nearby, used mainly during the working week and therefore potentially available for stadium use at other times. A further 900 parking spaces will be provided on the 3 hectare stadium site, served by a new major road.

Design concept

The 52,000 seat stadium has been designed to comprise five levels and meet the three key criteria listed below:

–   To keep spectators as close as possible to the action, while simultaneously ensuring 'C' values of not less than 60 mm

10.1 A number of sites in Melbourne were considered for the development of the stadium with the final decision taken to place the venue on a site in the docklands area of the city because of its urban regeneration potential. The site is also within 10 minutes' walk of the central business district (computer-generated image)

–   To provide best-practice standards of amenity and seating comfort
–   To maximise the provision of club and corporate accommodation, both of which make a disproportionate contribution to stadium revenues

Level 0, the basement level, accommodates services, storage, media production areas and competitor/performer and administrative facilities. Players, executives and VIPs can enter and exit from this level separately from the general public, as can goods and service vehicles, via a service road which runs all round the stadium at basement level.

Level 1 is a public level with four major entry points, longitudinal concourses, seats for up to 15,800 spectators and access points to the upper tiers. The lowest seating tier has been designed to move on tracks, either to surround a rectangular soccer or rugby pitch on four sides, or, when the tiers are retracted, to form an amphitheatre around a larger oval field suitable for Australian Rules football. Level 2 is the main club level. This has restaurants, dining rooms, bars and lounges, as well as seating accommodation for 11,800 spectators. Level 3 is the corporate and private box level. This has a total seating capacity of 2,700 and contains 58 private boxes, each seating 16 people, plus 20 further boxes, each seating between 20 and 30 people. There are also media broadcasting suites, bars, lounges and dining rooms on this level. Level 4 contains public facilities, with seats for up to 21,700 spectators and a skyline concourse offering spectacular views over the city.

There are four vertical circulation nodes denoting the points of entry into the venue. These are symmetrically placed around the circumference of the bowl and form prominent landmarks to help visitors orient themselves. Each is accessed from the external public concourse surrounding the stadium and contains ramps, stairways, and a passenger lift holding up to thirteen people, together with a 2,000 kg goods service lift.

As required by the brief, viewing standards are to a 'C' value of not less than 60 mm for all spectator seats, including those on the retractable lowest tier. Seating comfort is also in line with best current international practice, with tread widths of 800 mm and seat widths of 480 mm, measured from centre to centre for public seating, and of 500 mm on the corporate tier. All seats are self tilting, while those for club and corporate spectators are upholstered.

As mentioned above, the lowest seating tiers are mechanically operated movable sections, allowing the stadium to be configured for different sports. In the course of these reconfigurations the side tiers move 18 metres overall, and the end tiers 14 metres. Seating 12,800 spectators overall, the movable tiers are constructed from steel sections which run on tracks sunk in trenches below pitch level. When the seats are retracted

10.2

10.3

10.2 This is Australia's first opening-roof stadium and contains a wide variety of support and service facilities for use by spectators both before and after an event

10.3 The stadium is part of Melbourne city centre being used as a catalyst for further urban development

10.4 A seven-day-a-week venue designed to 'live' outside of normal event days by the use of extensive customer facilities

10.4

10.5a

10.5b

10.5 The dynamic interiors of the more exclusive areas in the stadium project the entertainment nature of the venue

10.6 Vertical spectator circulation is focused in the four corners of the building and these rigid cores are used to provide strength and support to the structure which supports the opening roof

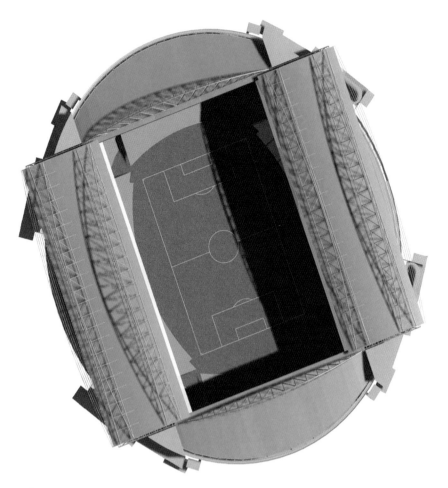

10.6

for the oval configuration (for Australian Football League (AFL) games), the exposed tracks are covered by palletised turf sections to maintain the smooth level of the grassed playing surface.

Because of the requirements for AFL games in which 10 officials and two teams, each of 21 players feature, the demands in terms of changing rooms and medical facilities quite exceed those of other sports. The extent and design standard for these facilities are therefore set by AFL needs.

Disabled provision is in line with best international practice. This totals 1 per cent of the seating capacity, of which half is allocated to people in wheelchairs, with a similar number of enhanced amenity seats designed for spectators with impaired mobility or other special requirements. This type of seating is provided

on all levels and on all sides of the stadium. Moreover, the seats are not grouped together, as is common practice elsewhere, but distributed throughout the building to provide a variety of viewing positions; at the top of the lower moving tiers, in the club tier and at box level. Unisex toilets for disabled spectators are located on concourses near to individual disabled seating positions, while food and other concession outlets feature lowered counters for wheelchair use. In its open position the roof covers 98 per cent of the 52,000 seats behind its drip line, with a 160 × 100 metre rectangular opening in the centre. This opening can be closed in 8 minutes by means of two equally sized roof sections which slide to the centre from each end on craneways supported by two upper arched trusses. The use of arched trusses for the roof construction reduces the size of steel sections required, and at the same time results in a bold, distinctive form and outline to the building. The four primary trusses spring from the four corner circulation cores, while secondary trusses spaced at 7.5 metre centres radiate from these primary trusses to the stadium perimeter.

The playing surface is natural turf, as required for rugby, soccer and AFL. However, because the roof line overhangs the field by up to 20 metres to allow for a practical size of closing roof, 35 per cent of the pitch will be in full shade for up to three months each year. During the same period the rest of the pitch will experience a moving shadow. The pitch will also be subject to periods when no natural light can enter the stadium, while the roof is closed. Similarly, those areas of grass around the perimeter will be deprived of light when the lower tier is moved forward for rugby and football. To maximise the usability of the grass surface in spite of these factors, the pitch construction is a reinforced sand profile system, capable of high rainfall infiltration and drainage, and allowing for a programme of turf replacement whenever necessary. In some areas it is estimated that the turf will probably need to be replaced several times per season.

Implementation

The project was delivered by a 'documentation and construction' contract, from August 1997 to February 2000. Owner/developers wishing to bid were given three months for a complete response. The chronology of these events is as follows.

In April 1997 tenders were called on the development. The bid documents comprised our sketch design documentation, a performance specification, outline materials and construction specification, facility brief and schedule of finishes. After one month of analysis, the State Government selected a preferred owner/developer consortium. Final negotiations were then held, and the preferred team was given two months to complete a documentation and construct package, detailing the building, ownership, financing and operation of the

stadium for a period of thirty years. The stadium had to be ready for use at the beginning of 2000. But the oval central playing area had to be in place a year before that, to allow for a healthy grass surface to develop by the time of the first match. In 2029 the stadium ownership will transfer back to the State Government.

When the above process started, the site had already been cleared of old railway tracks, had been partly decontaminated, and generally brought to a condition that allowed the selected developer to start work without delay. Early contract documentation was also completed for the initial packages of work, such as earth moving and piling contracts.

Conclusion

The procurement method for the stadium sought to encompass the development ideals of the State Government, whilst maintaining a profitable basis for the private ownership of the venue. This resulted in an unusual process that did not follow the more common design and construct method of building. In Melbourne's case, the builder will also be the owner of the stadium during its first thirty years' in operation. (A similar procurement method was also used for the Stadium Australia, the Olympic Stadium in Sydney, see Case Study 3.)

The project has been developed to the highest standards of design and facility planning. On completion it will certainly be comparable with other premium sports and entertainment facilities around the world, most specifically Australia's other brand new stadium in Sydney. But in one respect the Melbourne project is more advanced than any other yet to be designed, and that is in terms of its flexibility as a multi-functional venue. First, it is able to accommodate rectangular-based sports, rugby and soccer, and the larger sporting format of AFL, plus concert and exhibition events. Second, no event need ever be delayed or cancelled owing to the weather, thanks to the provision of a closing roof. Thus it could be said that the Colonial Stadium is indeed the first true example of what we have termed a 'fourth generation' stadium.

Site plan

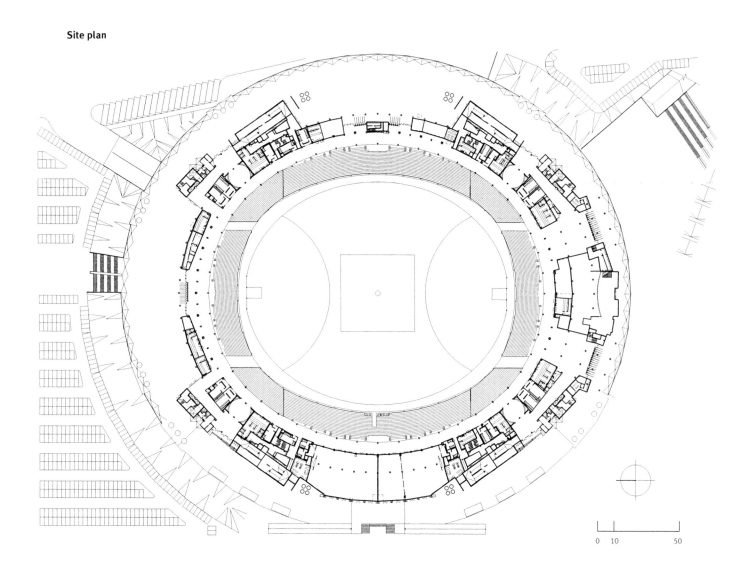

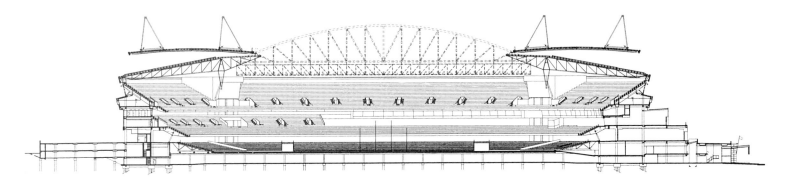

**Section with roof in
open position**

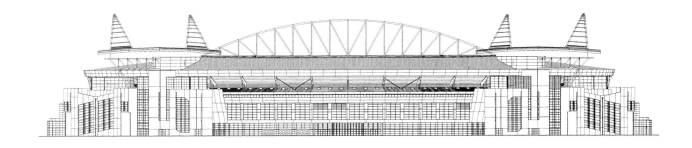

South elevation

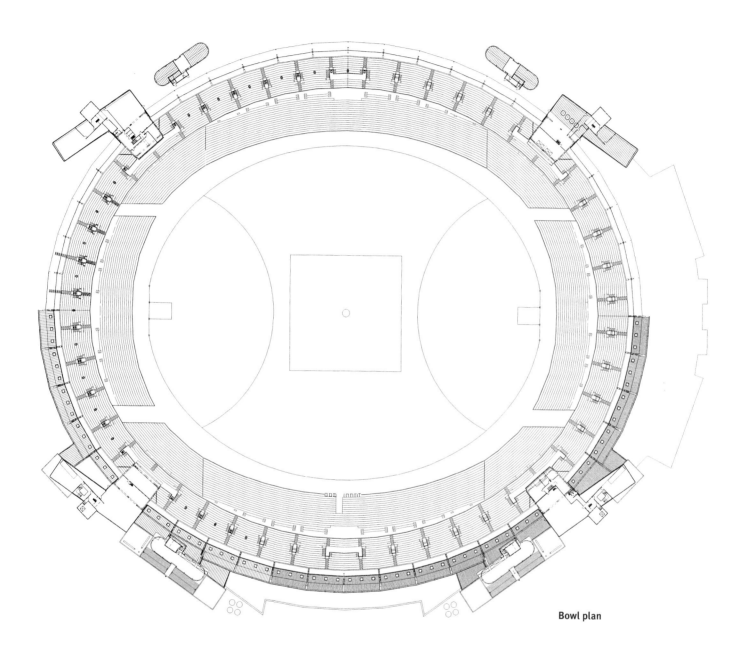

Bowl plan

Kempton Park

Redevelopment of existing racecourse

Project data	Consultants	Chronology	Project information	Economic information
Location:	*Structural engineer:*	*Design:*	*Site area:*	*Main building cost:*
Sunbury-on-Thames	*Jan Bobrowski and P*	*May 1996*	*250 acres*	*£8,000,000*
Owner:	*Services engineer:*	*Documentation:*	*Total parking spaces:*	*External works:*
United Racecourse Ltd	*Roger Fuller and P*	*August 1996*	*2,000 cars*	*£450,000*
Main contractor:	*Quantity surveyor:*	*Construction:*	*Total number of seats:*	
John Mowlem & Co.	*Davis Langdon Everest*	*January 1997*	*900, 14,500 standing*	
		Opening date:	*Total building area:*	
		December 1997	*11,060 square metres*	

Case Study

11

Background

There has been racing at Kempton Park, on the south-western borders of London, since 1878. For many years the course was one of four in the Greater London area. Now there are only two, both of which, at Kempton and Sandown, are owned by United Racecourse Ltd. In 1995 we were invited by the company to present our credentials for the masterplanning and redevelopment of Kempton. The site and buildings, developed piece-meal over many decades, had fallen behind rival racecourses in terms of atmosphere, consumer appeal, capacity and profitability, and the owners wanted an expert assessment of what could be done. Our response, as in all such cases, was to go back to basics by measuring the facilities against the three fundamental criteria we summarise as the SOP, that is, the needs of spectators, owner/operators and participants.

The brief

As has been stated many times in this book, a successful venue is one which entices customers to arrive early, use the full range of concourse and other facilities, thereby yielding a high spend-per-head, and leave late in a happy state of mind and with a desire to repeat the

experience. An initial assessment of Kempton Park from the racegoer's perspective identified some obvious strengths:

– Its location, which is 9 miles from central London, and its perceived status, as 'London's Racecourse', were definite assets
– The racecourse is also easily reached from points beyond London, via excellent motorway and rail-way connections
– Although situated on the edge of a suburban area, the facilities have a pleasing ambience, amid lakes and a green landscape
– The course is home to a major event on the racing calendar, the King George VI Chase, held each year on Boxing Day

But there were serious weaknesses also. For example, Kempton Park did not appear to have an identifiable main entrance, or front door. In our experience visitors want and need to see an inviting and emblematic main entry point giving access to the entire site. They also want clear and easy routes leading towards that entrance. Yet at Kempton there was no clear route from the nearby station, no weather protection along the way, and the entrance area was confusing, offering several low-key entrances instead of one obvious and attractive one. Having entered, the patron wishes to be welcomed by an attractive array of amenities and to find what they want easily, whether it be a viewing terrace, a betting hall, bar or restaurant. They want enough space for easy circulation and a minimum of queuing, yet at the same time, the facilities should be sufficiently concentrated to create that pleasant 'buzz' that arises when throngs of people are enjoying themselves in the company of others. At Kempton Park there was no genuine concourse. There were too few concessions covering too narrow a range of spending opportunities. Access and service standards were minimal, and people in the concourse areas had little contact with events on the racecourse.

Furthermore, a visitor from the corporate world, arriving to meet colleagues for a day of combined business and entertainment, was likely to be frustrated by the separation between private hospitality boxes and the course's other facilities. This was also true for committed racegoers. For example Kempton's parade ring was situated too far from the main viewing areas and was visually cut off by unattractive structures. The race starts were not clear, while support facilities in the grandstand, which dated from 1932, generally did not face the track. It was also impossible to circulate between the different buildings without going outside,

not always a desirable option on a cold or wet Boxing Day. Finally, whenever there was low attendance at races, spectators were too easily dispersed along the track to engender a good atmosphere. Arising from this analysis our message to the client was that Kempton Park was operating far short of its full potential.

This conclusion went beyond the course's facilities on race days. The modern racecourse, as we have stated in earlier chapters, retains horse racing as its core activity, but does not cater exclusively for racing fanatics. Nor can it survive solely on the race-day events. The ideal venue is one that is in use every day of the year, provided such use does not detract from the care and maintenance of the site and buildings. Yet the framework offered by Kempton Park in its existing form did not merely fail to assist the owners in developing this wider and more efficient range of facilities. It actually restricted such a process.

Design concept

Applying our analysis of the venue to the shortcomings outlined above resulted in the following proposals:

– To establish a clear and welcoming 'front door' that offers access to all events, and establishes clear

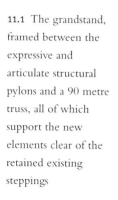

11.1 The grandstand, framed between the expressive and articulate structural pylons and a 90 metre truss, all of which support the new elements clear of the retained existing steppings

11.1

11.2

and convenient routes for arriving vehicles and pedestrians

– To establish a circulation route inside the venue that links all facilities in an effective manner, and is as clear and as visible as possible, in order to avoid the need for excessive signage

– To bring horses and customers much closer together, for instance at the parade ring

– To improve the quality of race viewing

– To knit facilities more closely together, in order to provide a 'critical mass' of enjoyment, instead of the current, loose arrangement of buildings

– To create additional catering and retail outlets, amusement arcades and function rooms, in order to attract and satisfy all identified customer types

(in addition to the racecourse's existing, more narrow range of regulars)

– To make provision for complementary facilities. Potential multi-use options identified were the use of the parade ring as an indoor sports arena, the staging of exhibitions and trade fairs, the use of the bar and concession areas as stand-alone entertainment attractions and the provision of a hotel on the site

– To make provision for the existing facilities to be extended and for new facilities to be added in future

For the racetrack itself we put forward a range of eleven alternative reconfigurations for the client's consideration,

11.2 One of the dramatic pylons that provided a signature for the new Kempton Park and which also minimises the apparent mass of the roof structure

11.3 The Sporting Index bar is one of the many facilities that serve the ground floor public concourse and exhibition area

11.3

11.4 The Champagne Bar is part of the Members' Lounge and banqueting facility

11.4

from which one was selected by the client. This configuration would provide more immediate viewing of the races, and at the same time allow for future developments.

Conclusion

The first phase of the masterplan commenced on site in early 1997, with completion late the same year. This phase involved a complete redevelopment of the main grandstand, plus the relocation of the parade ring to a site behind the redeveloped stand, closer to the core viewing areas of the racecourse. The architectural treatment to the stand's new roof structure was deliberately

conceived to 'put Kempton on the map' (in the words of United Racecourse's managing director, Sue Ellen). The redeveloped facilities had to make their mark and send out a message to both the racing community and the public alike that Kempton is changing for the better.

Fortunately, the new facilities' first day in use, in August 1997, illustrated beyond doubt that the effort had been worthwhile, and that the racecourse had adopted the right strategy of using modern, distinctive design to project a commercial message. On that day the racecourse's attendance was 20 per cent more than the previous year, helping to prove what we have claimed consistently over the years: that good design is also good business.

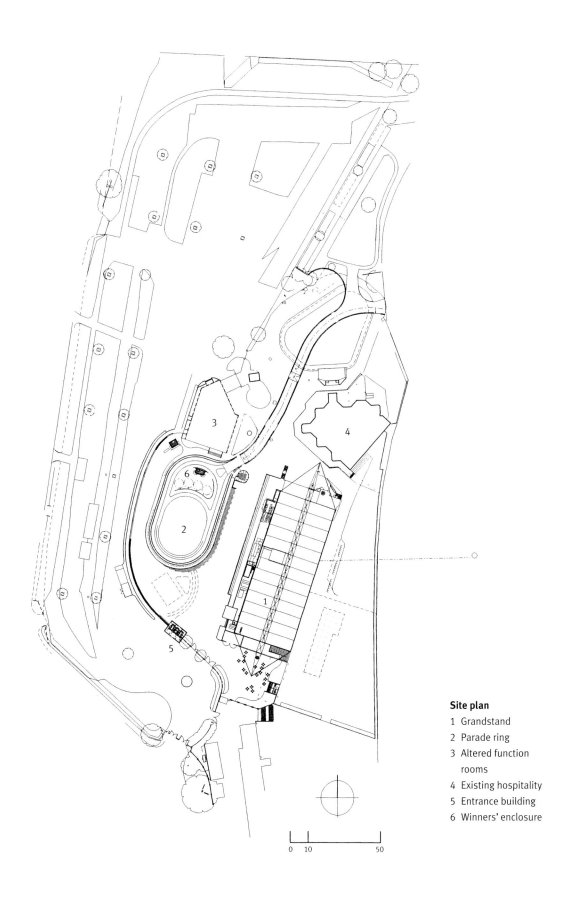

Site plan
1 Grandstand
2 Parade ring
3 Altered function
  rooms
4 Existing hospitality
5 Entrance building
6 Winners' enclosure

Section

1 Stepped restaurant
2 Bar
3 Banqueting hall
4 Betting concourse
5 Kitchen

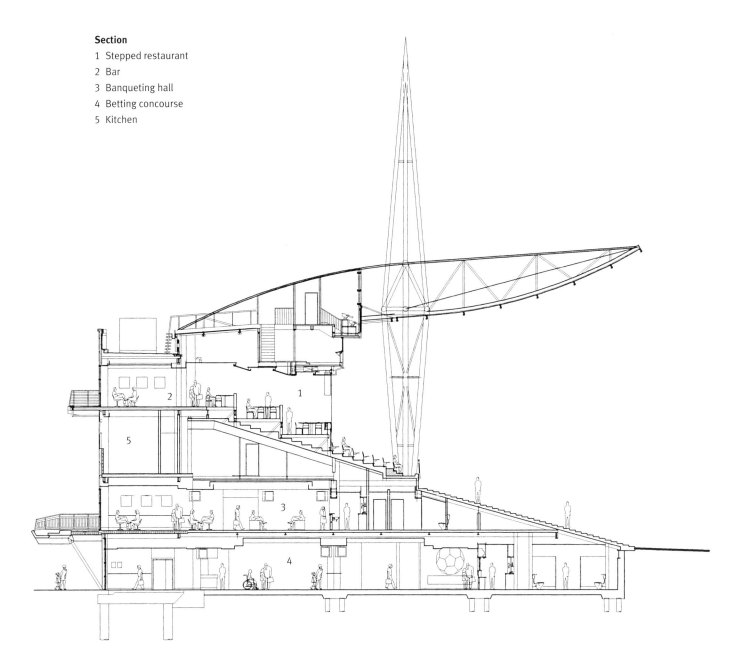

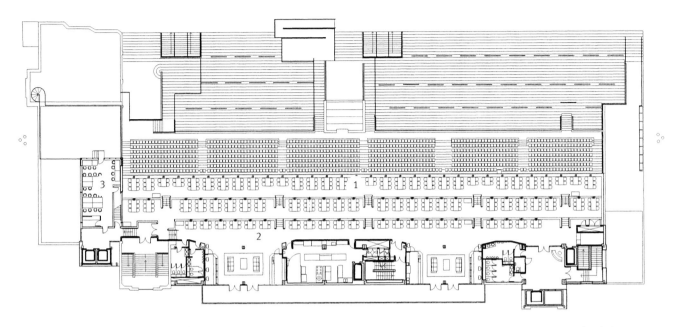

Restaurant level plan

1 Stepped restaurant
2 Bar
3 Press

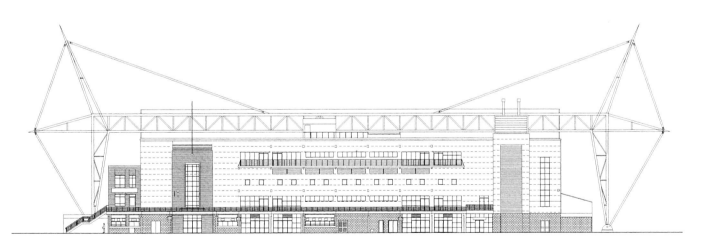

West elevation

Croke Park Stadium

Stadium masterplan

Project data	Consultants	Chronology (Phase 1)	Project information	Economic information
Location:	*Structural engineer:*	*Design:*	*Site area:*	*Main building cost:*
Croke Park, Dublin	*Hogan Lynch & Partners*	*September 1989*	*16.3 acres*	*£35,000,000 (Phase 1)*
Owner:	*Services engineer:*	*Documentation:*	*Total parking spaces:*	*External works:*
Gaelic Athletic Ass.	*J.V. Tierney & Partners*	*January 1993*	*200 cars*	*£2,000,000*
	Quantity surveyor:	*Construction:*	*Total number of seats:*	
	Seamus Monahan & P	*September 1993*	*90,000*	
	Project manager:	*Opening date:*	*Total building area:*	
	Seamus Monahan & P	*June 1995*	*50,000 square metres*	

Background

Croke Park has been the physical and spiritual home of Ireland's two distinctive field sports, Gaelic football and Hurling, for over a century. (Gaelic football was, incidentally, the precursor of that other characteristic game, Australian Rules football.) Since 1908, the stadium has been owned by the sports' joint governing body, the Gaelic Athletic Association. Before the southern part of Ireland declared independence from Great Britain in 1922, and to a large extent ever since, the GAA has acted as an ardent champion of both Gaelic sport and of Irish cultural identity. This is a direct throwback to the time when the Irish were effectively barred from participating in the established British sports of soccer and cricket. But while both Gaelic football and Hurling have substantial, dedicated support from within the Irish community, Croke Park itself suffered from a lack of investment over the years and, by the late 1980s, was in desperate need of redevelopment.

After a series of interviews we were invited to join the design team and work on a new masterplan for the grounds. Although this masterplan was intended to provide for the complete redevelopment of Croke Park, the work had to be carried out in phases, both for reasons of finance and in order to ensure that the stadium would remain in use during the redevelopment programme.

The brief

The two key features of Croke Park are its close proximity to the centre of Dublin, and, unfortunately, the limited availability of land to allow for its expansion. This latter constraint is significant, since the GAA hoped to increase the stadium's capacity from 63,000 to 75,000 and eventually to 90,000, all seated. To set such a high target was not merely wild ambition on their part. Attendance at GAA finals had regularly topped 70,000, while the ground record, set in 1961, was nearly 91,000. Even so, the GAA were aiming to create one of the largest all-seated venues in Europe, on a site suffering from severe constraints. Not only is the site limited in size, it is restricted at both ends by railway lines. Moreover, its other boundaries are defined by the road network around the site, and on the fourth side by a canal, over which one end stand of the new development would need to be located.

Design concept

To achieve the high capacity required by the GAA, a four-tier section was developed, consisting of a lower

12.1 The canopy roof was designed to create an elegant protective canopy over the fans at the GAA, where there is great passion for the games of Hurling and Gaelic football, while retaining an open-air feeling to the bowl

12.2 A number of design ideas were explored during the masterplanning stage to investigate the circulation and crowd flow options

12.1

12.2

and an upper tier of public seating, a middle tier of club seating, and a fourth tier for the exclusive use of box holders. Each of the public tiers was to have its own concourse immediately behind, containing all the food and beverage concessions, toilets and other public facilities necessary for a modern venue. The club level was to contain dining areas, lounges and bars, all of which offered superb views of the playing field. The lowest level was developed for servicing the venue, containing the catering, storage and engineering plant required to operate the facility.

The structural principles developed by the team were based on an *in situ* concrete frame, since this proved to be the most cost-effective structural material available in Ireland. Although comparatively slow to erect, its low initial costs were deemed to compensate for this shortcoming. The roof, which would be clearly visible from some distance across the city, was conceived as a lightweight structure of tubular steel framing which was cable-stayed from every second frame and tied down at the rear of the stand to resist wind pressure on the cantilever. The roof covering itself was designed as a series of barrel vaults of profiled metal sheeting, spanning between the main roof beams. This uniform sheeting was to be highlighted by the use of translucent panels covering the triangular roof beams themselves.

Conclusion

In the 1980s the GAA's plans were regarded by many as being far too grandiose and expensive. But their vision of how Croke Park could develop as a venue has always been consistent, as well as ambitious. As a result of this commitment, the implementation of the masterplan is now well under way, with the first phase, the construction of the new Cusack Stand, which holds around 24,000 spectators, being completed in 1996.

12.3

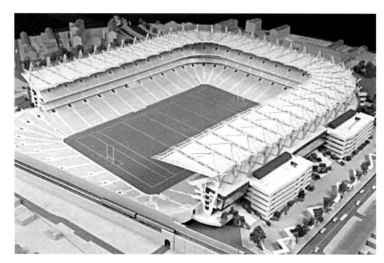

12.4

12.3 The first phase of development was the construction of the Cusack Stand on one of the long sides of the large pitch

12.4 A model of the final design shows clearly the difficulty of planning a large stadium on a site adjoining an existing railway line. The pedestrian ramps are used to provide spectators with access to all levels

The second phase, the continuation of the stand around the Canal End of the ground, followed soon after.

It is not uncommon to see a once proud venue slip into disrepair and become bleak and unwelcoming, however loyal its supporters. Yet to effect a real transition, to create a place where people can once again take pride in their surroundings, is often a difficult step to take, and one that requires almost superhuman tenacity and the clearest of visions. This was the vision of Liam Mulvihill, Chief Executive of the GAA. It has therefore been very pleasing for the team to see the masterplan at Croke Park taking shape; not only to see the beginnings of a magnificent new venue which will be comparable with the best in the world, but also to note how wonderful dreams can indeed be realised, despite the doubts of those without ambition.

Premium level plan

1 Restaurant
2 Bar lounge
3 Lounge

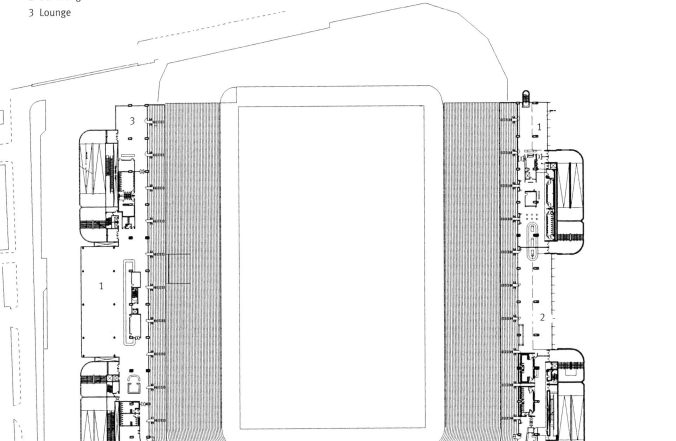

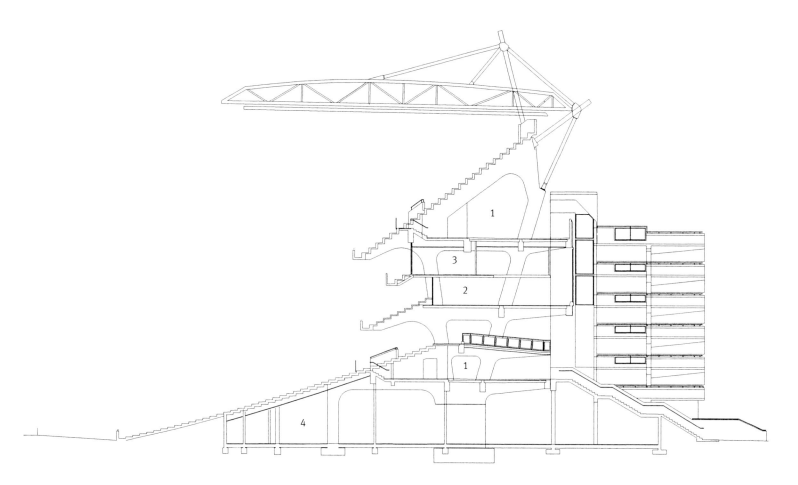

Section

1 Concourse
2 Season ticket
   concourse
3 Box
4 Team facilities

Reebok Stadium

New football stadium

Project data	Consultants	Chronology	Project information	Economic information
Location:	*Structural engineer:*	*Design:*	*Site area:*	*Main building cost:*
Bolton, England	*Deakin Callard & P*	*December 1995*	*513.9 acres*	*£24,000,000*
Owner:	*Services engineer:*	*Documentation:*	*Total parking spaces:*	*External works:*
Bolton Wanderers FC	*William Hannans*	*July 1996*	*5,000 cars*	*£1,500,000*
Main contractor:	*Quantity surveyor:*	*Construction:*	*Total number of seats:*	
Birse Construction	*O'Neil and Partners*	*October 1996*	*28,000*	
		Opening date:	*Total building area:*	
		September 1997	*34,000 square metres*	

Case Study

13

Background

Bolton Wanderers, one of England's oldest and most famous football clubs, entered a period of steep decline during the 1970s and 1980s, but then, during the mid-1990s, managed to stage a revival which saw them return to the highest level of the domestic game, the Premier League. In keeping with this renewed sense of purpose and vision, the club decided to sell their centrally located ground at Burnden Park, their home since since 1895, and move to a more suitable site where they could build an all-seated stadium, as required by the Taylor Report (Home Office 1990b). The aim of the move was to provide facilities more in keeping with their new image and more able to satisfy the needs of their supporters.

The opportunity to do this came about thanks to proposals for a 208 hectare site on the outskirts of Bolton, where a mixed leisure and retail development was planned. The site appeared to be ideal for accommodating a new stadium as it was spacious, had the potential for good public transport links via both road and rail, and offered the possibility of sharing the extensive car parks being planned for the retail site. The site was also directly accessible to a well developed road network, being a short distance from approaches to the nearby M61 motorway, which links the M6 and M62 motorways with Manchester. Another advantage was that the site was clearly visible from motorway approaches, offering the possibility of a high profile presence to millions of passing motorists.

The brief

The client's aspirations were for a football stadium holding a minimum of 25,000 seats, built to the highest affordable standards for viewing, comfort and safety. Given the club's recent return to the limelight, they were also keen for the stadium to make a bold architectural statement, one which might help transform their image from that of an essentially down-to-earth, rather traditional Lancashire club whose successes were all in the distant past, to one of a thrusting, ambitious outfit with an appeal to younger supporters and to a wider range of commercial interests and sponsors. (In this last respect they certainly succeeded, since the naming rights for the new stadium were eventually purchased by Reebok, the international sporting goods manufacturer whose origins were actually in Bolton.)

The stadium had to be multi-functional, using its many planned facilities for activities other than football.

13.1 The curved articulated trusses reflect the natural integrity of the structural elements following the stress patterns of the roof

13.1

It would have to accommodate restaurants, shops, conference facilities, exhibition spaces, a nursery and medical facilities. The local authority, which was highly supportive of the proposal, also desired that an indoor hall for sports such as netball and basketball be designed as part of the venue for use by the local community. This would have to be built under one of the stands, and be large enough to host exhibitions and shows on a commercial basis.

Finally, the stadium would be designed to act as the flagship for the new retail and leisure park, occupying the most prominent position within the site, although it would be physically linked to an adjoining, less dominating building in which an extensive network of related leisure facilities was planned.

Design concept

The Reebok Stadium design represents an incremental advance on our earlier award-winning design for the Alfred McAlpine Stadium in Huddersfield. Bolton representatives had visited this venue and were keen on emulating its exciting style, but they made one additional requirement: that the lower tier be designed as a complete, continuous bowl around the pitch. All 28,000 seats are under cover and within 90 metres of the centre of the field. They all have minimum 'C' values of 90 mm and there are no seats with restricted views. All treads are 800 mm wide, unusually large by most British standards, and 1000 mm wide for the boxes.

One of the key characteristics of the Reebok Stadium is the sheer amount of space available on the site (again, quite rare for sports venues in Britain). This space is fully exploited in the design's generous dimensions. For example, at ground level, surrounding the lower seating bowl, is a 25 metre wide pedestrian concourse. This fulfils several functions. It provides a circulation route between the various entrances, can accommodate external concessions and pre-match entertainment, and provides a clearly defined 'place of safety' in case of emergency.

13.2

13.2 The Reebok
Stadium on
completion
demonstrates a self-
assured authority as it
sits proudly in the
rural landscape

To respond to the client's ambition of achieving a 'landmark' structure, we developed a form of building visually focused upon a dramatic roof structure, oversailing a simple but articulate bowl. The bowl itself is in a large, oval plan form, providing constantly changing perspectives from any point of view. The roof consists of four leaning and tapering tubular towers, each providing support for floodlighting towers and for the main roof trusses, which span the full length of each side. The trusses themselves are curved both top and bottom to reflect the true viewing nature of the bowl below and the natural structural integrity of the main elements. The roof covering appears as a scalloped canopy, floating over the bowl, with each element fitting neatly to the other and being read as one unified form. From both inside and outside the stadium the visual impact of this assembly of roof components, angles, curved forms and textures is dramatic. Both elements apparently hard and soft are intended to lend the building as a whole a futuristic, yet instantly recognisable appearance; quite definitely a stadium, yet not like any other stadium, as it were.

Turning now to the main body of the stadium, the West Stand contains on level 1 a public concourse with its many associated facilities. Level 2 is a service and administration floor containing offices for the club and the stadium management, a boardroom and changing and warm-up facilities for players. Level 3 accommodates a second concourse, served by dedicated twin sets of scissors stairs, private boxes and a banqueting suite seating up to 450 people. Level 4 is another public concourse providing access to the upper tier. Level 5 is a plant area containing engineering services.

The East Stand houses most of the stadium's community facilities, with levels 1 and 2 accommodating the large, double height 2,000 square metre column-free exhibition space which has a sprung floor for community sports activities. Level 3 is devoted to facilities for club seats and private box holders. Level 4 is the public concourse and level 5 again contains plant and engineering services. The North Stand is the 'home' end, which is reserved for Bolton Wanderers' supporters and backs on to a car park with 5,000 spaces (a huge number, unrivalled by any other

13.3

13.3 A reception which is welcoming and inviting: the Reebok's main (West) stand

football club stadium in Britain). Level 1 accommodates the public concourse, plus concession outlets. Level 2 is planned for food and beverage areas. Level 3 accommodates a concourse and facilities for private box holders.

Finally, the South Stand is reserved for visiting supporters, and also backs on to its own car park. Internal circulation is similar to that of the North Stand, except that the space can be subdivided into sections, to allow for varying numbers of visiting fans. Plans are in progress to incorporate a hotel into the South Stand. Emergency escape time for all the stands is calculated at below 8 minutes from any seat to a

'place of safety' which, at the Reebok Stadium, is the wide public external concourse surrounding the venue.

Conclusion

There was a five year gap between our design for Huddersfield and our subsequent work in Bolton, and although the two designs share many similar elements, there are clear differences also. Huddersfield's stadium was designed for two less successful clubs with fewer financial resources. Hence it was built in two distinct phases, to lower specifications. Bolton's greater access to

13.4

13.4 Floodlight towers were designed as an integral part of the roof composition and are used to good effect in illuminating the entire structure

13.5 Night-time view of the Reebok Stadium

funds enabled them to complete their stadium in one main phase, leaving only individual areas to infill at a later stage, without the need for major structural additions. It is possibly true to say that the Reebok Stadium might not have evolved as it did had it not been preceded by Huddersfield. But that is not simply because of the shared structural and technological elements. Rather, it is because the largely positive reactions to Huddersfield's pioneering stadium design paved the way for other clubs to take a similar leap of faith. In a country where football clubs have traditionally been extremely conservative, and even cautious in their approach to stadium design, Huddersfield demonstrated what could be achieved if only designers were allowed to interpret their clients' wishes in a more expressive manner. In this respect, the Reebok Stadium has shown that Huddersfield was not a 'one-off' experiment, but instead the beginning of a new era in football-related architecture.

As far as Bolton is concerned, the Reebok Stadium also provides confirmation that the Wanderers have emerged from their past to become a modern, progressive and forward-looking club. They now have a stadium that is not only much enjoyed by their supporters but is also widely admired as an arresting landmark set against the undulating hills of Lancashire.

13.5

Site plan
1 Stadium
2 Retail, leisure and
  commercial zones
3 Motorway M61,
  junction 6

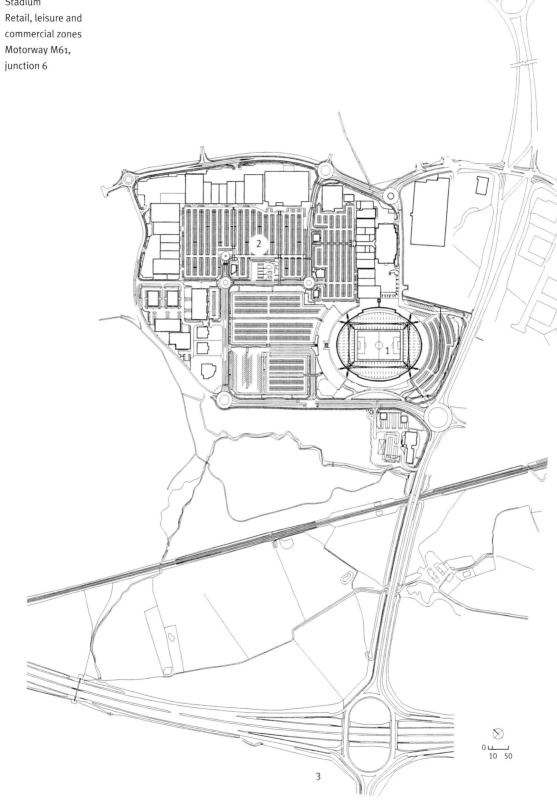

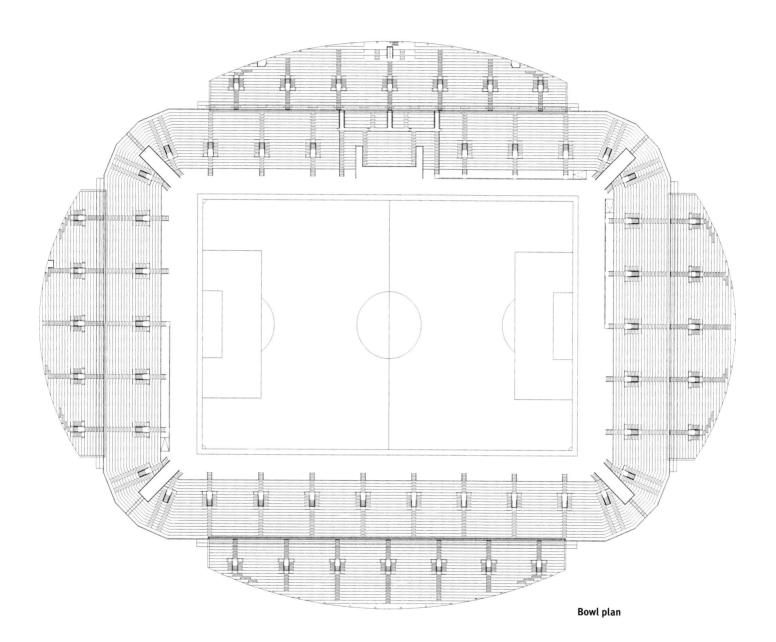

Bowl plan

178

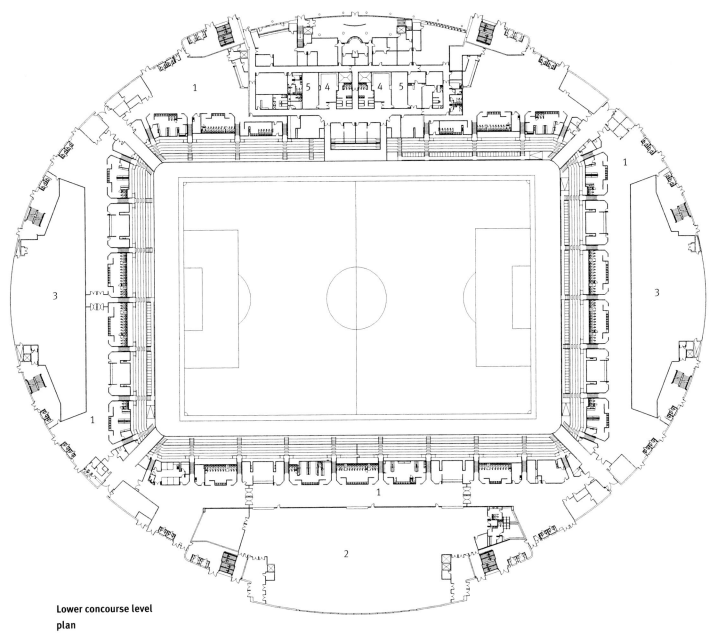

Lower concourse level plan

1 Concourse
2 Exhibition space
3 Future fit-out
4 Changing rooms
5 Warm-up rooms

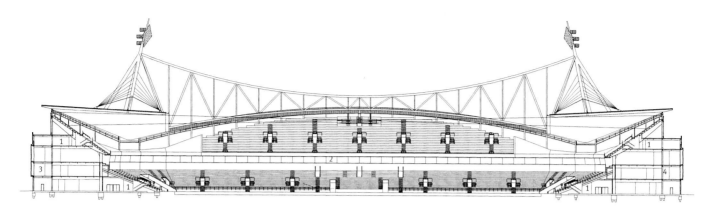

Section

1 Concourse

2 Boxes

3 Hotel development

4 Future fit-out

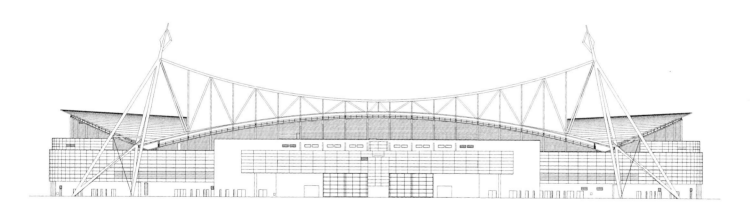

East elevation

Blue Wings Stadium

Football stadium design competition

Project data	Consultants	Chronology	Project information	Economic information
Location:	*Structural engineer:*	*Design:*	*Site area:*	*Main building cost:*
Suwon, South Korea	*Modus*	*February 1997*	*76.5 acres*	*K$161,000,000*
Owner:	*Services engineer:*	*Submission:*	*Total parking spaces:*	*External works:*
Samsung	*Short Ford*	*May 1997*	*980 cars and 50 coaches*	*K$20,000,000*
	Quantity surveyor:		*Total number of seats:*	
	Davis Langdon Everest		*43,000*	
			Total building area:	
			80,000 square metres	

Background

During the bidding stage for the rights to host the 2002 FIFA World Cup, South Korea and Japan were keen rivals. Never before had the finals been staged in an Asian country, and although South Korea had a superior record as a footballing nation, Japan were regarded by many as favourites to win the vote. Meanwhile, both nations put forward a series of exciting proposals for stadium developments. There were therefore many raised eyebrows when FIFA announced that, for the first time in the tournament's history, the 2002 finals would be shared between the two countries.

This required both of the bidders to modify their development proposals, while at the same time both remained firmly committed to the aim of providing world-class facilities that would be eminently impressive to the massive worldwide television audience. At the end of 1996, the national Samsung project team proposed a new World Cup stadium for the Suwon area. Three international firms of architects, including HOK LOBB, were invited to submit a design scheme for a new stadium.

The brief

The client sought a stadium capable of providing 43,000 spectators in its World Cup format, after which it would revert to 30,000 seats as the home of the Blue Wings football team. The main requirements of the design brief, as set out by the client, were relatively simple. However, we evolved the brief to provide for a truly advanced stadium which would result in a mix of leisure and entertainment facilities built around the central focus of the football venue. In South Korea such multi-functional facilities are often given the name 'spolex' short for sports and leisure complex. Thus our design envisaged both a stadium and spolex linked on the same site.

Design concept

The design of the structure uses a rigid concrete frame without bracing planes, in order to maintain flexibility and adaptability in use. The combined use of *in situ* concrete, pre-cast concrete and steel has been proposed to allow for simultaneous on-site construction and off-site pre-fabrication, as the most efficient use of time and of each type of material. The use of an inverted 'shell' form of roof is also extremely efficient. As well as being designed to complement the form of the seating bowl, the distinctive shape and high degree of shelter offered by this form creates a visually stunning effect, without compromising the roof's functional requirements. It also allows the client to incorporate a moving roof system if and when required.

A responsible attitude to Environmentally Sustainable Development pervades all aspects of the design approach, and is particularly important for a showcase stadium likely to be seen by so many viewers around the world during the World Cup. The key environmental strategies we adopted for the design include the following:

- Containers that store rainwater for irrigation and retain storm water runoff
- A dual reticulation system to recycle waste water
- Gas co-generation of electricity and hot water to minimise energy consumption
- Passive design measures to provide ventilation, natural cooling and warming, and natural lighting to minimise energy consumption
- Eco-profiling of building systems to ensure environmental friendliness
- Use of subterranean temperature for winter heating and summer cooling

Roof design

The roof is the visually dominant element of a stadium, and is also of critical importance to the performance of the venue. Generally speaking the roof form determines to a large extent the level of crowd atmosphere experienced, the degree of exposure to the elements and the quality of broadcast television pictures. The chosen form of roof design has a number of inherent advantages.

The form is structurally efficient and visually appealing. The structural lines are straight and simple to construct while the inverted shell form of the main roofs allow rainwater to drain to the middle so that the roof slopes down rather than up. With the front pencil beams this lowers the front edge significantly and allows a considerably higher degree of weather protection. The roof is able to span over all of the seating, providing

cover to the drip line and the form has acoustic benefits, important for the retention of atmosphere within the spectator areas.

Arena lighting can be suspended from the underside of the roof structure, minimising light spill to surrounding areas. The proximity and distribution of light fittings also allows for improved light quality and reduces the number of fittings needed, compared with lighting towers. Gantries are provided around the length of the roof edge, to provide for the fixing of and access to the floodlight fittings and public address speakers, for the fixing of a moving camera rail, and for the hanging of ceremonial flags.

The shadows from the roof's large pencil beams have been carefully calculated to avoid problems with overshadowing – an important consideration for both the live and TV audience. Certainly they will be less uneven than the shadows formed by, for example, an exposed lattice roof structure. Dramatic effects are possible within the stadium by lighting the inside of the roof beams, which are perforated and therefore allow light to seep out.

Finally, the design allows for the future installation of moving roof sections, so that the stadium can be entirely covered, should this be desired. The advantages of retractable roof systems are that they allow events to be staged almost regardless of weather conditions; they expand the event calendar; they avoid light and noise spillage, and they greatly assist television coverage by effectively turning the whole stadium into a giant TV studio. However, such roof systems also have knock-on environmental effects upon natural turf surfaces. Nevertheless, we believe that it will not be long before moving roofs are able to justify their extra capital cost and will thus become an integral part of future stadium design.

Spectator viewing

The cross-section of the seating bowl is fundamental to the composition of the Blue Wings Stadium. There are two seating tiers for general admission, separated by two intermediate tiers for corporate and membership seating. Each general seating tier is directly served by its own concourse level, at level 1 for the lower tier, and at

14.1 Two circular trusses which span the full length of the stadium not only support the roof and its moving panels but also house the lighting, public address, CCTV and other support services

14.2 The four-tier bowl allows a range of seating capacities to be used to provide flexibility in the type of event which could be staged at the venue

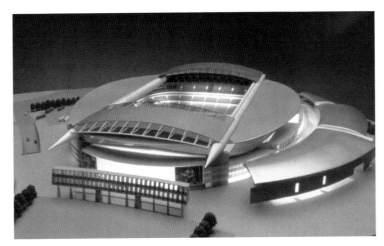

14.1

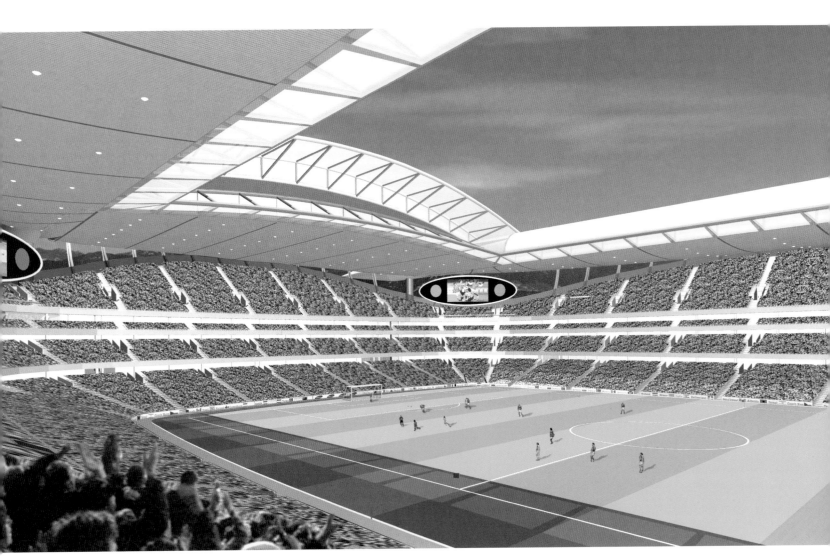

14.2

14.3 An extensive range of related sporting facilities are designed into the venue including a multi-tiered golf driving range at one end

14.3

level 4 for the upper tier. To improve crowd flow, and yield further cost and efficiency benefits, in post-World Cup mode there are no vomitories offering access to the lower tier. It is also worth noting that the design allows for the client to raise the capacity of the stadium back up to the 43,000 level, should this be necessary at a later date. The North Stand is also designed to allow for the optional provision of retractable seating, so that the venue could be reconfigured, if needed, when it is being used as a concert venue.

The seating is designed to be as close to the action as FIFA recommendations allow. This close proximity is a feature most associated with British football venues, and is a characteristic much admired, though not often implemented, by other soccer-loving nations, many of whom still build stadia with tracks or large neutral areas separating the fans from their heroes. All seating profiles in the design have been drawn by our computer software, which calculates the riser height for each and every row to a high degree of accuracy. The profiles are constructed to a true curve, by the simple method of varying the height of the support stools for each pre-cast unit. To simplify pre-casting, the risers of the units are measured uniformly in groups of five or six, with the gaps between units varying slightly. The use of a true curve, rather than one created in facets, contributes to the efficiency of the seating bowl's cross-section by

lowering the height of the overall stadium and therefore reducing costs, yet without compromising viewing standards. Indeed a minimum 'C' value of 90 mm is achievable for each seat in both the stadium's World Cup and post-World Cup modes.

Seat specifications

Individual seats in the general admission areas are allocated a tread depth of 800 mm, with seat widths set at 500 mm centres. These widths are extended in the VIP and members' areas to 560 mm lateral spacing. To accord with World Cup demands, media representatives are given spaces equivalent to three seats, to allow for the installation of writing desks, plus telephones, faxes, laptop computers and television monitors.

One unusual feature of our proposal concerns the provision of 'smart seats'. These advanced forms of seat allow for a number of services to be available to each spectator, usually through the arm rest. For example, a communications port can provide a link up to the stadium's own radio or information service. The seat can also offer an LCD flip screen and keypad, a card swipe (for purchases), service and emergency call features and so on. Wiring ducts built into the design allow these systems to be progressively installed throughout the stadium, and modified as the technology (or budget) develops. We proposed that at the very least it should be possible to fit smart seats in the corporate and members' areas of the stadium, with cup-holders and slip-on padding to the bases and backs as standard fittings. Certainly we predict that such seats will become standard in certain areas of most 'fourth generation' stadia during the early part of the twenty-first century.

Services, media provision and circulation issues

For maximum efficiency, at basement level a service road provides vehicle access to the lowest levels of the stadium and spolex, for servicing and parking. The concentration of services in the basement allows for the separation of staff functions and spectators to avoid overlap, while the provision of service lifts means that the public and staff need never cross paths. Passenger lifts serve each grandstand. There are also food lifts to the East and West Stands, 'dumb waiter' lifts to the North and South Stands, with a pair of escalators serving each floor level of the East and West Stands. Access to the spolex is via escalators and lifts. Also at basement level, there are secure parking spaces for 580 cars and two team coaches. Service vehicles can be parked in the North Stand. An additional 400 parking spaces are available under the pitch.

Meanwhile, the circulation system for the media is also designed to be independent throughout the complex, with a lift and stairway which links the media facilities and the commercial facilities to each level of the West Stand and the media seating. Spaces for outside-broadcast vehicles and two support trucks are provided in the basement, with direct vertical access by lift and stairs to the commentators' and camera positions. Media access to players' areas is limited to the basement interview rooms, unless otherwise permitted.

Conclusion

When architects draw up submissions for design competitions they sometimes gain an opportunity to design to a looser, more open-minded brief. The design competition for the Blue Wings Stadium was certainly one good example of this, allowing us to come up with a progressive design, combining our experience of the past with our vision for the future. Realistically, the Blue Wings design is unlikely to reach fruition. Nevertheless, members of our design team seldom regret entering competitions of this nature, if only because they provide us with an excellent opportunity to explore and develop ideas. Indeed it could be argued that competitions in effect form the vital research and development work so necessary for architects to keep pace with modern ideas. Of course it is even better when they are paid for their efforts, as was the case in Suwon, but none of the work we did on this project will be wasted. We are always learning. In this respect, the Blue Wings Stadium may well turn out to be the blueprint for an altogether different project of the future.

14.4 Public access to the site is largely by public transport which is accessed through an underground tunnel system with its bubble-like entrance canopy

14.4

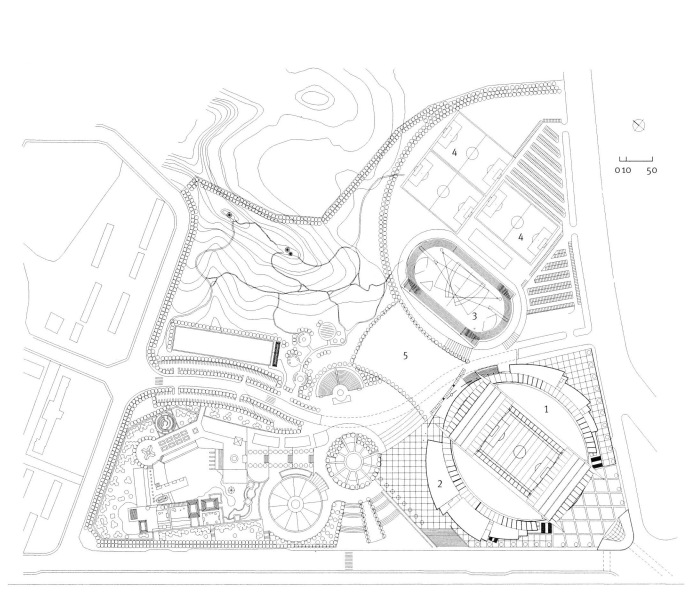

010   50

Site plan
1 Stadium
2 Sports and leisure
   complex (spolex)
3 Training field
4 Practice pitches
5 Golf driving range

186

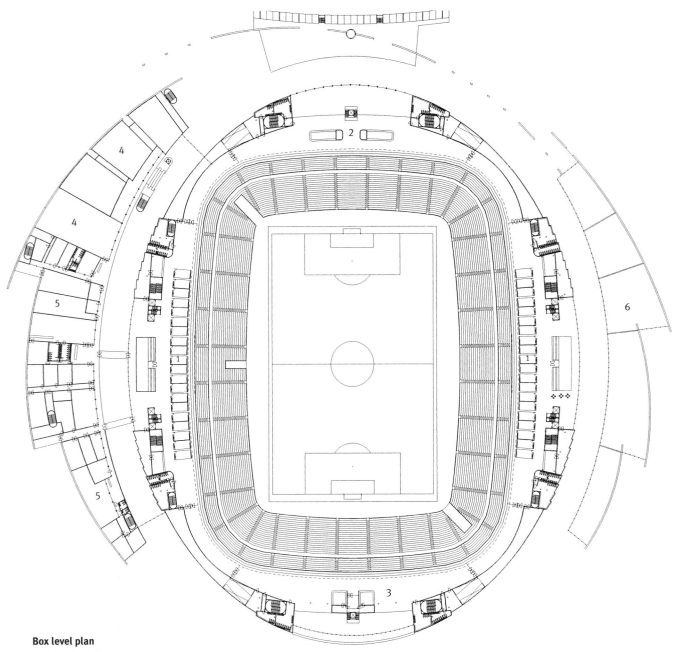

Box level plan

1 Executive suite
2 Sports bar
3 Restaurant
4 Cinema
5 Spolex facilities
6 Future spolex

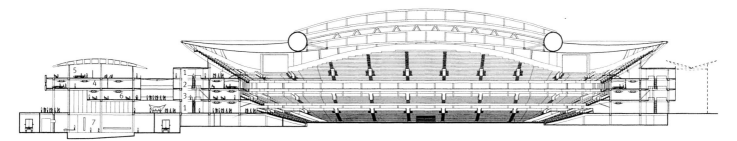

Section

1 Concourse
2 Box
3 Club
4 Executive
5 Media
6 Cinema/cafe
7 Swimming pools

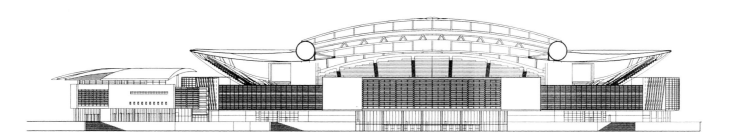

South elevation

Robin Park Athletics

New athletics stadium

Project data	Consultants	Chronology	Project information	Economic information
Location:	*Structural engineer:*	*Design:*	*Site area:*	*Main building cost:*
Robin Park, Wigan	*Thorburn Colquhoun*	*January 1996*	*15.37 acres*	*£1,680,000 (Phase 1)*
Owner:	*Services engineer:*	*Documentation:*	*Total parking spaces:*	*£3,460,000 (Phase 2)*
Wigan Met. Bor. Council	*Thorburn Colquhoun*	*February 1996*	*390 cars, 6 coaches*	
Main contractor:	*Quantity surveyor:*	*Construction:*	*Total number of seats:*	
Phase 1 – ERDC Ltd	*Frank Whittle*	*March 1996*	*1,000*	
Phase 2 – Birse Ltd	*Project manager:*	*Opening date:*	*Total building area:*	
	CTP Limited	*December 1997*	*3,600 square metres*	

Case Study

15

Background

The northern town of Wigan is best known for two things. First, 'Wigan Pier' was immortalised by George Orwell, in his famous socialist tome of the 1930s. Second, Wigan Rugby Football Club have dominated the English Rugby League scene for over a decade. But in athletics circles, the name of the town's local running track is also well known. Robin Park has for years been a major centre and focal point for sports and recreation in the northwest region.

But the venue was in acute need of redevelopment. Indeed Britain's failure at the 1996 Olympic Games in Atlanta only proved that more attention and funds must be concentrated upon training facilities such as this. At the same time, improvements were needed if Robin Park was to continue serving the local community in Wigan adequately.

The new athletics stadium came about as the result of a successful partnership between Wigan Metropolitan Borough Council, Wigan City Challenge and two development companies based in Manchester and Scotland. These combined to undertake the wholesale redevelopment of the 140 acre park area, to include not only the new athletics stadium but also other sports, leisure and retail outlets.

The brief

Originally commissioned by the Wigan Metropolitan Borough Council early in 1995, the new Robin Park Athletics Arena was conceived to provide athletes in the northwest of England with one of the best training facilities in the country, and more specifically to act as a base for the well-known athletics club, the Wigan Harriers. The facilities would also have to be good enough to attract leading coaches to the area, thereby benefiting both the Harriers and individual athletes from other clubs and schools within the region. In addition, our design set out to encourage increased usage of the facilities by individuals on a casual, recreational basis. It was further intended that schools in the area would benefit from the enhanced facilities and use them as part of their extra-curricular activities.

Design concept

The first phase of the project was completed in November 1996 and comprised an eight-lane polymeric running track, full-size grass and synthetic sports pitches, together with four new multi-court synthetic sports pitches for five-a-side hockey and tennis. This

15.1 A modest sports complex reflected in the simplicity of materials and detailing here showing the southwest corner of the main grandstand building

15.1

first phase also involved major landscaping to the River Douglas and various external works to provide practice areas for field athletics and areas for parking.

The construction of a new grandstand and other specialist training facilities formed Phase 2. Changing facilities for individuals and groups were also provided to serve both the track and the synthetic sports pitch complex. One feature of the grandstand is the inclusion of an indoor sprint-training track, which accommodates both high jump and pole vault practice areas, as well as an indoor throwing circle. Private viewing lounges, lecture rooms and offices for the Council's Sports Development Unit complete the first floor accommodation, which is located at the rear of the covered seating tier. This tier holds 1,000 spectators.

A third phase is also planned, to provide an indoor recreation facility designed to complement the overall development at Robin Park.

Due to the significant expanse of the site we deliberately accentuated the visual impact of the

grandstand by the addition of two cylindrical masts, 25 metres high, to provide a point of focus and to assist in orientation. Further visual emphasis is created by two aerofoil roofs, which cover the majority of the building accommodation as well as the spectators. The curved form of these roofs is also defined by a band of clerestory glazing, which appears to detach the roofs from the external envelope of the building, lending them an appearance of weightlessness.

The building sits on a plinth of textured architectural masonry, with metallic silver panels providing a clean, articulate finish at an economic cost. The blue clad rectilinear form of the specialist gymnastics training area creates a striking contrast to the rest of the building. This is treated as a secondary element in the massing of the complex, as it slides under the grandstand roof to announce the entrance of the building.

From the parking area immediately in front of the building, pedestrian walkways have been created in the

15.2

15.2 The main entrance with its blue-clad gymnastics training centre and the roof masts providing a point of reference to the site

15.3 The trackside view from the 400 metre start to the sweeping aerofoil roof. The eight-lane track is a 13 mm non porous Polymeric surface

paving and hard landscaping, in order to identify routes to the entrance.

The internal layout is a result of the multiplicity of uses the facility accommodates. The central reception area controls the access of both athletes and the public to these internal areas and is designed to accommodate both crowds attending event days and individuals with specific day-to-day appointments. The building serves the community with a variety of function rooms, regular fitness and aerobic classes and a communal bar area. From the reception area on the ground floor, access is afforded to a physio treatment

15.3

room, with its own waiting area, and to changing rooms and various training facilities housed within the double height, single-storey part of the building. Also accommodated in the main part of the building are offices, toilet facilities, changing rooms for officials and access to the track, synthetic pitches and the seating tier, via vomitories.

The training area and its main constituent, the indoor sprint-training track, also houses a club room (for the Harriers athletics club), gymnastics training, weight training, high jump, throwing circle and internal and external equipment stores for first-, second- and third-tier athletics events. Community and function rooms are accommodated on the first floor and have views over the indoor training area and the athletics track. In addition to regular event-day use, the layouts of the private viewing box, plus other rooms for the press and timekeepers, are designed for a wide variety of flexible use throughout the week. Administration offices and the Council's Sports Development Unit are housed at this level. Lecture rooms, bar/kitchen facilities and lounge areas provide further flexible spaces for use by clubs and the community.

Conclusion

Partly funded by lottery grants, the new Robin Park Stadium and complex came about as the result of local people's sheer enthusiasm for sport and the attainment of sporting excellence. It has been this enthusiasm and vision that has directly led to the development's success and to the support it has received from the best training programmes and coaching staff. The client's enthusiasm is not just limited to the facilities themselves, but also to our architecture, which has received many flattering plaudits from local politicians. All that can be hoped now is that the fruits of such facilities as these might be reaped on the distant tracks and fields of Olympics venues. George Orwell once wrote of the hardships to be encountered along the Road to Wigan Pier. Let us hope that the road to success from Wigan's Robin Park is a good deal smoother.

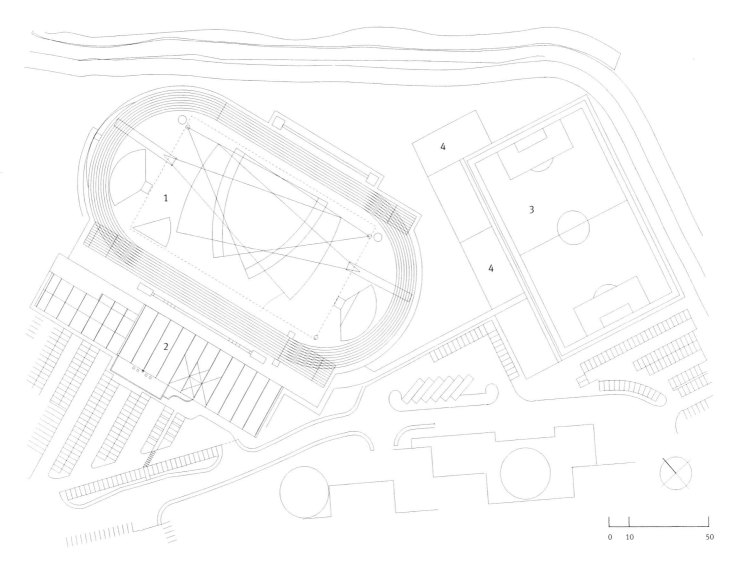

Site plan

1 Athletics arena
2 New grandstand
3 Synthetic sports pitch
4 Multi-courts

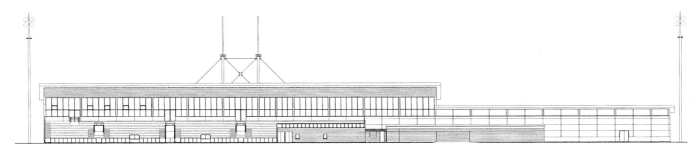

East elevation

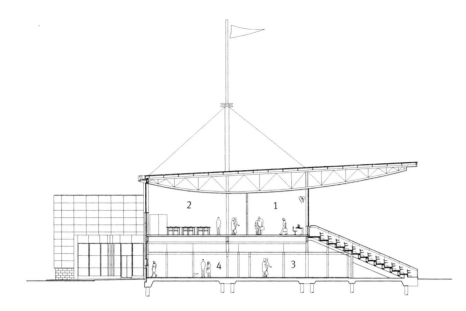

Section
1 Time-keeper
2 Lecture/VIP rooms
3 First aid
4 Officials

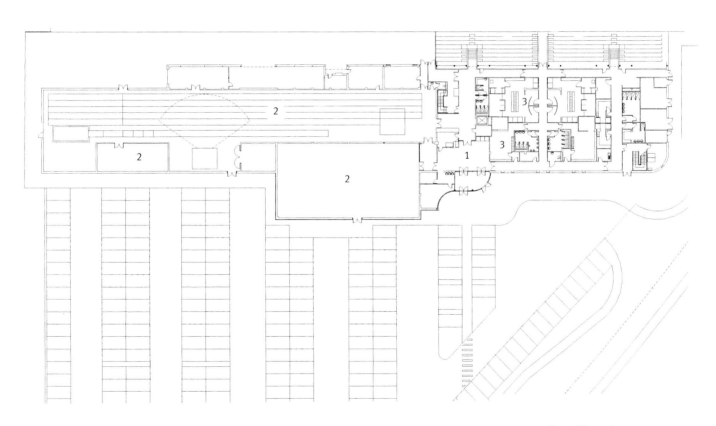

Ground floor plan
1 Reception
2 Training areas
3 Changing rooms

Millennium Stadium

Cardiff Arms Park

Project data	Consultants	Chronology	Project information	Economic information
Location:	*Structural engineer:*	*Design:*	*Site area:*	*Main contract cost:*
Cardiff, Wales	W.S. Atkins	January 1996	13.7 acres	£94,000,000
Owner:	*Services engineer:*	*Documentation:*	*Total parking spaces:*	
Millennium Stadium Ltd	Hoare Lea & Partners	October 1996	239 cars	
Main contractor:	*Quantity surveyor:*	*Construction:*	*Total number of seats:*	
John Laing Construction	Bute Partnership	April 1997	72,500	
	Project manager:	*Opening date:*	*Total building area:*	
	O'Brien Kreitzberg	June 1999	80,000 square metres	

Case Study

16

Background

Rugby football has been played on the site of Cardiff Arms Park since 1876, but the more modern National Stadium which replaced the original ground was built in phases over a 16-year period, beginning in 1968. Once completed in 1984 this new stadium, with its horseshoe of two-tiered stands and its seamless, cantilevered roof, was rightly considered to be one of the world's leading rugby venues. Yet how quickly standards evolve.

Within less than two decades of its inauguration, this pride of Wales was overtaken by developments in design, in safety codes and, just as importantly, by other rugby venues around the world, such as Twickenham in London, Murrayfield in Edinburgh and the Stade de France in Paris. The Cardiff Arms Park bowl still offered good views and a wonderful atmosphere, but in all other respects the venue was seriously lacking, particularly when it came to important revenue-earning facilities such as food and beverage outlets and corporate hospitality facilities. For ordinary spectators, too, the facilities were poor, particularly the toilets and the stark stairways and narrow approaches from street level.

Another serious drawback was its capacity. When completed in 1984, the stadium held around 65,000 spectators, of which nearly half were standing spectators, concentrated at the one end which had not been substantially redeveloped. But, as the years passed and safety standards grew ever more stringent, this reduced to 53,500, still with 8,000 standing. After the Taylor Report in 1990, which required the ground to be all-seated by 1994, the stadium's owners, the Welsh Rugby Union, calculated that the existing stadium could only hold 47,500, if the remaining terrace was converted to seats. This was much less than the capacities of rival rugby stadia such as Twickenham (75,000), and certainly too small to cope with the ever increasing demand for tickets whenever the Welsh Dragons were playing at home.

In 1995, therefore, Cardiff County Council and the Welsh Rugby Union commissioned HOK LOBB to develop a concept design for a new multi-purpose, 75,000 seat venue. This proposal would then form the basis of an application for funding from the Millennium Commission (which distributed monies raised by Britain's new National Lottery). From the beginning, the decision was made that, if at all possible, the new stadium would be built on the same site as its predecessor, even though this would require the acquisition of several adjoining sites in order to create more

16.1

room. By retaining the stadium in the centre of the city, the huge income which Cardiff's many shops, hotels and businesses derived from match weekends would be retained. (One study in 1992 reckoned that the Arms Park's twelve events that year had been worth a staggering £35 million to local businesses.) Second, a new stadium incorporating enhanced facilities for leisure and entertainment would help to galvanise the city centre throughout the year, not only on match days.

16.1 Across the River Taff, the view to the plaza entrance from Wood Street Bridge is a dramatic approach to the stadium

Finally, its location, just to the west of Cardiff city centre, bounded on its western side by the River Taff and easily accessible from the nearby bus interchange and railway station made it ideal for the majority of spectators to arrive by public transport. As we have already noted in our case studies of the stadia in Wellington and Melbourne, this factor alone made the existing site quite desirable in environmental terms.

The brief

Primarily, the new stadium is the new home of the Welsh Rugby Union, and specifically, the main venue

for the Rugby World Cup in 1999. The stadium is also likely to continue as the de facto national stadium for the Wales national soccer team. In addition to these two sports, the stadium had also to be able to offer world-class facilities for other entertainment, cultural events, concerts and festivals.

To meet these diverse needs the brief included a number of key requirements, one of which – the realignment of the pitch to a more suitable north–south orientation – meant that a number of key sites adjoining the existing grounds would have to be purchased, and several substantial buildings demolished. Possibly the boldest requirement of the brief was for the roof to

16.2 A seating bowl which we have designed to retain the ambience and crowd-pleasing atmosphere of the former Arms Park

16.3 From above the Millennium Stadium its neighbour, the Cardiff Athletics Club, can be seen adjacent to it

16.4 One of four 93 metre high masts which support the roof and are the highest building points in Cardiff

16.5

be capable of closing completely over the pitch, in order to ensure environmental control of the venue and guard against disastrous delays or even postponements of major events, such as occurred in South Africa during the Rugby World Cup in 1995.

One final part of the brief was that the new stadium had to accommodate the needs of the adjoining ground belonging to the Cardiff Rugby Club, one of whose stands was physically and structurally linked to the back of the stadium's existing North Stand.

16.5 River walk at night from the banks of the River Taff

16.6 Longitudinal section through the three-tiered seating bowl looking east

Design concept

Unlike the existing stadium, which is largely hidden from view and to some extent landlocked and difficult to access, the new venue is conceived as a prominent and attractive landmark building, well served by pedestrian routes, which positively invite the public to approach and stroll around the perimeter. Apart from clearing adjacent sites, this enhanced circulation system has also required the widening of a walkway immediately alongside the stadium, along the River Taff, and the opening up of a northern access route to pedestrians.

As the two main sports to be held at the stadium are rugby and soccer, the playing surface obviously had to be natural turf, albeit capable of all-year use for sport and for other events scheduled at the venue. It is only in recent years that natural grass pitches have been expected to withstand this kind of extended usage, and so considerable research for this and several other similar projects has been conducted to investigate all aspects of this important area. The issues addressed by the design team for Cardiff included temperature, humidity and air movement (which could be generated either naturally or by mechanical means). We also studied the effects on grass which is enclosed on all sides by a spectator bowl, and is then covered part of the time by a roof, thus increasing the level of shade and restricting natural light and ventilation. The research also looked into the best types of grass to use in such artificial situations, and into current developments of which there

are several concerning the use of movable or interchangeable turf sections.

Finally, the design team decided that the best solution for Cardiff was to use a fully palletised system of interlocking turf modules which could be lifted out easily to replace those worn or damaged. Built into the modules, sub-surface air and water channels enabled control of the root zone temperature and extension of the growing season as required. Mechanical ventilation units would be installed, plus state-of-the-art automatic irrigation and drainage systems. The original brief called for a bowl capacity of 75,000 but as the project developed, achieving this figure became less important than solving the many restrictions resulting from the site and its immediate surrounds. One of the most acute limitations caused by these restrictions affected the safe exit times achievable. As a result of these difficulties, the target capacity was reduced to 72,500.

In designing any viewing bowl there are a series of factors which need to be balanced in order to achieve the optimum configuration. In the case of Cardiff these factors included bowl dimensions to accommodate the required numbers while offering excellent sightlines, seating comfort and safety; the number and positions of private boxes; provision for disabled people; and, last, the creation of the kind of atmosphere that would be likely to draw top performers and large audiences. Having considered all these factors, the bowl configuration was finally settled as having three tiers, with private boxes positioned behind the middle tier.

16.6

16.7

16.7 South elevational view across the entrance plaza from the transport interchange. Excellent public transport links are provided via the adjacent bus and railway station

The roof had to provide complete shelter to all spectators, as well as achieving good acoustic conditions when the venue is used for concerts. This is no easy objective in a building of this size, particularly one fitted with a movable roof. One of the greatest challenges facing the design team was the provision of a whole range of high quality consumer services within the limited and fixed budget available. This was particularly important to the client after the failure of the previous stadium design to cater for such facilities. These services were to include:

–   Food and beverage concessions covering the full range of options, from fast food to reserved table restaurant
–   Private hospitality facilities, evenly distributed around the venue
–   Corporate seating areas and dining areas
–   Family attractions, play areas and crèches

–   Spaces and facilities for disabled people and their carers
–   Merchandising franchises, a museum and other retail outlets, for daily use
–   Extensive toilets and child care areas
–   Future flexibility to enable the venue to flourish in a competitive environment

On the basis of all the above considerations, the design evolved along the following lines. Level 1 contains the main service circulation network around the stadium, plus areas for the officials, points for service deliveries and general support areas. Level 2 is a mezzanine level containing the players' changing rooms, press facilities, media centre and much of the back-of-house areas required for the catering system. Level 3 is the main public concourse with a range of spectator services and entrances to the upper levels while level 4 contains the corporate facilities and has direct access

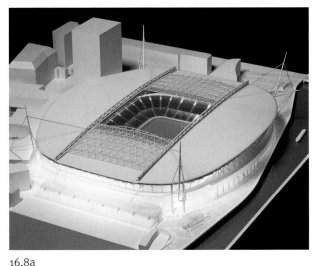

16.8a

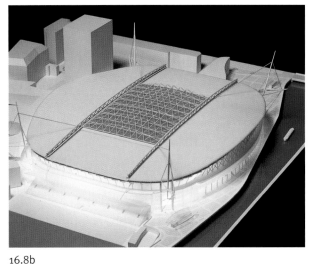

16.8b

16.8 Cardiff model showing retractable roof in opening (a) and closed (b) positions

to the middle tier, where corporate seating is located. Level 5 is the private box level at the back of the middle tier, and is accessed by escalator banks in the centre of each of the two long sides. Level 6 is the upper tier concourse with further spectator service facilities and level 7 accommodates services engineering plant.

Conclusion

The new Millennium Stadium in Cardiff is not only the first stadium in Britain to feature an opening roof, it is also the largest such stadium in the world. It is able to function in all seasons and weathers, hosting a range of activities from conventions to opera and major cultural festivals, thus bringing new life into one part of Cardiff city centre. In these respects, both as an advanced technological building, and as a focus of urban activity and renewal, the new stadium can well and truly be considered as one of the first of the 'fourth generation' stadia we described earlier in this book. It is therefore only fitting that it should be called the Millennium Stadium. It opened for the 1999 Rugby World Cup, only three months before the dawning of the new millennium, and it will undoubtedly be a stadium of the twenty-first century.

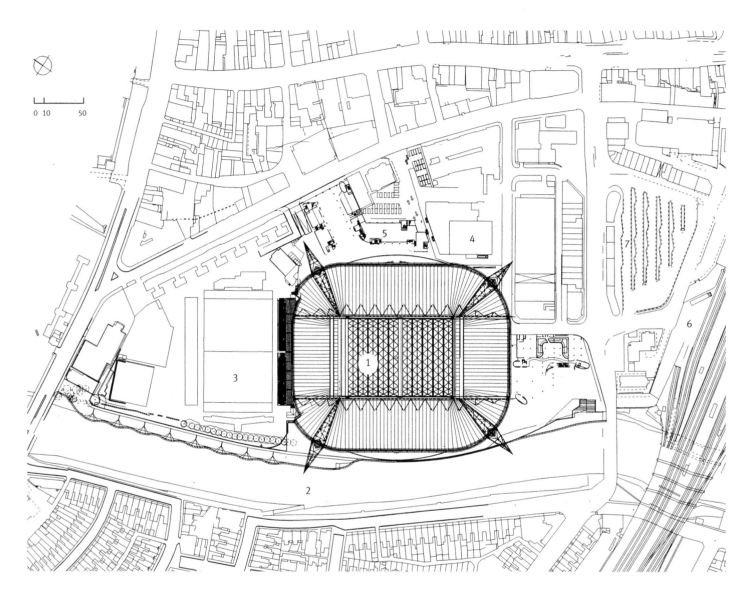

Site plan

1 Stadium roof in a
  closed position
2 River Taff
3 Cardiff Athletics Club
4 British Telecom
5 Proposed hotel
6 Railway station
7 Bus station

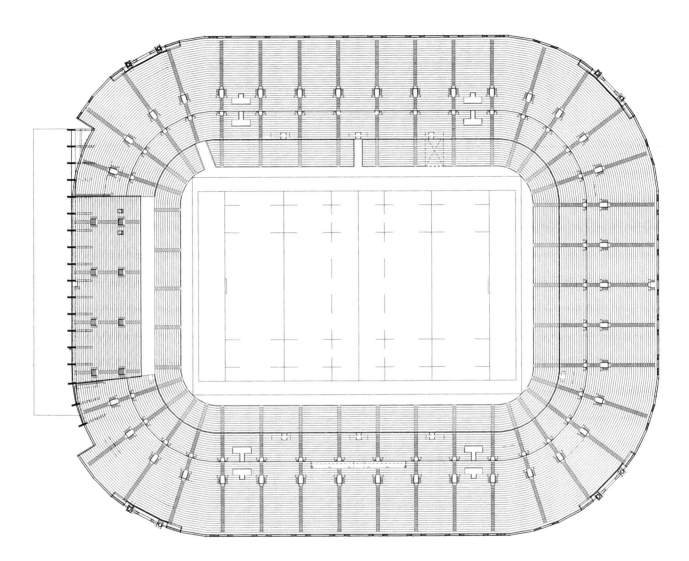

Bowl plan

Southwest corner:
elevation detail

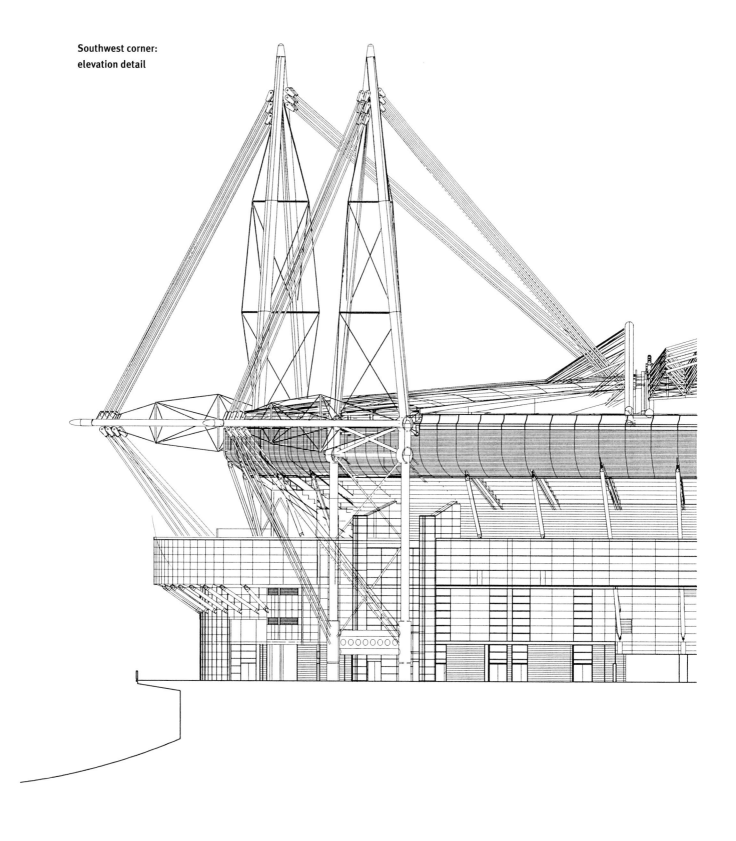

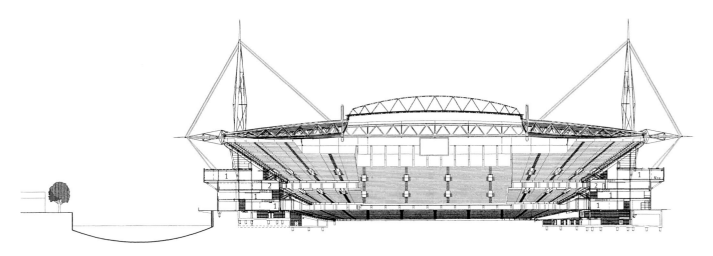

Section west–east
1 Concourse
2 Box

The Future **Part III**

Wembley
Arena 2020

Wembley

English National Stadium

1 Clarity of shape and form will direct spectators into the lower concourse at podium level to enjoy food and beverage facilities before, during and after the event

2 The sense of enclosure provided by the new bowl retains the atmosphere for which Wembley is renowned

1

2

Wembley is probably the best-known stadium in the world and in 1997 it was decided that it needed redevelopment if it were to maintain its status as one of the world's premier venues. Our team, including Foster and Partners, was commissioned in 1998 to design the new stadium that would be the centrepiece of England's bid to host the 2006 World Cup and will be completed in 2003. A range of design options have been developed

with one of the most striking being to support the large roof area on a 130 metre high arch which will replace the existing twin towers. It will provide a new symbol of a dynamic and exciting future for Wembley and will create a unique profile against the skyline visible for miles around. The new 90,000 seat stadium will also feature a partly retractable roof to allow the sun to reach all parts of the pitch and a platform athletics track to be

3

3 The spectacular approach along Olympic Way where the crowd will be directed by the 130 metre high arch which will be seen for miles

inserted when needed thus allowing seating for pitch sports to remain close to the action.

For visitors to Wembley the most memorable view of the stadium is that from Olympic Way and the new design presents a dramatic new frontage to this axis, providing the same thrill for future generations of fans as the old stadium has done for past generations. The main facade follows the model of the old stadium with a large banqueting hall placed at its centre overlooking Olympic Way. From each side, escalators rise around the facade of the stadium, taking spectators from the main concourse level to the upper concourses. These rise over stepped accommodation that wraps around the stadium. Ensuring that the pitch quality can be maintained within a stadium which is considerably taller than the existing one, and placing fans closer to the pitch, has been a key challenge for the design team. The objective is to find a way of exposing the pitch turf to an adequate amount of daylight for healthy growth and the solution the team developed is based on expanding the size of the roof aperture. This allows moving sections of the roof to be retracted to allow extra daylight onto the pitch. The roof panels will be left open between events and during fine weather to allow the pitch to be exposed to sunlight. When nec-

essary, the roof can be closed within 15 minutes to cover all seating for events.

The design of the new stadium bowl and its enclosure aims to provide spectators with the same highly charged atmosphere as the existing stadium. An important aspect of the stadium's atmosphere is its acoustics. Crowd noise recordings have been made at the 1999 FA Cup Final and at an England v. Sweden football international to act as a benchmark for the acoustics within the new stadium. We will use sophisticated computer modelling techniques to tune the acoustics of the new stadium interior to recreate the 'Wembley Roar'. The geometry of the new seating bowl is designed to significantly improve sightlines and comfort. The curved seating rows will focus spectators on the event and enhance the sense of intimacy within the crowd.

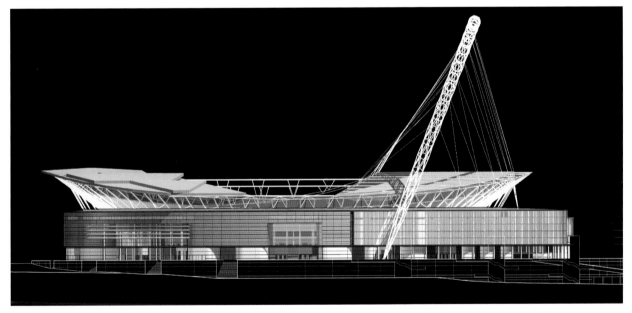

4

4 The world's best known stadium is to become the world's most spectacular stadium in 2003

Arena 2020

A 24 hour a day venue

The Arena 2020 project is a conceptual mixed-use development that explores the concept of a major sports leisure facility as a nucleus for urban regeneration and revitalisation. As previous developments of this nature tend to tear unsustainable holes in cities and isolate themselves from their surrounds, 2020 seeks to establish links, open up new opportunities and provide a seed for the renewal process.

The project incorporates a central multi-use event space that may be utilised as a stadium for rugby and football (30,000 seats), an indoor multi-event arena and a convention exhibition centre. The central event space is surrounded by a band of urban park-land that links the arena to a perimeter building which contains both support facilities for the event space as well as retail, commercial and accommodation facilities that serve both the arena and the city. In this sense, 2020 is a functioning entity of city fabric where people can be seen every day of the week not just on event days. Arena 2020 has a number of guiding principles.

Urban regeneration

The Arena 2020 project will be a central element in an urban renewal strategy. The concept is to create a critical mass of sports, leisure and entertainment facilities which will act as a catalyst for the regeneration of the surrounding area. The presence of the new facility and the new associated working, living and event populations will contribute to a new vitality in the surrounding area.

It will integrate with surrounding city fabric and not be isolated from its surrounds. The surrounding support facility structure will contain functions that are both complementary and stimulating to the surrounding cityscape. With a facility geared towards full time use and not geared only around a series of events.

The leisure and commercial facilities are contained within an open public space as the project is conceived first as an inner city park that contains a dense arrangement of leisure facilities. It is envisaged that the core leisure activity of the development will be the enjoyment of open public space.

The availability of public space in future cities will be at a premium, and building footprints will have to be

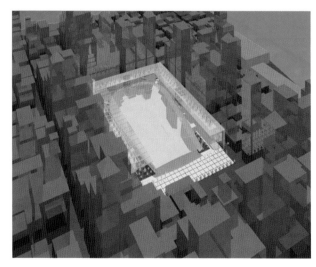

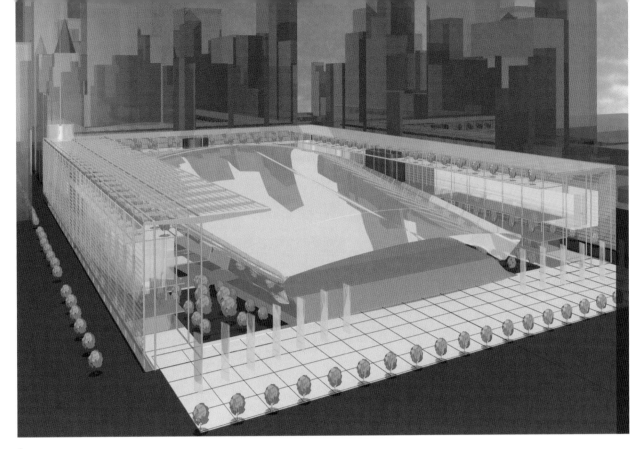

2

minimised to increase the availability of open public space. The Arena 2020 project amalgamates a convention exhibition centre, stadium and arena into a multi-purpose event facility that economises on space and maximises flexibility.

It is both flexible and adaptable in order to maximise its potential usage over time. The event space will be able to be adapted for a myriad of sporting, cultural and social events while the surrounding support structure will provide a framework into which different types of facilities can be grafted and renewed over time.

The project is to work on zero emission principles with passive environmental controls, having a double building skin to control heat loss and gain. Passive power generation will be incorporated such as photovoltaics and wind generators, while vegetation and planting will be maximised throughout the development to enhance the city oxygen supply, and natural light and ventilation will be maximised in order to reduce energy costs.

1 Aerial view of Arena 2020 set amidst the urban landscape

2 Main entrance elevation showing the permeability of the 'building' dissolving into existing built context

3 Internal view showing the 'arena' set within an inner city park and linking to perimeter accommodation

3

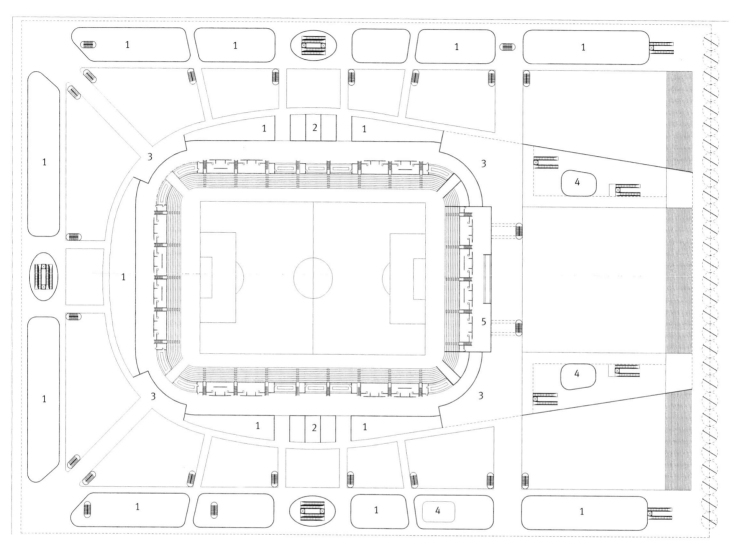

Ground level plan

1 Retail
2 Player/VIP entrance
3 Turnstiles
4 Office/hotel
   circulation core
5 Sliding stand

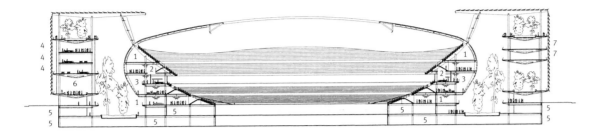

Cross-section

1 Concourse
2 Box
3 Club
4 Offices
5 Retail
6 Fitness centre
7 Residential

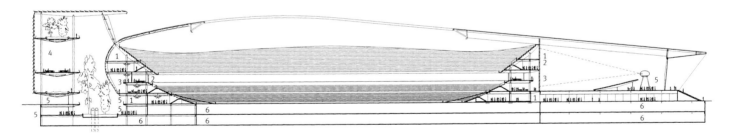

Long section

1 Concourse
2 Box
3 Club
4 Banqueting
5 Retail
6 Car park

Finis

The future starts now, but to be able to act upon our ideas and put our plans for the future into effect, to build our vision, we have to spend time developing our understanding of that future. Having devoted the past twenty years developing that understanding of the design of sports and leisure buildings, we can see a clear vision of these buildings in the future.

The three guiding stars will be technology, money and social change as they have been for our design business. We have seen these factors change our own business and we can safely attribute a large measure of our success to the jumbo jet and the microchip. Quite simply, Boeing and Intel have completely transformed our lives as architects.

It goes without saying that the availability of faster and more comfortable air travel has allowed us to seek, and accept, work in all parts of the globe. Like many professionals working in the international arena we now think little of catching a 747 for a meeting on the other side of the world, at short notice.

Computers have equally transformed the way we work. Indeed we contend that digitally processed information will become the single largest force for change in stadia design during the next ten years. To explain our thinking, we recall being asked, several years ago, how the coming of computers and computer-aided design was likely to change our working practices. We concluded that the question was akin to a river asking, 'How is my arrival at the ocean going to affect me?' The answer is that the rules which have guided the river to the ocean simply no longer apply. Once in the ocean, there are no more river banks, no limits.

Once one fully grasps this concept, one should be able to work with and appreciate the new tools of design more easily, more freely and more productively. For architects and clients alike, the drawing board is no more. In the same way that the microchip has revolutionised the way we work and the way we approach our business, so too will the same technology shape our buildings of the future. Our own conversion to computerisation took place in 1989 and since those early years we have moved to a fully PC-based operation for both drawing and design. Using a Windows environment our specification writing, project planning, staff resourcing and accounting are now entirely coordinated throughout the practice.

Some of the applications we use are highly specialised and have led us to produce our own software, dedicated to tackling the specific problems of stadium design. This is an example of how our single-minded focus upon this building type has allowed us to research the subject more deeply than if we had remained a general architectural practice. Among the software programs we have developed are those able to predict crowd flows and to calculate exit times; to calculate numbers and distribution of turnstiles, entry points, toilets and concessions; to calculate sightlines from every seat in the venue. We construct full three-dimensional models of any given stadium design in the computer, and then display this model in a wide range of three-dimensional images, including walk-through videos and views taken from any seat.

Above all else, we love the work we do and believe in the changes we are helping to bring about. We now operate from three offices in London, Kansas City and Brisbane in three very different parts of the world, but our staff have retained a common bond, stemming from the enjoyment we all feel for sport, music and the leisure business as a whole. When not busy designing venues, we can be found visiting them, and when not wearing our professional hats, we like to be part of the crowd. We know what it is to be an ordinary fan, elated or deflated, buying our tickets to delight or despair. It is also extremely important to us that we design successful buildings; not just large ones or expensive ones or ones that comply with other, usually meaningless criteria. We know full well that statistics alone are no indicators of success. In 1995 the Adelaide Formula One Grand Prix attracted some 500,000 spectators during the course of four days, which at the time was a world record. Yet when the bidding came round again, Adelaide lost the event to its neighbour Melbourne simply because the 1995 event had been widely perceived as unsuccessful. In short, venues need more than just people at an event in order to succeed.

We must also accept that the technology of today will soon be overtaken by the discoveries of tomorrow. In this respect we should all take heed of the words of NASA astronaut Jim Lovell, following his colleagues' successful manned landing. 'Gentlemen', Lovell was reported to have declared, 'Imagine what an amazing time we live in, when man can walk on the moon and an entire computer can fit into a single room.' That was in 1969, the year I first started studying architecture in Australia. That same year Concorde and the Jumbo Jet flew for the first time. It was also the year that saw the creation of the Internet. And yet now, over three decades later, while the Jumbo is still flying and the Internet and the exchange of digital information is changing our lives, there is many a production line automobile that boasts more computing power under its bonnet – in a unit smaller than a matchbox – than the Apollo team used.

On a different level, but encompassing the same dramatic time-frame of scientific development, this book is one attempt to illustrate some of the changes in which we have played a part, and of the many changes yet to come that we fully intend to develop in our work for the future. Like the cathedrals of the medieval period and the great engineering works of the Victorian era, the stadia of the twenty-first century look set to become classic expressions of their time. They will exude an image of grace and power. They will be at the cutting edge of technology. They will stand as proud emblems of their host communities, while broadcasting their wares to a worldwide audience. If you are as excited by these possibilities as we are, you may take comfort from the knowledge that there is even more to come in the future. This most rewarding form of architecture, which has well and truly become both our passion and our life's work, is still developing and the new venues it will produce are even more exciting than those of the recent past.

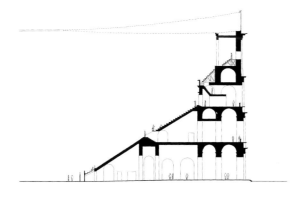

The Colosseum, Rome

Concorde

Bibliography

'A blueprint for British Stadia' (1993) *Sports Industry* September–October: 3–4.

Collins, Pippa (1990) 'Playing safe: Rod Sheard and Geraint John talk about the changing design of stadia', *Atrium* April.

Comitato Olympico Nazionale Italiano (1990) 'The stadiums of 1990 FIFA World Cup', *Spaziosport* 9 (2).

Comitato Olympico Nazionale Italiano (1994) 'The stadiums of 1994 FIFA World Cup', *Spaziosport* 13 (2): 1–128.

Croker, Ted (1979) 'The Secretary's column: Ted Croker looks at the possibility of covered stadia in England', *FA Today* 1 October: 8–9.

Fédération Internationale de Football Association, Union of European Football Associations (1991) *Technical Recommendations and Requirements for the Construction of New Stadia*, Zurich: Fédération Internationale de Football Association.

Football Association (1991) 'The control of crowds at football matches', *FA Handbook 1990/1*, London: Football Association.

Football Stadia Advisory Design Council (1991a) *Football Stadia Bibliography 1980–1990*. London: Football Stadia Advisory Design Council.

Football Stadia Advisory Design Council (1991b) *Seating: Sightlines, Conversion of Terracing, Seat Types*, London: Football Stadia Advisory Design Council.

Football Stadia Advisory Design Council (1991c) *Stadium Public Address Systems*, London: Football Stadia Advisory Design Council.

Football Stadia Advisory Design Council (1992a) *Designing for Spectators with Disabilities*. London: Football Stadia Advisory Design Council.

Football Stadia Advisory Design Council (1992b) *Digest of Stadia Criteria*, London: Football Stadia Advisory Design Council.

Football Stadia Advisory Design Council (1992c) *On the Sidelines, Football and Disabled Spectators*, London: Football Stadia Advisory Design Council.

Football Stadia Advisory Design Council (1992d) *Stadium Roofs*, London: Football Stadia Advisory Design Council.

Football Stadia Advisory Design Council (1993) *Terraces, Designing for Safe Standing at Football Stadia*, London: Football Stadia Advisory Design Council.

Football Stadia Development Committee (1994a) *Design-Build: A Good Practice Guide Where Design-Build is Used for Stadia Construction*, London: Sports Council.

Football Stadia Development Committee (1994b) *Stadium Control Rooms*, London: Sports Council.

Football Stadia Development Committee (1994c) *Toilet Facilities at Stadia*, London: Sports Council.

Happold, Edmund and Dickson, Michael (1974) 'The story of Munich, Zodiac 21', *Architectural Design* 6: 330–44.

HMSO (1975) Safety at Sports Grounds Act 1975, London: HMSO, esp. Ch. 52.

HMSO (1988) Safety at Sports Grounds Act 1975 (rev. edn), London: HMSO.

HMSO (1990) Safety at Sports Grounds Act 1975 (rev. edn), London: HMSO.

Home Office (1985) *Committee of Inquiry into Crowd Safety and Control at Sports Grounds. Chairman: Mr Justice Popplewell. Interim Report*, Cmnd 9595, London: HMSO.

Home Office (1986) *Committee of Inquiry into Crowd Safety and Control at Sports Grounds. Chairman: Mr Justice Popplewell. Final Report*, Cmnd 9710, London: HMSO.

Home Office (1989) *The Hillsborough Stadium Disaster, 15 April 1989. Inquiry by Rt Hon. Lord Justice Taylor*, London: HMSO.

Home Office (1990a) *Guide to Safety at Sports Grounds*, London: HMSO.

Home Office (1990b) *The Hillsborough Stadium Disaster, 15 April 1989. Inquiry by the Rt Hon. Lord Justice Taylor, Final Report*, London: HMSO.

Home Office/Scottish Home and Health Department (1976) *Guide to Safety at Sports Grounds: Football*, London: HMSO.

Home Office/Scottish Office (1986) *Guide to Safety at Sports Grounds*, London: HMSO.

Home Office/Scottish Office (1990) *Guide to Safety at Sports Grounds*, London: HMSO.

International Association for Sports and Leisure Facilities (1993) *Planning Principles for Sports Grounds/Stadia*, Koln: IAKS.

Inglis, S. (1982) 'Football Grounds of Great Britain; Football Grounds of Europe; The Ibrox Stadium Redevelopment (GB)', *Acier Stahl Steel* 2: 59–7.

Inglis, S. (1990) *The Football Grounds of Europe*, London: Willow Books.

Inglis, S. (1992) *The Football Grounds of Great Britain*, London: Collins Willow.

John, G. and Spring, M. (1987) 'Where are our big arenas going?' *Baths Service and Recreation Management* 46: 128–9.

Laventhol and Horwarth (1989) *Convention Centres, Stadium and Arenas*, Washington, DC: Urban Land Institute.

Luder, Owen (1990) 'Sports Stadia after Hillsborough', Papers presented at the Sports Council/Royal Institute of British Architects Seminar, RIBA, 29 March. London: RIBA/Sports Council in association with the Football Trust.

Millbank, Paul (1968) 'Olympic Stadia, Mexico City: Building for the XIXth Olympic Games', *Building* 6 September: 87–90.

Millbank, Paul (1975) 'Football clubs: time to open their gates to all sports', *Surveyor* 16 May: 12–13.

Panstadia International (1992) *Panstadia International – Leading the Field. A Worldwide Guide to Stadium Newbuild and Management*, Harrow: Panstadia International.

Petersen, David C. (1996) *Sports, Convention and Entertainment Facilities*, USA: RICS Books.

Schmidt, T. (1987) 'A Stadium which reflects the Games: architectural history of the Seoul Olympic Stadium', *Olympic Review* 239 (September): 441–4.

Rich, Ben R. (1995a) *Skunk Works*, London: Little Brown & Co.

Rich, Ben R. (1995b) *Skunk Works X12 S/W*, London: Little Brown & Co.

Schmidt, T. (1988) 'Building a stadium: Olympic stadiums from 1948–1988, Part 1', *Olympic Review* 247 (June): 246–51.

Sheard, R. and John, G. (1997) *Stadia, A Design and Development Guide*, 2nd edn, London: Architectural Press.

Shields, A. (1989) *Arenas: A Planning, Design and Management Guide*, London: Sports Council.

'Setting new limits at Toronto's Skydome', *Athletic Business* 12 (September): 35–6.

Sports Council, Royal Institute of British Architects, UIA Work Group for Sports, Leisure and Tourism (1990) *Sports Stadia in the 90s*, London: Sports Council, RIBA, UIA.

Sports Council (1992) 'Planning for stadia', in *Planning and Provision for Sport*, London: Sports Council.

Geraint, John and Campbell, Kit (eds) (1993) *Handbook of Sports and Recreational Building Design, vol. 1, Outdoor Sports*, 2nd edn, Butterworth-Heinemann for the Sports Council Technical Unit for Sport.

Spring, M. and John, G. (1987) 'Sporting new arenas', *Building* 17 April: 42–4.

'Stadia development in San Siro and Bari', *Impanti* (2).

'Stadia', *Spaziosport* March 1989.

Index

Italic page numbers refer to illustrations.

13. Feb. 2001 HHI 67.50 (75.65) 799738